BUILDING, LEADING, AND MANAGING STRATEGIC ALLIANCES

BUILDING, LEADING, AND MANAGING STRATEGIC ALLIANCES

How to Work Effectively and Profitably with Partner Companies

Fred A. Kuglin
with
Jeff Hook

AMACOM
American Management Association
New York • Atlanta • Brussels • Buenos Aires • Chicago • London • Mexico City
San Francisco • Shanghai • Tokyo • Toronto • Washington, D.C.

This publication is designed to provide accurate and authoritative information in regard to the subject matter covered. It is sold with the understanding that the publisher is not engaged in rendering legal, accounting, or other professional service. If legal advice or other expert assistance is required, the services of a competent professional person should be sought.

Library of Congress Cataloging-in-Publication Data

Kuglin, Fred A.
    Building, leading, and managing strategic alliances: how to work effectively and profitably with partner companies / Fred A. Kuglin with Jeff Hook.
        p.   cm.
    Includes bibliographical references and index.
    ISBN 0-8144-0683-1
    1. Strategic alliances (Business)   I. Hook, Jeff.   II. Title.

HD69.S8   K83   2001
658'.044—dc21

2001055226

Printing number

10   9   8   7   6   5   4   3   2   1

Contents

Acknowledgments   *vii*

Introduction   *ix*

1. What Is an Alliance?   1

2. Great Idea, but How Do I Get Started?   23

3. 3G Wireless Networks: The Future Is Now . . . or
Is It?   49

4. Telecom Providers and 3G Wireless Device
Manufacturers: A $1 Trillion Investment, yet
Where's the Value?   74

5. Mission Impossible? From Intense Competitor
to Alliance Partner!   98

6. Transportation: Win-Win Must Mean Profit-
Profit   124

7. Health Care: Alliances and a Healthy Supply
Chain   151

8. Software Companies and Consulting Firms:
Alliances Viewed from Both Sides   189

9. Know When to Hold, and Know When to Fold   214

10. Critical Success Factors in Establishing Alliances   238

11. The Alliance Hall of Fame   251

Index   *269*

Acknowledgments

The inspiration to write books comes from many sources. This book was inspired by my passion for alliances and the growing value of alliances in our ever-changing global economic world.

I want to thank my wife and children for their patience, support, and understanding throughout the writing process. This book came at a difficult time for me given the health issues with my Mom and the passing of my Dad, and it placed an intense time burden on my wife, to whom I am very grateful for her ever-present support.

In addition, I want to thank Phil Robers for sharing with me the passion to write and for his support to make this book a reality, and Dr. Les Waters for his ongoing mentoring and support. Also, I want to thank Jeff Hook of i2 Technologies for his contribution of Chapter

Eight. The book is definitively strengthened as a result of his contribution. It was a pleasure to work with Jeff, who is a business associate and a friend.

Also, I want to thank Diane Richey for her contributions to Chapter One; my many contacts in Telecommunications and High Tech for material in Chapters Three and Four; my daughter Heidi for her research contributions to Chapters Three and Four; Stephen Justice of Lockheed for his input, contributions, and permission for material in Chapter Five; David Keirsey for his advice and his permission for material in Chapter Five; my many friends in the trucking industry for their contributions to Chapter Six; and Lydon Neuman and Ken Gottesman of CGE&Y for their contributions for Chapter Seven. I also want to thank the anti-capitalists from my May Day experience in London for their contributions to Chapter Nine, and General Electric and Cisco, whose outstanding commitments to hall-of-fame alliances formed the basis of Chapter Eleven. Finally, all quotations not specifically referenced in the endnotes come from my personal interviews.

Lastly, I want to thank my Mom and Dad for giving me the encouragement to be the best I can be. My Dad passed away on July 24, 2001 after a long bout with complications from heart surgery. He was not only a strong coach in life, but a best friend as well. My Dad had a philosophy to learn every day of one's life, and to make the choices necessary to continue to both learn and add back to others. Despite his physical absence, I will continue to draw support and strength from his coaching and advice. I am also thankful for having had him as a Dad for forty-eight years.

—Fred A. Kuglin

Introduction

Alliances have been around for some time. In fact, alliances were formed among ancient peoples as they banded together to fight common, sometimes dominant enemies. In modern times, we see alliances in war (the Desert Storm coalition, or the NATO forces in Kosovo), in politics (coalitions in government), and in the business marketplace. As commonplace as alliances have been in our history and our current world, they are often misunderstood and misused.

Early in 2001, I was visiting a highly regarded CEO of a major global company based in Europe. As we discussed his favorite topic—how to drive the shareholder value of his company to new levels—the subject of alliances surfaced. He rose from his chair, pointed to the flipchart that had the words "strategic alliances" on it, and said, "I want one of those. Get me one this quarter, so that I can announce it at the next shareholder meeting. And please, make sure that there is a small 'e' in front of a catchy name for this alliance. That will get the analysts' attention."

Needless to say, I was flabbergasted as to how little regard this CEO had for alliances. In addition, he displayed a surprising naiveté that totally underestimated the degree of difficulty involved in setting up an alliance. Unfortunately for his company, the security analysts have come to their senses about valuations of technology start-ups and alliances with small e's in front of catchy names.

It is attitudes like those expressed by this CEO that are responsible for alliances being announced solely for the purpose of hyping the company's stock and feeding the ego of the CEO. These "empty press releases" frustrate security analysts, employees, and customers—as well as alliance partners. If you want to have fun, track the press releases around major trade events, and then follow-up six months later with the PR departments of the companies releasing the press releases. You may be surprised by how many companies are very liberal in their interpretation of a valid reason to issue a press release.

The problem lies with the understanding of what an alliance is, the value of an alliance, when to use an alliance, and when not to use an alliance. Many large, successful companies like Cisco Systems, IBM, and General Electric are using strategic alliances in significant numbers with wonderful results. Many others recognize that other companies are doing alliances, but do not have a clue for how to start an alliance. Still others do not even consider alliances, and adhere to a "not invented here" philosophy.

This book is intended to provide you with a road map on how to do alliances. It is designed to walk you through a series of events, with each event presented in a separate chapter. In each chapter, a specific industry is showcased, with examples used to support the industry and the events. Let's take a brief look at each chapter and at how the construction of a successful alliance is connected throughout the book.

Chapter One introduces the definition of alliances. It also introduces the five types of alliances, and how to determine each alliance type. These five types of alliances are sales, solution-specific, geographic-specific, investment, and joint venture. Chapter One also introduces the framework to determine the need for an alliance. This is critical for anyone considering starting up an alliance, because it provides a basis of need for the initiation of an alliance. The chapter then ties this framework to the type of alliance needed through a second framework that helps to determine what type of alliance is needed. This chapter also focuses on the appliance industry.

Chapter Two addresses the start-up of alliances. In this chapter, the framework on how to create an alliance agreement is introduced, as well as the process to approve alliance agreements. This chapter also presents the guidelines on knowledge sharing and knowledge transfer with alliance partners, especially in hypercompetitive industries. (Are there any industries today that aren't hypercompetitive?) This chapter focuses on the automotive industry, and it contains a specific discussion on Covisint, the automotive Business-to-Business (B2B) marketplace.

Chapter Three addresses the start-up and emergence of alliances. This chapter introduces the definition of 3G Wireless Networks, and covers the frenzy that is engulfing the telecommunications industry and mobile device manufacturers. It also looks at current activity with alliances in the telecommunications industry and mobile device manufacturers, and maps these alliances into the five types of alliances introduced in Chapter One. Chapter Three also introduces the process on how to construct a memo of intent (MOI) with an alliance partner. Memos of intent are used to initiate work with an alliance partner while a more permanent agreement is negotiated and executed.

Chapter Four covers the emergence and rapid growth of alliances. This chapter covers the need for companies to look hard at the 3G wireless technology introduced in Chapter Three, and the need to base their adoption of 3G technology on the business value it produces. In this chapter, the Networked Value Chain is reintroduced as a framework for companies to anchor their 3G technology decisions on business value. (The Networked Value Chain was first introduced in the book, *The Supply Chain Network @ Internet Speed*, published by AMACOM in October 2000 and copyrighted by Cap Gemini Ernst & Young.) The Scan, Focus, and Act process is introduced as a way to creatively brainstorm solutions that support the two main value drivers in the networked value chain. In addition, the chapter introduces the process to construct a nondisclosure agreement.

Chapter Five reviews how intense competitors can and sometimes must become alliance partners. This chapter highlights the development of the F-22 Raptor, and examines how a program like the F-22 can span three decades. Throughout the F-22 program, competitors spent years chasing the pot of gold at the end of the Pentagon rainbow. After several years spent intensely competing with each other, the competitors were suddenly required by the Pentagon to team and present teaming bids. What an alliance challenge this was for all involved! Connecting to this challenge, this chapter reviews the softer side or the people issues relating to alliances. The Keirsey Temperament Sorter is used to show how different personality types interact and to show readers how they can "connect" with others on an alliance partner team.

Chapter Six focuses on the mature stage of alliances and covers the financial considerations involved with alliances. In addition, the transportation industry is highlighted. In this chapter, we look at typical costing of transportation shipments, and at how innovation and alliances have impacted the costing trade-offs between modes of transportation. This chapter also introduces the framework on how to construct an alliance business plan. The alliance business plan is usually an addendum to the alliance agreement introduced in Chapter Two. Alliance compensation is also addressed in Chapter Six.

Chapter Seven focuses on the high growth and mature stages of alliances, with a highlight on the health care provider industry. The Health Care Adaptive e-Supply Chain is introduced, along with its four guiding principles. Content and strategic sourcing are addressed in a health care provider environment. The five-step strategic sourcing framework is introduced. In addition, this chapter also introduces how to construct a solution-based definitive agreement.

Chapter Eight introduces a view of alliances as seen from a leading global software company. Jeff Hook, vice president of consulting alliances with i2 Technologies, writes this chapter from the point of view of how alliances are formed to penetrate the software marketplace. He covers how and why alliances have worked and have not worked with i2, and what are the lessons learned that should be shared with the readers.

Chapter Nine focuses on the decline stage of alliances. The five forces of alliance blues are reviewed, along with the lifecycle of alliance management. The stages of the lifecycle of alliance management are discussed (start-up, emerge, high growth, mature, decline, and disband), with the alliance agreements and documents mapped into each stage. This chapter introduces the Framework to Determine the Need to Disband an Alliance, which builds on the Framework to Determine the Need for an Alliance presented in Chapter One. The chapter also introduces the Framework to Disband an Alliance when it is determined to be the best course of action for alliance partners. And finally, the need for character and integrity in alliances is covered in this chapter.

Chapter Ten focuses on the complete process for successful alliances by introducing the seven critical success factors that support a successful alliance program. This leads naturally into Chapter Eleven, which looks closely at the two companies whose distinguished track record with alliances has earned them entry into the Alliance Hall of Fame.

This book offers you a road map on what it takes to successfully develop an alliance with another company. The company examples will help you identify what types of alliances have worked in what situations and scenarios. The frameworks will help you follow a path to create the alliance. The legal document examples identify what legal documents are necessary and in what business context, and they will help you understand the complexity of the documents and what is entailed to create them. By default, I hope that these documents also provide you with an appreciation for legal teams and their involvement in successful alliances. All too often, executives trying to create alliances view the legal teams as inhibitors to the process. In reality, legal teams can be effective enablers while protecting the assets of the company.

Alliances are a way for companies to quick-start sales through accessing new markets and solutions, reduce costs through strategic relationships matching core competencies, leverage fixed assets through shared services, accelerate working capital turns through supply chain and financial alliances, and lower effective tax rates. They can be strategic or tactical, with many opportunities available in the marketplace. Is your company prepared to address how to achieve a successful alliance? The leading companies are doing alliances right, and the market is moving fast. Let's begin the journey through the alliance process.

BUILDING, LEADING, AND MANAGING STRATEGIC ALLIANCES

CHAPTER ONE

What Is an Alliance?

Toto, We're Not in Kansas Anymore!

One of my recent business trips to Europe took me to Paris, Brussels, Helsinki, Amsterdam, and London. In each city, I had the pleasure of interfacing with executives of top global and European companies. As a global alliance partner with a leading global professional services firm, it was my role to work with clients and extend the joint service offerings we developed with our alliance partner. It was also my role to work with the many members of our alliance partner organization and other members of my firm to both educate and promote the value of the alliance.

While I was in Helsinki, I checked my voicemail to stay in touch with the day-to-day events back home. I have a very competent staff, and everyone has my reach numbers when I travel. (After this trip, I will also have an international cellular phone to make sure that I am reachable 24/7.) When I was retrieving my messages, I was surprised to find an excited message from the CFO of one of our alliances, who had picked up rumors that my firm had invested in one of the alliance's top competitors. Before I finished retrieving my messages, there was a second message from the CFO asking whether I had found the answer to his question.

The CFO message was puzzling at best. First, the CFO was a consummate professional who was almost always controlled with his actions. Second, I had a greeting on my voicemail that informed the caller that I was out of the country on firm business. Third and most important, our firm had made not only an investment but also a commitment to our alliance partner to exclusively focus on a specific industry sector with their technology solutions. Our firm is very large, and the chance of someone developing competing alliances was always present. However, when it comes to exclusivity in an industry, the industry sector leader has to approve all alliances. In addition, any investment has to go through our new investment group.

Quickly I sent to both the industry sector leader and the new investment leader an urgent voicemail asking whether the rumors were true. Their replies came back negative, just as I had anticipated and hoped they would. However, there was an event that triggered the rumors. A separate company had decided to spin off an in-house technology solution that was similar to the one with our alliance partner. Our industry sector leader was approached with the opportunity to invest in the new spin-off. Despite the attractiveness of investing in a pre-IPO spin-off, our industry sector leader declined the offer.

Needless to say, I was relieved with the answers I received. However, I knew that in our firm's matrix organization, the chance of someone violating the terms and spirit of our alliance agreement was always present. It did not happen frequently, but when it did, the energy to fix the violation was exceeded only by the energy to calm executive anxieties.

This scenario also reinforced the ever-present belief that it is a small world. When I investigated what had happened with this separate company and its spin-off, I was informed that only its three most senior people knew of the firms that they had invited to be investment partners. If I add the two people within our firm, then the sphere of influence and knowledge of this offer was five people. Despite this small inner circle of people in the know, word leaked out and reached our investment alliance partner at Internet speed! The lesson here is that alliance behavior has to be consistent at all times.

The reason for alliance behavior to be consistent at all times is that successful alliances are built on trust. It takes a long time and personal relationships to build up trust. It takes only one event to destroy this trust, no matter whether the event was intentional or unintentional. One set of behaviors in the face of the alliance partner and another set of behaviors behind the partner's back are a recipe for mistrust—and a failed alliance relationship!

Definitions of "Alliance"

The definition of the word "alliance" varies from executive to executive, company to company, and industry to industry. Often I find that companies that have entered into an alliance don't necessarily agree on what is meant by "alliance." The fact is that there are many different types of alliances. Another fact is that companies must approach them in vastly different ways.

Webster defines the word "alliance" as: *1. An allying or close association, as of nations for a common objective, families by marriage, etc. 2. An agreement for this 3. The countries, groups, etc. in such association.*"[1]

Another way to define "alliance" is to look at synonyms. According to Webster's *Thesaurus*, "alliance" can be defined by the following synonyms: "(The state of being allied) connection, membership, affinity, participation, cooperation, support, union, agreement, common understanding, marriage, kinship, relation, collaboration, partnership, coalition, affiliation, bond, and (The act of joining) fusion, combination, and coupling . . ."[2]

Webster's *Dictionary* definition and the *Thesaurus* words used to describe "alliance" appear to be as broad and as deep as one would want.

It is important to understand the common objective of an alliance before one seriously considers entering into an alliance agreement. The first step has to be the categorization of the types of alliances in order to connect the concept of an alliance with the successful creation and implementation of an alliance. Let's look at one way to categorize the types of alliances.

Types of Alliances

There are five basic categories or types of alliances.

✧ Sales alliance
✧ Solution-specific alliance
✧ Geographic-specific alliance
✧ Investment alliance
✧ Joint venture alliance

Let's take a look at each alliance type and its definition. (Please note that in many cases, alliances between companies can involve two or more categories or types of alliances.)

Sales Alliance

A "sales alliance" occurs when two companies agree to go to market together to sell complementary products and services. For example, i2 Technologies (i2), which sells eBusiness and Advanced Planning and Scheduling (APS) technologies, goes to market with a professional services provider like Cap Gemini Ernst & Young (CGE&Y) that will provide program management and systems integration services. This type of "sales alliance" usually revolves around targeted clients or targeted industries.

Exclusivity is not a requirement around a sales alliance. For example, i2 has multiple sales alliances with professional services providers, while CGE&Y has multiple sales alliances with similar technology providers. Where the trust factor comes into play is the partnership agreements around specific clients or specific industries.

The focus of a sales alliance is to create sales. Usually this revolves around joint selling activities with specific clients. As such, the "rules of the road" are usually client- and sales-process-related.

Solution-Specific Alliance

A solution-specific alliance evolves when two companies agree to jointly develop and sell a specific marketplace solution. For example, Whirlpool, Hearst, and Boston Consulting Group joined together in an alliance to develop and sell an Internet eMarketplace that was to be an objective, comprehensive information source for appliance buyers. This eMarketplace, called Brandwise.com, was intended to provide up-to-date information on products—their performance, availability, and prices. Retailers who would become part of the eMarketplace alliance would pay Brandwise.com a percentage of the sale (e.g., 5 percent) for any referrals that became sales. As such, Hearst, Boston Consulting Group, Whirlpool, and the retailers who formed Brandwise.com were all part of a solution-specific alliance.[3]

Exclusivity may or may not be "in play" with a solution-specific alliance. Many times, one alliance partner will own the solution developed, whereas the other alliance partner will have a "preferred partner" designation as a result of the joint solution development work. At times, the ultimate customer may like the solution and *one* of the partners but may not want to do business with the other partner. A solution-specific alliance may provide for this scenario and the "sale" of a solution, despite another, nonjoint development partner being selected by the customer. For example, let's go back to the agreement (an extension of their alliance agreement) entered into by i2 Technologies and CGE&Y to jointly develop and sell an eFulfillment solution to the marketplace. Although many clients are approached jointly by i2 and CGE&Y, there are clients that prefer to work either with one of CGE&Y's competitors or with one of i2's competitors. In this agreement, as long as there is a register for what clients are joint clients and what clients are "open," there exists a mutual understanding and expectation of how each company will behave in the marketplace. This builds the foundation of trust on which both companies can operate.

Again, the focus of the solution-specific alliance is joint selling of a jointly developed solution. Usually this type of alliance has specific parameters and incentives to maximize the return to both parties for their part of the joint development effort, regardless of other competitors potentially participating at clients' requests.

Geographic-Specific Alliance

A geographic-specific alliance is developed when two companies agree to jointly market or co-brand their products and services in a specific geographic region. This type of alliance has existed for years in the beer industry. For example, Fosters is a very popular beer brewed by the

Foster Brewing Company of Australia. Rather than export its beer to North America and incur the high cost of shipping from Australia to North America, Foster's entered into an alliance with Molson Canada. Foster's licenses its beer brands through a licensing agreement with Molson. Molson brews the Foster's beer, according to Foster's precise formula and distributes it through its normal distribution channels. Foster's avoids having to pay for the export supply chain or spend the capital to build a North American brewery, while gaining access to an important geographic market. Molson gains additional product volume in both its brewery and its distribution network, driving efficiencies in both manufacturing and distribution.[4]

Another example is in the global appliance industry. When Maytag announced in November 2000 that it was looking at expanding into Europe through potential strategic alliances, it was rumored that this alliance would be with AB Electrolux of Sweden. According to informed sources, this was only a rumor. If it was true, this would be a solid example of a geographic-specific alliance. However, rumors do have a way of getting out of hand when alliances and competitors are mentioned in the same sentence![5]

Care must be taken to verify the validity of rumors. There are empty press releases, rumored alliances, and even merger discussions between companies (and even competitors) that are called off yet continue to live on in the media and the rumor mill. The marketplace is tough enough without having to deal with rumors on top of everything else.

Sometimes a geographic alliance such as the Fosters/Molson Canada involves some sort of investment in plant and equipment if the specified products to be co-manufactured involve different manufacturing processes. In this case, these strategic geographic alliances would be investment alliances as well.

Investment Alliance

An investment alliance occurs when one company makes an investment in another company while at the same time developing an agreement to jointly market their products and services. Let's go back to the Brandwise.com example. Hearst and Boston Consulting Group actually entered into both a solution-specific and an investment alliance with Whirlpool and Brandwise.com. According to Wall Street analysts,

Whirlpool and their partners invested approximately $10 million in Brandwise.com.[6]

Another example of an investment alliance is viaLink, a company that provides data synchronization and scan-based trading solutions to the consumer products, retail, and other industries. Hewlett Packard, i2 Technologies, and Cap Gemini Ernst & Young have all invested in viaLink. CGE&Y and i2 are actively working with viaLink to jointly sell the viaLink solution in the marketplace, while HP provides the hardware infrastructure for the viaLink solution.

As such, an investment alliance includes an investment of capital and possibly of resources. It also involves some sort of joint effort to co-market and/or co-develop the products and services.

Joint Venture Alliance

In a joint venture alliance, two companies come together and form a third company to specifically market and/or develop specific products and services. It usually means setting up a separate organization and financial structure, with ownership interests and incentives specified as the joint venture is established. The positive aspect is that there is a financial and legal commitment between the two companies. The negative aspect is that in a joint venture, failure can be as painful as a divorce. With a sales alliance, either party can cancel the alliance in a specified period of time and just walk away. With a joint venture, there is the responsibility of a separate company and the financial implications that are tied to the performance of both companies.

In the early 1990s, Northern Telecom (now Nortel) formed a joint venture with Motorola to market wireless infrastructure equipment on a worldwide basis. This joint venture collapsed when each partner refused to help each other out in different regions of the world. Although each company on its own was extremely successful, either this joint venture underestimated the challenge of merging organizations in culturally diverse regions of the world, or their joint metrics did not cross-incent the joint venture partners to behave in a win-win manner.[7]

In summary, then, there are many definitions for the word "alliance." Each definition has its own costs and benefits to the executive. The road to a successful alliance is not necessarily a short one, and it requires a significant amount of planning and negotiating.

Sometimes, alliances are thrown together with nothing more than a couple of meetings and a press release. When done wrong, alliances can be worth no more than the paper that the press release is printed on. Alliances done wrong can actually carry a negative marketplace perception for both companies, and can impact a company's business beyond the specific market tied to the alliance. On the flip side of things, alliances that fail can actually produce a positive marketplace impression, if the failed alliance was focused on innovation or leading-edge solutions.

Real World Examples

Brandwise.com: Solid Investment Alliance, yet Out of Business!

The eMarketplace start-up Brandwise.com was conceived during the height of the dot-com frenzy. In 1998, many executives were fearful of having their markets dis-intermediated by the Internet. The thought of creating a Web site that would demystify the research around an appliance purchase for an appliance buyer appears on the surface to be a very intriguing idea. Not only would the buyer benefit from the extensive information available on appliance products, availability, and pricing, but also retailers would benefit from referrals of buyers to their stores. There even was the promise of the value of the buyer purchase data, matching the "what was bought" to the "why it was bought."

From published reports, it appears that Whirlpool, Hearst, and Boston Consulting Group worked very well together in their investment alliance. However, the life cycle of Brandwise.com was only two years. It was conceived in 1998, launched in 1999, and shut down in May 2000. What went wrong?

It appears that the intent of Brandwise.com was to connect appliance buyers to product information, and to influence the buyer behavior through comprehensive product, price, and availability data. However, the planning around Brandwise.com appeared not to address supply chain execution and real-time product promising and order status.

One of the driving forces behind customer behavior in major appliance sales is speed from order to delivery. Without coordinating the networked supply chain to meet customer fulfillment, delivery became a big negative in retaining and subsequently attracting customers to Brandwise.com. Customer fulfillment is the battleground for control of customer relationships. By focusing on influencing customer demand based on inventory visibility and not focusing on coordinating the networked supply chain to meet customer fulfillment, Brandwise.com missed connecting with the driving forces behind customer behavior, especially speed from order to delivery.

However, even the ability of Brandwise.com to influence demand based on inventory visibility was inhibited by its reliance on retailers for on-line, up-to-date data on products, their specifications, inventory availability data, and price data. In many cases, the data either did not exist or was not in a clean or ready format to populate Brandwise.com's Web site from the retailers.[8]

Maytag.com and Cart-to-Cart Shopping

In January 2001, Maytag.com announced its Cart-to-Cart shopping option for consumers. From home, a buyer can fill out an online questionnaire and receive a purchase recommendation. Once this recommendation is in the "shopping cart," it is then referred to the dealers in the buyer's geographic area. The buyer then receives real-time pricing and product availability from the retailer or dealer. Once the payment method is finalized, delivery and installation are scheduled.[9]

This online shopping option is a step in the right direction. Maytag.com connects both to influencing customer demand, based on inventory visibility, and to coordinating the networked supply chain to meet customer fulfillment. Cart-to-Cart shopping does utilize the Internet to enhance the shopping experience for the buyer, and it addresses supply chain execution with real-time product promising and order status. The only drawback with Cart-to-Cart shopping is that it does not connect the manufacturer of the appliance to the actual customer order.

Perhaps the biggest driving force is installation and service. Sears and their successful "Brand Central" program can attest to the value of installation and service in appliance sales. The local stores coordinate the Brand Central program, yet Sears Home Central executes the service through nonstore service centers. Sears is successful in protect-

ing the customer touchpoint, yet providing scale in their service operations.[10]

The Battle for Control of Customer Relationships

Brandwise.com, Maytag.com, and Brand Central are all competing for
a share of the customer's wallet. The biggest factor missed by Brand-
wise.com appears to be who owns the customer relationships in the
marketplace. For appliance sales, it is the major appliance retailers who
"own" the customer relationships. These retailers have the on-site appliance inventories (or knowledge of their regional warehouse inventories) and can commit to specific delivery dates and times. The
appliance retailers are accustomed to commit-to delivery dates due to
installation/hook-up needs and other time-sensitive factors (e.g., moving into a new home, the replacement of a broken appliance). Frequently, these retailers are in a geographical area close to the buyers.
This also allows for personal access in case of service or delivery fail-
ures. Maytag.com and Brand Central included retailers in their solution designs, whereas Brandwise.com did not.

Diane Ritchey, executive editor of *Appliance Magazine*, furthers
these perspectives. "Why would appliance retailers help set up *Brand-
wise.com* through investments, then pay a 5 percent referral fee for
customers they already have? In addition, the appliance retailers are
the customers for appliance manufacturers. If they perceived that they
were being dis-intermediated by an appliance manufacturer going direct to their customers, they would switch suppliers quickly. The appliance manufacturer would then be selling to a small number of online
customers, while the appliance retailer has taken his or her orders for
hundreds or thousands of appliances to a competitor. The lack of connectivity to the customer/consumer relationship that drives appliance
sales contributed to Brandwise.com being a bad idea."

Ms. Ritchey adds, "Appliances will for the most part not sell over
the Internet. Information on appliances is good for the consumer, but
most of it is readily available today. There exists appliance.com and
the Web sites of all the major appliance manufacturers to offer product
information to consumers. As such, the market for appliances on the
Internet is in my opinion only for retailers who are not currently selling appliances."[11]

In an industry that has experienced few major innovations since

Hurley Machine of Chicago came to market with the first electric washing machine in 1908, Brandwise.com was a bold and refreshing move. However, the mistakes made in the planning and execution of Brandwise.com suggest that more emphasis should have been placed on execution and buyer behavior in the appliance industry. The rise and fall of Brandwise.com provides a solid case study of how executives should approach alliances. There are two distinct frameworks for executives to follow when considering alliances. These frameworks are, one, the framework to determine the need for an alliance, and two, the framework to determine what type of alliance is needed. Let's look at both frameworks.

Framework to Determine the Need for an Alliance

This framework consists of the following six steps.

Step 1. Business and Market Strategy

The first step in determining whether an alliance relationship is needed by an organization has to be the review of the company's business and marketing strategies. The mission and vision of the corporation, as developed and adopted by the CEO, the board of directors, the employees, the critical stakeholders, the suppliers, and the major customers, will serve as the foundation for the major objectives. These major objectives will then serve as a foundation for the company's marketing strategy.

The company's marketing strategy should include the product portfolio, its strategy and capital expenditure support, and the associated marketing programs to support it. All of this should be anchored around the customers' needs, desires, and behavior on what products they are willing to pay for.

Knowing the customers and their behavior is critical. What is also essential is to know how the company's products are incorporated into a total "customer solution." Specific knowledge of the customer, his or her buying behavior, and, most importantly, the total solution being sought by the customer, are all critical to satisfying actual customer demand—and whether an alliance will be beneficial from a customer-centric viewpoint.

Step 2. Marketplace Scan

The second step in assessing the need for an alliance relationship is to scan the marketplace for competitor activity. There are four stages to this step.

1. The first stage is a review of existing competitors and their current market positioning. In this stage, current products and services as well as current market share should be identified. For example, in this stage a lawn mower company would identify all other lawn mower manufacturers, their products, and their market shares. A professional services firm that specializes in technology-enabled supply chain solutions would identify similar or like consulting firms.

2. The second stage is a review of existing competitors against the identified total "customer solution." This bundling of products and services into a total customer solution frequently resets the table as far as competition is concerned. In this stage, care must be taken to identify what companies have the customer touchpoints, the organization speed to change from selling products to bundled solutions, the technology, and the operating or execution efficiencies to meet the customers total solution needs. In this stage, the lawn mower company would broaden its definition of competitors to all landscaping product manufacturers (e.g., trimmers, edgers, tillers). The professional services firm would identify all supply chain consulting firms that also perform systems integration services as well as technology companies that perform supply chain consulting services and integrate their own systems applications.

3. The third stage involves the identification of new competitors drawn into the marketplace by the bundling activity. For example, our lawn mower company should identify a total customer solution as a "garage solution." In this case, if Company A sells lawn mowers, in the future they may be competing against not only their existing landscaping accessory companies, but perhaps all car dealers, parts and supply companies (oil, filters, grass refuse bags, etc.), and even perhaps all storage racking companies. The professional services firm may find

competitors drawn into technology-enabled supply chain consulting from other "connected" solutions, such as SAP or Oracle and their Enterprise Resource Planning (ERP) systems.

4. The fourth stage involves the identification of non–total-customer solution providers that are intermediaries in the marketing process through technology. For example, our lawn mower company may also compete with someone like JC Penney through their eRetailing Web site. The professional services firm may find itself competing against a technology hardware company like IBM (or partnering with a firm like IBM or Cisco) that develops a consulting capability around the technology infrastructure or componentry that connects company to company and people to people in the supply chain network.

An executive can be overwhelmed in this stage with the possibilities. What matters here is that the companies with total solution products other than what your company carries, the companies with the best technology, the companies with the strongest brands, and the companies with the best financial health—all be identified as future or new potential competitors.

Step 3. Product Portfolio Assessment vs. Marketplace Scan

Once Step 1, Business and Market Strategy, and Step 2, Marketplace Scan are completed, it is critical to execute Step 3, Product Portfolio Assessment versus Marketplace Scan. In Step 1, the foundation is established in terms of where the board of directors, major stakeholders, and senior executives believe they want the company to be in a specified period of time. In Step 2, there is a determination as to where the competition is in terms of marketplace positioning. Step 3 identifies what the current products and services are in the company's product portfolio, and compares them to the current and perceived future positioning of competitors and their products and services.

In a world moving at Internet speed, many companies in this Step 3 find that a few key competitors are using technology and network supply chain methodologies to rapidly leapfrog their company and their existing products and services. Sometimes, companies discover that competitors have actually progressed beyond the company's vision of their current state, creating a precarious scenario for the company's senior executives. Imagine being a CEO and having the embarrassment of informing your shareholders and your employees that achieving your vision in two years will position your company behind where your key competitor is today!

In Step 3, the gap between the Business and Market Strategy, the Marketplace Scan, and the current Product Portfolio of the company is identified. More times than not, it is imperative to have speed in closing or eliminating this gap for the company to regain its competitive positioning in the marketplace.

In addition, in today's world, the creation and application of technology that transforms business processes in what seems to be an overnight time frame is frequently what creates this gap. Having access to the technology and its new products quickly can be one solution to close the gap in the marketplace with speed.

Let's revisit Northern Telecom/Nortel. Nortel entered into an alliance with Juniper Networks to have Nortel sell Juniper routers to Nortel's telecommunications customers. The Juniper routers were of high quality, were on the market today, and were configured into the Nortel solution. Nortel had a choice—either to compete with Juniper or to develop an alliance with Juniper. They decided to develop the alliance for reasons of speed to market and customer satisfaction.

Step 4. "Build Internally" vs. "Acquire Externally"

In Step 3, we discussed having access to technology and its products as one solution to help close the gap between the company's current product portfolio and the competitive positioning surfaced in the marketplace scan. The executive is faced with three choices.

1. Choice number one is to do nothing, and cede the specific market segment in question to a competitor. This is frequently not a very good choice, but sometimes a necessary and shrewd one. Nokia ceded the analog cellular telephone market to Motorola, to focus solely on the digital cellular telephone market. Due to the rapid pace of change in the technology, Nokia was able to leapfrog Motorola in the mobile communications device market when digital overtook analog.

2. Choice number two is to create or build the needed technology or products internally. Some companies, especially ones in the technology or high-tech industries, have the capability to internally build

capabilities at speed to match or lead the marketplace competition. For other companies, they either do not have the capability, the speed, or the "vision" match to accomplish this. For example, Nortel had the capability but did not have time on its side to develop and go to market with routers that Juniper already had. In another example, a professional services firm would not necessarily build a supply chain network suite of products internally because the marketplace starts to drive supply chain network innovations through collaborative planning and execution software. With the life cycle of technology software products, their solutions would be outdated by the time the firm went to market with them. Besides, if the vision of the professional services firm is to be the leading supply chain network solutions provider, then why would they want to get themselves into the software development business?

3. Choice number three is to "acquire externally" access to the technology products and services that drive the gap between the total customer solution and the company's existing products and services. Above and beyond a total acquisition of a company with these products and services, a company gains access to these products and services through alliances.

One element that must be considered in all three choices is the cost/benefit analysis. Nokia could have built internally the best-in-class analog cellular telephone and competed head-on with Motorola, but where was the return? In another scenario, if it is cheaper to acquire externally, then why build internally? Or vice versa? If build internally is an option, then you must complete a cost/benefit analysis.

Step 5. Organizational Readiness and Speed to Market Demand

Another area that needs to be explored quickly is the organizational readiness to build internally and create these needed products and services with Internet speed to meet the current and anticipated market demand. For the executive, this Step 5 is usually a quick, decision-tree process. For the products and services in question, the answer is usually a clear "yes" or "no" for executives as they assess the organizational readiness of their organization. Ask yourself how fast your organization is in responding to or leading your competition in technology-enabled innovative solutions in the marketplace?

Speed to market may be more beneficial than a lower cost but a longer time-to-market connected to "build internally." The capability to build internally, the connectivity to the vision of the company, the cost/benefit associated with build internally, and the organizational readiness to move at Internet speed to meet the market demand all play a role in the decision to build internally or acquire externally.

Step 6. Proceed to "Build Internally" or "Acquire Externally"

The answers gathered in Steps 4 and 5 will provide a clear choice for either building internally or acquiring externally. To acquire externally, a new process must be followed to ensure that the right products and services that complete the total customer solution are accessed in a manner that the market positioning of the two companies are simultaneously enhanced and the company's operations are enriched and not degraded by the relationship.

Framework to Determine What Type of Alliance Is Needed

The framework to determine what type of alliance is needed is a high-level framework that will be discussed throughout the book. You can get a flavor of how to determine the type of alliance your company needs by answering the five questions listed in Exhibit 1-1. Each question is reflected in a separate step in the framework, with the last step pulling the framework together.

Step 1. Do You Need an Alliance That Is Sales-Based?

All alliances must be directly or indirectly sales- and client-based. Alliances must generate additional sales for both alliance partners in order to be successful. This includes solution-based alliances, geographic-specific alliances, investment alliances, and joint ventures. If the answer to this question is "no" to any type of alliance, then the potential

Exhibit 1-1. Framework questionnaire: What type of alliance is needed?

Question	Type of Alliance				
	Sales	Solution	Geography	Investment	Joint Venture
Do you need an alliance that is sales- and client-based?	Y	Y	Y	Y	Y
Is there the need for joint solution development?	N	Y	N	Y	Y
Is the need geographic-based?	N	N	Y	N	Y
Is there a necessity for a direct investment in the external company?	N	N	N	Y	Y
Is there an overriding reason to set up a separate company to acquire the needed products and services from the external provider?	N	N	N	N	Y

alliance partner should consider a "work for hire" arrangement with the other company. For the matrix in Exhibit 1-1, all blocks should be filled in with a "Y" for yes to the question, "Do you need an alliance that is sales-based?"

Step 2. Is There a Need for Joint Solution Development?

In Step 2, the field begins to narrow. There is no need for joint solution development in a sales alliance. There is also no need for joint solution development with a geographic-specific alliance. For these two questions, an "N" is entered in the appropriate spaces.

However, there is a need for joint solution development in a solution-specific alliance. In addition, investment alliances and joint ventures rely on joint solution development as a cornerstone for their alliances. As a result, a "Y" is entered under solution-specific alliances, investment alliances, and joint venture alliances.

Step 3. Is the Need Geographic-Based?

Sales-based alliances usually focus on products and services, although there are occasions when a sales-based alliance can be geographic-based. Solution-specific alliances are not geographic-based. Investment alliances are generally not geographic-based as well. Geographic-specific alliances and joint ventures usually have needs that are geographic-based. As such, an "N" is entered under sales, solution-specific, and investment, and a "Y" is entered under geographic-specific and joint venture.

Step 4. Is There a Necessity for a Direct Investment in the External Company?

Sales alliances, geographic-based alliances, and solution-specific alliances do not require direct investments. Investment alliances and joint ventures generally do require direct investments in an alliance partner. An "N" is placed under sales, solution-specific, and geographic-specific, and a "Y" is entered under investment and joint venture. Direct investment should be defined as an investment in capital for this framework.

Step 5. Is There an Overriding Reason to Set Up a Company to Acquire the Needed Products and Services from the External Provider?

There are many reasons why alliance partners may need to set up a separate company. We will cover these reasons throughout this book. Here, when there is an overriding reason to set up a separate company, a "Y" should be entered under joint venture.

For all other columns, an "N" should be placed in answer to this question. There is no overriding reason why a sales, geographic-specific, solution-specific, or an investment alliance needs to set up a company to acquire the needed products and services from the external provider.

Step 6. Pulling Together the Answers from the Framework

To pull the answers together from the matrix in Exhibit 1-1, first look horizontally at the type of alliance applied to the question, and then look vertically by alliance to see the makeup of each alliance as framed by the questions. The completed matrix should follow the key in Exhibit 1-1, with the pattern of "Y's" and "N's" directing the framework user to the type of alliance that is needed by the alliance partners.

Real-World Examples

Lost in Space!

Two companies that two years ago entered into a solution-specific alliance could not wait to join forces and jointly develop a next-generation technology solution. Their two teams got together, mapped out the solution at a high level, and even crafted a joint press release announcing their alliance. However, they forgot one important item. They did not consider the need for a sales or client-based alliance. Before the alliance agreement was executed, the executives of one company demanded a sales plan for the alliance. When a sales plan could not be provided, the alliance was postponed. Had these two companies used the above framework, they would have placed an "N" for sales- or client-based under the solution-specific column. The lack of a match to the framework would have raised a red flag as to the validity of the type of alliance needed by these two companies.

Heading in Different Directions?

A very different challenge faced two other companies that decided several years ago to create an alliance based on the creation of a small but important piece of technology. One company invested in the alliance, and the two companies set out working with each other in a variety of ways.

One year into the two-year alliance agreement, very little progress had been made with the alliance. The creator (and CEO of one company) of the small piece of technology was getting nervous, because he knew that he only had little time left to be first to market with this new technology. The other company was bewildered as to how this small piece of technology fit into a business solution model to drive measurable business value to clients.

As a result, one company was attempting to steer the alliance into a sales mode, while the other company was trying to steer the alliance into a joint solution development direction. While these two companies were progressing in different directions, time was moving on. The marketplace was moving, and so was the timeline for the alliance agreement.

The two companies did get together and mapped out what type of alliance was needed. The answer was a difficult one, but they agreed to proceed along parallel paths in two directions. They agreed to jointly develop a marketplace solution that encompassed and embraced the new piece of technology. They also agreed to target a select number of accounts to actively begin sales cycles while they were jointly developing these marketplace solutions.

It is a difficult position to be in when you are in the middle of an alliance agreement and discover the need to start over. There was a lot of pressure on these two companies to pull this alliance out of the ditch, so to speak. But luckily, there was enough executive support to place the proper resources on the parallel activities to create a success out of a troubled relationship. However, in today's fast-moving environment, it is not advisable to rely on heroic actions to create successful alliances.

The two companies would have benefited immensely from following the two frameworks outlined in this chapter. The framework to determine the need for the alliance may have been done internally by each of these companies. They should have shared at a high level the reasons for creating the alliance, developed their concentric areas of need, and proceeded through the framework to determine what type of alliance was needed. This would have placed emphasis on developing both a joint solution with the small but important piece of technology and an aggressive sales plan to protect the "first to market" status for the technology. It would have also allowed each alliance partner to generate early momentum for the alliance agreement within each of the alliance partner's organizations. Instead, the only momentum that was created was a momentum of crisis management. The lesson learned here is not to pass out fire extinguishers instead of ceremonial pens when both parties sign an alliance agreement!

Summary

In a world moving at Internet speed, fewer and fewer companies can survive and thrive by being all things to all people. The days of total vertical integration are rapidly diminishing as the pace of technology creation and innovation accelerates. The need to rapidly recognize the need for alliance partners and then select the right alliance partner may mean the difference between being a world-class company and an average company. It may even mean disappearing from the competitive landscape in the worst-case scenario!

The Framework to Determine the *Need* for an Alliance provides a road map to determine whether or not an alliance is needed. When it has been decided that an alliance is needed, the Framework to Determine What *Type* of Alliance Is Needed provides a road map into the five types of alliances. The combination of the two frameworks provides a sound way to begin the journey to establish successful alliances.

The ability to know how to create, implement, and disband alliances is a critical success factor for world-class companies. This ability is an art and a science. This book is designed to demystify the process to establish successful alliances, and to provide the reader with the frameworks and the real world examples to establish their own successful alliances. Let's begin the journey!

Notes

1. *Webster's New World Dictionary and Thesaurus* (New York: Simon & Schuster, 1996), p. 16.
2. Ibid.
3. Amy Kover, "Why *Brandwise* Was Brand Foolish, *Fortune* magazine, November 13, 2000, pp. 201–8.
4. www.molson.com/home/main.ghtml.investorrelations.
5. Christopher Bowe, "Maytag Brings in Former Chief to Replace Ward," *Financial Times*, November 10, 2000, p. 25.

6. Kover, pp. 201–8.
7. Adam Lashinsky, "Valley Keiretsu: Beware 'Alliances,'" *Fortune* magazine, November 13, 2000, p. 451.
8. Kover, p. 208.
9. News release: "Maytag.com Gives Consumers the Ride of Their Lives with Cart-to-Cart Shopping," Maytag Appliances, Newton, Iowa, January 31, 2001, pp. 1, 2.
10. www.sears.com/SearsHomeCentral.
11. Interview with Diane Ritchey, Editor, *Appliance Magazine,* April 2001.

CHAPTER TWO

Great Idea,
but How Do I Get Started?

The meeting started on time, which was amazing because of the weather. It was a snowy February day in a suburb of Detroit, and people had to travel from all over the Detroit area to attend the meeting. Representatives from all the major automotive assemblers were in attendance, in addition to key automotive parts suppliers. Some of the attendees had flown in from warm Los Angeles, cold Stuttgart, and chilly Tokyo, especially for this meeting.

The purpose of the meeting was to review the possibility of an aftermarket parts exchange or marketplace. The concept was to have multiple companies share in an infrastructure that would enable the acquisition and movement of aftermarket parts from manufacturer to customer. This infrastructure would be technology-enabled, and follow the networked supply chain design.

The opening of the meeting consisted of introductions. The atmosphere was light, dominated by small talk about families, the snow, and the new cars hitting the marketplace. For people who like concept cars, there is no better place in the Americas than Detroit. For that matter, there may be no better place in the world for people who love cars, period! No matter what meeting, the talk in the Motor City will usually migrate to cars, then the weather.

As I looked around the meeting room, I noticed that there were almost as many lawyers in attendance as there were company attendees. The lawyers tended to be quiet—even in the face of some lawyer jokes—usually just stating their names and the companies they were representing.

After the introductions, the two key executives who coordinated the meeting started discussing the meeting agenda. They had worked feverishly with each meeting participant to establish a collaborative agenda, designed to address nonmarketplace differentiating infrastructure issues around the aftermarket parts networked supply chain. Before they were done discussing the agenda, one of the lawyers asked to speak. He then stated that he was advising his company representative not to proceed with the meeting for several reasons. At the top of his list were the lack of the proper nondisclosure agreements and the risk of violating antitrust laws.

Before the two executives could address his concerns, a few more lawyers raised the same concerns. The executives from the competing companies became quiet as if so instructed, and their silence was deafening. The meeting had come to a close before it had even started.

The two executives had taken great care in establishing the agenda and avoiding what they thought were issues surrounding collusion or antitrust. But in spite of being directionally correct, they had failed in two areas. First, they had failed to involve their legal departments when they began to work with direct competitors. And second, they had established an agenda that focused on getting operational as quickly as possible, but in a rush to create immediate cash flow had minimized the proper planning steps.

The concept of establishing an industrywide global networked supply chain for the physical movement of aftermarket parts is a great idea. The physical infrastructure (warehouses, material handling equipment, parts containers, tractor-trailers) and the systems infrastructure (data centers, servers, network architecture, and systems applications) are both expensive and nonmarketplace differentiating. The idea to build a common physical and systems infrastructure for all competitors to share would reduce everyone's costs—without providing a marketplace differentiator to any one selected competitor. The only exceptions would be the competitor who already has a world-class aftermarket parts infrastructure or the competitor who makes the decision not to join the consortium.

Covisint: Competitors Becoming Partners the Right Way!

There is a real-life e-business trading exchange within the automotive industry that took the right steps to get operational. This e-business trading exchange is called Covisint.

Covisint was announced in February 2000 by founding partners DaimlerChrysler, Ford Motor Company, General Motors, Renault/Nissan, and other Technology Partners, Technology Providers, a Consulting Partner, and Business Partners (see Exhibit 2-1). The intent of Covisint is to provide the automotive Original Equipment Manufacturers (OEMs) and suppliers the ability to reduce supply chain costs and improve efficiencies in their business operations. Areas of focus are the procurement process, production requirement visibility, and collaborative product design.[1]

In September 2000, Covisint announced that the Federal Trade Commission (FTC) had concluded its investigation, clearing the way for Covisint to be operational. "The completion of the FTC review represents a significant milestone in our efforts to establish a transformational business-to-business entity. After a thorough investigation, the FTC understood that the parties forming Covisint have always intended to operate in full compliance with the antitrust laws," said Alice Miles, Covisint Executive Planning Team.[2]

In December 2000, Covisint announced its transformation from a planning organization to a Delaware LLC (limited liability corporation), called Covisint LLC. It is now a multimember joint venture,

Exhibit 2-1. Covisint Partners.

Founding Partners	*Business Partners*
DaimlerChrysler	AK Steel Corporation
Ford Motor Company	ArvinMeritor, Inc.
General Motors	Autoliv Inc.
Renault/Nissan	BASF
	BorgWarner, Inc.
Technology Partners	Collins & Aikman Corporation
Commerce One	Dana Corporation
Oracle	Delphi Automotive Systems
	DENSO International America
Technology Providers	Dura Automotive Systems, Inc.
Documentum, Inc.	Federal-Mogul Corporation
Engineering Animation, Inc.	Flex-N-Gate Corporation
NexPrise, Inc.	Freudenberg-NOK
	Johnson Controls, Inc.
Consulting Partner	Lear Corporation
Cap Gemini Ernst & Young US LLC	Magna International Inc.
	Tower Automotive, Inc.
	Visteon Corporation
	Yazaki North America, Inc.

Source: *www.Covisint.com/info/partners*, pp. 1–8; and confirmation conversations with Covisint executives in February 2001.

with DaimlerChrysler, Ford Motor Company, General Motors, Nissan, Renault, Commerce One, and Oracle as members.[3]

The game isn't over, but experts are betting that Covisint has the right plan, the right financial backing, the right partners, and the proper legal clearance to succeed. Imagine, an e-business trading exchange succeeding with competitors as founding partners of the joint venture. How did Covisint get this far while so many other e-business trading exchanges have failed?

Covisint carefully mapped out its concept, announced its intentions to form an e-business trading exchange, and then detailed its business plan for review by the FTC. The founding partners took all the necessary precautions to create Covisint within the confines of the antitrust laws and the Federal Trade Commission. In addition, Covisint took care to select the right technology partners, technology providers, consulting partner, and business partners as they progressed from announcement to FTC clearance to corporate entity. In other words, they took the right amount of planning time before they initiated their operations.

Select the Right Partner, then Construct the Right Alliance Agreement

Taking the proper time to plan is absolutely essential for success in establishing an alliance. The selection of the right partner and the construction of the right alliance agreement will make or break any solution that an alliance is designed to support. (As my Dad always told me, do it right or do not do it at all!) We discussed earlier in Chapter One the process to determine the type of alliance needed. The review should then proceed to look at companies that have complimentary products and services to comprise the potential marketplace solution.

Constructing an Alliance Agreement

Once the type of alliance has been determined and a potential partner has been identified, the process should shift to constructing an alliance agreement. The alliance agreement template presented at the end of this chapter outlines in detail many of the basic sections, provisions, and items found in most alliance agreements. It is intended to be a guideline and to illustrate the types of terms and conditions that must be discussed and agreed upon before going to market as "alliance partners."

The construction of an alliance agreement takes time and involvement from both the leaders of the parties and the lawyers. In addition, the business terms must be defined before the lawyers work their magic with the legal terms.

An alliance agreement also helps companies get started with alliances and allows alliance partners to evolve from a start-up stage to an emerge stage. It sets the guidelines for how the two alliance partners will behave organizationally, and sets the base for all other alliance documents to be developed.

It is absolutely essential that alliance partners take the proper time and care to construct the alliance agreement in the right manner. It is this document that everyone will rely on to do business and guide the joint behavior of the alliance employees. As we will see in future chapters, the operations of alliances involve doing business in multiple ways. The alliance agreement will provide a business and legal anchor for the future business opportunities between the two alliance partners. As such, it is important that the right process be used to approve all alliance agreements. Let's take a look at a suggested process for companies to approve alliance agreements.

Process to Approve Alliance Agreements

In addition to the proper time and care to construct an alliance agreement, companies must also have a solid process to approve alliance agreements (see Exhibit 2-2). A process to approve alliance agreements needs to include the following steps in order to be consistently successful.

Alliance Approval Committee

There needs to be an alliance approval committee that governs the entire alliance process. This committee should consist of a cross-section of leaders from multiple departments and divisions, and include representation from the legal department. This committee should meet either as needed, or on a regularly scheduled basis (e.g., every two weeks). It should review the business need, the legal compliance, and the proper approvals of the leaders from the submitting and impacted departments. This committee should also recommend the makeup of the alliance performance steering committee.

There are those companies that rely on a single strong-willed individual to accomplish all of this in lieu of a committee. In some respects, this might work. However, people do get sick, take vacations, and sometimes switch jobs. The downside to having one person do all of this is that the process is only as good or as available as the person!

Business Need Review

The alliance approval committee must review the business need for the alliance. This review may include the results of the framework to

Exhibit 2-2. Process to approve alliance agreements.

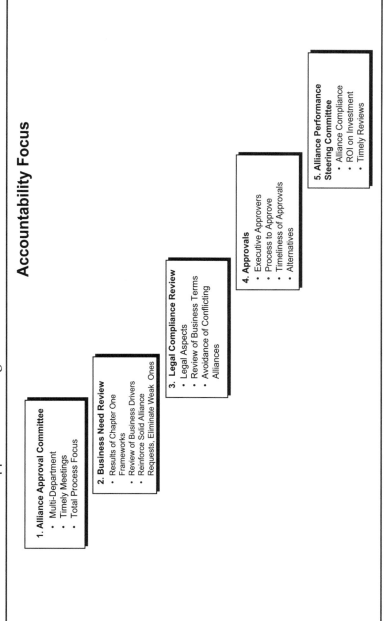

Accountability Focus

1. Alliance Approval Committee
- Multi-Department
- Timely Meetings
- Total Process Focus

2. Business Need Review
- Results of Chapter One Frameworks
- Review of Business Drivers
- Reinforce Solid Alliance Requests, Eliminate Weak Ones

3. Legal Compliance Review
- Legal Aspects
- Review of Business Terms
- Avoidance of Conflicting Alliances

4. Approvals
- Executive Approvers
- Process to Approve
- Timeliness of Approvals
- Alternatives

5. Alliance Performance Steering Committee
- Alliance Compliance
- ROI on Investment
- Timely Reviews

Source: Cap Gemini Ernst & Young.

determine the need for an alliance, as introduced in Chapter One. It may also include a detailed review of the business drivers behind the request to form an alliance. In either case, the process to present the business need for an alliance will strengthen a solid alliance request or eliminate a weak alliance request.

Legal Compliance Review

The lawyers must perform their review, and they should be included from the initial discussions with an alliance partner. Lawyers will have to do two sets of reviews. The first set has to do with the legal aspects of the alliance, many of which were discussed earlier in the chapter. In addition, the lawyers must perform a business terms review. This is necessary to ensure that the legal terms of an agreement map to the business terms desired by the executives of the company. As such, leading companies usually have the lawyers perform their legal reviews, and then have their lawyers be part of the alliance approval committee to participate in the review of the business need for the alliance.

Approvals

Companies do want accountability for alliances. It is critical to align these accountabilities with executives. This is generally done through the authorization of approval authority for alliances, which must be established at the start of the process. The approval levels in a company will vary company by company. They will be known, however, within the executive ranks of most companies. These approvals will also vary by type of alliance. For example, a vice president of sales and marketing may have the highest business approval for a sales alliance, whereas joint ventures may have to be approved by the chief executive officer or the board of directors.

What is also needed is a process to secure these approvals in an expedited manner. For example, one company places the approval process for all programs and alliances on an internal Web site for all executives. These programs and alliances are placed on the Web site over the weekend, and are available for the first approver on Monday morning. The executive has twenty-four hours to approve or deny the request. Any executives who fail to get on the network, access the Web site, and enter their approvals or denials are skipped in the approval process. A preapproved vote through the office of the chief financial officer on the Friday before the posting of the programs and alliances is the only way executives can vote in absentia. Otherwise, they lose their privilege to vote through inaction.

The chief executive officer of this particular company decided to institute this process because she felt that the executives were not demonstrating a sense of urgency to respond to marketplace opportunities. I know that some of these executives missed voting early in the process, and found themselves accepting outcomes they wished were different. However, it generally took only one miss on a critical program or alliance to instill a sense of discipline in the process!

Alliance Performance Steering Committee

During the alliance approval process, the members of the alliance performance steering committee need to be selected. This committee should meet on a periodic and timely basis, and should focus on measuring the effective return on their investments into the alliance.

The performance of alliances should be measured in two ways. The first way is the straight-up way with hard numbers on both the investment and the return sides of the equation. The second way is more subjective. It should answer the question, "Is my firm better off with the alliance than without the alliance?" Both measurements are important, and must be calculated or answered through the alliance performance steering committee.

Alliances—Not for the Weak-Hearted

The multicompany group that came together to discuss the industry-wide business to business (B2B) marketplace for automotive aftermarket parts had another chance for a second meeting. This time, the lawyers were briefed in plenty of time to make things happen from a legal standpoint. With some advanced warning, the lawyers were able to keep a good idea afloat and maintain momentum with the participants.

However, as we have seen, the construction of an alliance agreement does not happen overnight. An alliance agreement takes a concentrated effort on both sides to identify and establish the business and legal terms for the alliance partners to operate. Preparation is critical to the success or failure of any alliance. The old advertising slogan, "Pay me now, or pay me later," really does apply. The effort to carefully craft an alliance agreement will pay immense dividends for all involved as the alliance grows and expands. Conversely, a poorly planned alliance agreement can cause a company significant monetary and resource penalties if troubles arise.

There are also the normal business cycles with day-to-day business. During a recent alliance review at a Mediterranean seaside resort with members of one of our alliances, my mind drifted to the start-up of the alliance two years before that meeting. At this time, our firm was the newcomer, joining a very crowded alliance group. We struggled to get an equal share of mind and attention, and although our intent was positive, our newness relegated us to an opportunistic versus strategic alliance.

During the year preceding the review meeting, our firm had made a major acquisition, which in essence doubled our size. Conversely, our alliance partner's growth rate had slowed down considerably. As such, I felt during this meeting by the Mediterranean that our alliance partner was actively pursuing us with the intent on expanding our strategic relationship. This was the exact opposite of the relationship we had a year ago.

Was the change in our relationship attributed to our doubling in size? Was it the new demographics of our firm? Was the slowdown in growth of our alliance partner responsible for their willingness to expand our alliance relationship? Perhaps it was a combination of all of these factors that contributed to this change in attitude. However, there was an even greater factor involved.

Privately, one of the senior executives told me that his company was very opportunistic in its high-growth days, and that it was not the best of partners. He went on to say that with growth slowing, his company started taking a longer-term view of its partners, and desired to invest into their alliance relationships. He stated that he wanted these alliance relationships to truly be strategic, and to focus on the joint strengths of both alliance companies. When his company reviewed its alliance relationships, they decided to pick the firms that had dedicated people to their alliance for enhanced, strategic relationships. He also told me that the fact that our firm had kept the same alliance leaders in place during the past two years was a sign of strong commitment to their company regardless of good or bad times.

Thus, there were several factors involved in the change in the alliance relationship. However, there is a strong message here. As you embark on establishing an alliance with another company, answer the following question:

> Is my company willing to commit the time, energy, and resources necessary to make the alliance a long-term success?

The construction of the alliance agreement should evolve around the answer to this question. The alliance agreement should reflect whether the intent of your particular alliance is short-term and opportunistic, or longer-term and strategic. If it is the latter, then your company should dedicate the proper resources and be prepared to stick with the alliance through good times and bad throughout the duration of the alliance agreement. No matter where in the world business is done, the nature of alliances is relationship-driven. Relationships do transcend deals over time (although deals are necessary to keep all of us employed short-term). The return on an investment in alliance relationships, if done properly with the right companies, the right leaders, and the right economic environment, should be in the form of consistent, repetitive revenue flows. All of this is important to remember when constructing an alliance and its associated alliance agreement with another company.

Summary

There are a lot of alliances announced in press releases every week. It seems that not a week goes by without someone announcing in *The Wall Street Journal* or on the Financial News Network an alliance that will come close to solving world hunger or finding a cure for cancer. Frequently, this is the last we hear about these alliances. Do you ever wonder what happens to these alliances post–press release?

It is evident that many companies are run by very strong, operationally focused executives who want immediate action and immediate results. Alliances can significantly reduce the amount of time a company can get to market with a solution, and, as such, can significantly reduce the amount of time from solution concept to generating results. However, without the right amount of planning and construction of an alliance agreement, the risk of failure with an alliance increases significantly.

Alliances are focused on influencing the behavior of others for the benefit of both the customer and the companies that are the alliance partners. It is not about utilizing command and control directives to "execute or else" against a set of objectives handed down from above. The alliance agreement will help establish the set of guidelines for companies to work together. A right alliance agreement will free up employees from both companies to focus on the marketplace solution, and avoid having these same employees try to command and control each other every time an opportunity surfaces. The world is changing, and there is a pot at the end of the rainbow for those who know how to create and execute strong alliances.

The selection of the right alliance partner and taking the right amount of time to construct the alliance agreement should both be complemented by establishing the right process to approve the alliance agreement. This process to approve the alliance agreement should lead to the commitment to either an opportunistic or strategic alliance.

Once again, the alliance agreement outlined in this chapter is a template for your use. The actual alliance agreement that you would use may in fact only resemble a part of what is discussed in this chapter. It is absolutely critical that you work with your legal departments and secure from them the alliance template that your company would want to use. Each company and each industry has its own unique situations that need to be addressed. The lawyers are usually well trained in what works and what doesn't work for their respective companies. Don't wait until deadlines are upon you before involving the lawyers. In addition, ask them to help explain the alliance agreement templates and the intent behind each item. This will help immensely as you embark on alliance discussions with your potential partner.

Alliances are also all about relationships. These relationships are company-to-company, solution-to-solution, and culture-to-culture. Most importantly, successful alliances are driven by executive-to-executive and salesperson-to-salesperson relationships. These relationships are built over time, and require consistent, dedicated executives who are present during good times and bad times. The critical nature of relationships within alliances should not be lost during the construction of the alliance agreement. In fact, it should be front and center throughout the process.

How to Construct an Alliance Agreement

The following is a step-by-step process that covers many of the basic sections of a legal, formal, alliance agreement . This process is designed to give you a template for constructing the draft of such an agreement. *(Author's note: You should always work with your legal department or legal counsel to get the right legal support for your company, your alliance, and your protection before entering into a formal, legal alliance.)*

Opening Paragraph

The opening paragraph should state the legal names of the parties entering into the alliance agreement. It should also identify the agreed-to execution date of the agreement.

Background

The background statement should clearly state the intent of the alliance agreement. For example, "Company A desires to enhance its professional services revenues by offering services in connection to Company B's software products." Another example may read, "Company A and Company B desire to formalize their relationship by entering into this agreement to deliver integrated transformational solutions to their mutual customers."

It is advisable to state the intent of the alliance agreement from more than one viewpoint. It is entirely probable that the two examples identified above could be used together to describe the intent of one alliance agreement. The more specific the statement describes the intent of the alliance agreement, the less chance there is to dispute the intent in the future.

1. Definitions

To a layman like myself, the "definitions" section represents a boring description of the obvious. To the lawyer, this is a critical section to keep people like myself out of trouble. The following terms are representative of terms that could possibly be included in the "definitions" section.

Agreement Date represents the official date of the execution of the document. *Products* and *Services* describe in detail the products and services involved in the alliance agreement. These two are critical items, because the next item— "proprietary information"—builds on the detailed description of the products and services and identifies how each party can ascertain the nature of what is "proprietary."

Many alliance agreements further describe what is proprietary by identifying what is NOT proprietary. (Confucius lives on!) Two examples of this are as follows:

> Information is not Proprietary Information to the extent that it was in the public domain at the time of the party's communication thereof to the other party.
>   and
> Information is not Proprietary Information to the extent that it is approved for release by written authorization of the originating party.

These two examples are important to review. The first example establishes public domain as a safe harbor for both parties to work with each other's products and services. This is why it is very important to have internal safeguards as to what information to hand out to customers, what information should be placed on Web pages, and so forth. When in doubt, don't distribute sensitive information to a third party without an agreement. Even when working with alliance partners, mark sensitive information as "sensitive—material owned by Company A."

The second example involves written approval to have and use what would be otherwise termed "proprietary information." By securing written approval, an alliance partner is released from liability connected with having possession of this material.

2. Authorization

In this section, the two parties come to agreement on several items. The first item is usually an agreement on the authority to use each other's names. This authority can be given for internal communications, for external marketing programs, or for external sales-related activities. Usually, the authority granted to use each other's name is governed by communications standards provided by each partner and is subject to the terms of the overall agreement.

Another item covered in "Authorization" is the subject of exclusivity. The parties in the agreement can enter into one of three types of arrangements—exclusive, preferred, or general—depending upon the business need and the competitive environment. If not exclusive, the parties need to include language that protects concepts and proprietary and/or confidential information gained through working with each other.

A third item, which is very important, is the subject of contracting with customers. This section provides the language that covers how each party in the agreement will work with the other when contracting with customers. There are three scenarios that must be considered. The first is where Company A is the prime contractor with the customer, and company B subcontracts to Company A. The second is where Company B subcontracts to Company A. The third is where both Company A and Company B work together to provide a complete solution to a customer, but they each contract separately with the customer for their respective products and services.

3. Services and Responsibilities of Company A

For this example, let's say that Company A sells software. This section would cover several services and responsibilities. Software licenses can be granted to Company B for demonstrations to clients, for internal training, for evaluation purposes, and for support of the delivery of the products to the customers. The product support and maintenance for software provided to Company B should be covered as well.

Consideration should be given to Company B regarding the early release of software by Company A for evaluation and training purposes. In conjunction with this, language may be established concerning the certification of Company B employees on the new software.

Another critical area is software product support for sales pursuits and marketing events. This is important, because a technology-driven business solution needs software product support and business solution expertise. Actual customer sales pursuits and marketing events should both be included in the agreement.

Another item that can be covered here is the dedication of personnel to support the alliance between the two companies. By placing the commitment in print, the assignment of personnel becomes the responsibility of Company A. This is important, because business conditions do change.

4. Services and Responsibilities of Company B

In this example, let's say Company B provides business or consulting services. This section would cover training and the responsibilities around certification. The two companies can agree on training expenses and "rules of the road" regarding the placement of trained personnel on competitor projects.

This section can also address the control of Company A software under the control of Company B. It should also address how Company B should present Company A software to customers. The agreement can range from a complete reselling agreement with pricing authority granted to Company B to a very limited condition for presenting Company A software without the presence of Company A personnel.

This section should also cover the services and responsibilities of Company B in the business solution expertise support in sales pursuits and marketing events. Just as technology-driven solutions need software product support, so do software product sales need business solution expertise.

The dedication of Company B personnel to support the alliance activities should also be included in this section. This commitment of personnel should be collaboratively linked to the dedication of personnel by Company A, as committed to in Section 3. Remember, nothing happens until people make it happen. As such, it takes people to make things happen!

5. Services and Responsibilities of Both Parties

There are several items that need to be covered under services and responsibilities of both parties. The sharing of pertinent market information should be included, as well as the process to communicate this information on a timely basis. In addition, new product information and other pertinent events should be shared as they occur.

The development of a joint business plan is a solid example of a joint responsibility. This section should detail how the joint business plan should be developed, what it should contain, and the goals of the plan. The parties should also agree on how often the business plan should be reviewed and modified, and how the business plan should be communicated throughout each other's organizations.

6. Representations, Warranties, Disclaimers, and Limitations

Just like the "Definitions" section, this section is important, though boring to nonlawyers like me. The representations and warranties section represents and warrants that each party has the right and power to enter into the agreement. It also ensures that entering this agreement does not violate the terms and conditions of other agreements. It also provides for each party to warrant that the information provided does not infringe upon any proprietary right (copyright, trademark, etc.) of any third party.

This section also covers limits of liability. This is especially important for alliance partners as they join forces to jointly sell solutions to the marketplace. Frequently, liability is limited to direct damages, lost profits, and other damages to a specific level. The exceptions are for breach of confidentiality, unauthorized use of proprietary or confidential information, death or personal injury due to negligence or willful misconduct, and other related events and actions.

7. Term and Termination

This section usually covers four main items. The first item is the initial term of the agreement. The initial term commences on the *agreement date*, or agreed-to execution date (see opening paragraph). The initial term expires on an agreed-to date, frequently on a yearly anniversary (one year, two years, etc.) of the agreement date. For large, long-term efforts like Covisint, it is not uncommon to have the term of an alliance agreement run five years or longer. It all depends upon the nature of the alliance and the potential marketplace opportunity for the alliance partners.

The second item to be covered in this section is the *renewal term*. Usually there is a period of time preceding the expiration date (say thirty days) during which the two parties will decide to renew or terminate the alliance agreement. Renewal can depend upon the success in attaining the goals in the joint business plan or upon the continued potential value of the alliance partnership. Some alliance agreements call for expiration of the agreement unless the two parties agree to renew the agreement. Other alliance agreements call for the reverse—automatic renewal of the alliance agreement unless the two parties agree to review potential expiration or termination of the agreement. Either approach will work, depending upon the business needs of the companies and the past practice of their legal departments.

The third item covered is *termination* of the agreement. One area that must be included in the agreement is termination due to cause or material breach of the agreement. Frequently, one company will give the other company a period of time (thirty, sixty, or even ninety days) to fix the material breach before exercising the termination option. This notice to fix a material breach is almost always done in writing.

Another cause for termination is the material change of the company. Mergers, acquisitions, investments into each other and into competing companies and substantial asset sales are all material changes to a company. Sometimes, after a merger or acquisition, a company will "assign" alliance agreements to the new corporate entity. However, when the new entity takes on a different corporate identity and or its mission is not aligned with the old company's identity and mission, it may significantly alter the value of the alliance relationship and agreement.

Beyond the events mentioned above, there is usually an *exit* clause that allows either party to terminate the agreement without cause. There is normally a lengthy written notice clause attached to this clause (90 to 120 days) to protect one company from the other's actions.

The fourth item is the terms covering the *effect of expiration* of the agreement or termination. The wording in this item usually calls for the cessation of all joint marketing and advertising, in addition to any activities that suggest a continuing relationship under the agreement. The return of materials furnished to each party is also covered in this item. Under these terms, there are usually clauses that protect the alliance relationship on an ongoing basis when customers are involved. In addition, certain items usually survive the expiration or termination of the agreement. These items include representations, warranties, disclaimers, limitations of liability, the term and termination, the relationship of the parties, intellectual property rights, confidentiality of proprietary information, and general provisions. Some of these items will be covered in the upcoming sections.

8. Relationship of Parties

There are a few items in this section that are critical to how the two parties behave in the marketplace. The first item covers whether the two parties are "business partners" or "independent contractors." *Business partners* have the right to either represent or commit to the performance or delivery by the other party. There are tight restrictions that usually govern this behavior (e.g., schedule of rates for agreed-to products and services). *Independent contractors* do not have the right to represent or commit the other party. Sometimes, there is language that governs the use of the words "partner" and "joint venture," which may indicate the authority to commit the other party.

The second item builds on the first item and refers to *distribution rights*. Frequently, this section of the alliance agreement covers the issue of pricing with customers. The two parties can either agree to negotiate pricing with customers for each other (again on a mutually agreed-to schedule of rates for defined products and services) or specify that each party has the sole responsibility to negotiate their own pricing. *This is a critical item that governs alliance behavior!* Be specific and clear when agreeing to the issue of pricing for one's products and services. It can mean the difference of profit or loss, and even, in extreme cases, survival.

The last item covered in this section has to do with subsidiaries and affiliates. They are either included in the agreement by mandate from the corporate office, or party to the alliance agreement through a "subsidiary" or "affiliate agreement" that attaches to the alliance agreement.

9. Intellectual Property Rights

Another critical section of the alliance agreement covers the subject of intellectual property rights. From companies that are world leaders in the application for patents (e.g., General Electric) to networked supply chain content leaders (e.g., Cap Gemini Ernst & Young US LLC) to supply chain software application leaders (e.g., i2 Technologies) the protection of trademarks, service marks, and logos is critical to the protection of the intellectual content behind these items. Frequently, authority is granted to use certain items that are involved with co-marketing or joint advertising of products and services. There is usually a clause that calls for written permission to use each other's trademarks, service marks, or logos beyond the identi-fied boundaries described in this section.

There is also language in this section that should cover the joint creation of new intellectual property that relies on existing intellectual property owned by either or both parties. For ex-ample, Company A may contribute their process flow method-ologies and Company B may contribute their networked supply chain technology to create a wireless networked supply chain. In this agreement, there should be language for Company A to retain the rights to their process flow methodologies and for Company B to retain the rights to their networked supply chain technology. This language should consider this intellectual property as "confidential or proprietary information." As far as the newly developed wireless networked supply chain, the two parties could co-own what was co-developed and be free to use what was co-developed, as long as it did not include the intellectual property that was considered "confidential or pro-prietary information."

Consideration should also be given to how the two parties will handle working with each other's intellectual property. In joint solutions to customers, it may be necessary to modify each other's intellectual property to "customize" a solution for a customer. The two parties need to narrow the acceptable range of working on each other's intellectual property so that there is no infringement on the intellectual property rights of the company owning the rights.

There is also a related issue surrounding the creation of a competing product or service. For example, take a huge com-pany like General Electric, with its many diverse and autono-mous divisions and subsidiaries—including GE Capital, which makes investments in numerous companies and industries. It would be entirely possible for one GE company to have an alliance with an outside company, while another GE company or GE Capital investment creates a competing product or ser-vice with the outside company alliance partner. There should be language in the agreement that protects large companies like General Electric if this occurs. (General Electric, which does work very hard to avoid this situation, is used only as an exam-ple because of its size and diverse divisions.) However, there should also be language that calls for the substantiation behind the development of the competing product and service that proves the development was independent of the knowledge and transfer of intellectual property that resulted from this alliance agreement.

One cautionary note. There are companies in the marketplace that are very astute at absorbing intellectual property, repackaging it, and reintroducing it to the marketplace under their service marks or trademarks. Be very careful when entering into alliance agreements. It is better to be careful and protective on the front end and avoid a very bad and potentially damaging situation later on. You may be frustrated with the slowness or deliberate speed of your lawyers, but the investment in time to do it right is absolutely essential to protect your crown jewels—your intellectual property.

10. Confidentiality of Proprietary Information

In a few sections, we discussed "confidential or proprietary information." In this section, "confidential information" should be defined. In some cases, this task may be easy, when one or both companies provide lists of specific products or materials identified as "confidential information." In other cases, this task may not be so easy. There should be language that refers to materials that are reasonably understood to be confidential. The more specific the two parties can be, the better for the agreement and the alliance.

The two parties need to agree on language that acknowledges receipt of the specified information and agree not to publish, copy, or disclose the confidential information outside the boundaries of the alliance agreement (e.g., outside joint customer needs.) The two parties should also agree that disclosing confidential information may cause irreparable damage to the other alliance partner, and that legal proceedings may be appropriate if the provisions covering the handling of confidential information are breached.

The issue surrounding confidential information is serious. Once the two parties agree on what constitutes "confidential information," each company should be proactive in communicating this information to all involved, including providing instructions on how to handle this information when an individual comes in contact with it or receives it.

11. General Provisions

There are several items that need to be included in an alliance agreement that do not fall into sections 1 through 10. The following items are meant to be representative and not all-inclusive.

✧ The first item is *nonsolicitation*. Most of the time, alliance partners agree that personnel working directly or indirectly with each other under an alliance agreement will not be recruited or "solicited" for employment by the other party. There are times when it does make sense for both companies to have a person or persons go to work for the other company. In those cases, it will be done with full knowledge of both companies, and with the purpose, the role, and the structure of the new position fully described in writing.

In a second scenario, a person going to work for the other company can be a big negative. For example, Company A may have two to three alliances in the same marketplace. A person working for Company B could go to work for Company A, but take on a role working directly with a competitor of Company B's.

A third scenario involves job positions or employment opportunities that are published in newspapers, journals, or listed on the Internet. Usually opportunities that are available to the general public are not considered solicitation.

✧ The second item involves *notices*. Notices are official exchanges of information that are intended to change, modify, terminate, or extend the alliance agreement. For this item, the parties agree to exchange notices in writing, and to specify to whom and at what address such notices are to be sent.

✧ The third item is *governing law*, where the companies usually agree that the laws of a specific country or state of the United States will govern the agreement.

✧ The fourth item is *alternative dispute resolution.* The two parties in the agreement can agree to a stair-step resolution process (executive review committee, voluntary mediation, then binding arbitration) or a one-step resolution process (e.g., a six-member committee with internal binding arbitration—and no outside arbitration allowed). The two parties can agree on almost any combination of dispute resolution that is legal and which is acceptable to both parties.

✧ The fifth item is *amendments.* Simply put, modifications to the agreement are usually not acceptable unless they are in writing and signed by both parties.

✧ The sixth general provision item is *severability.* If any item is found to be invalid, the item will be considered severed from the agreement. All other items and provisions would then be interpreted using the "intent" of the parties for the agreement.

✧ The seventh item, *nonassignment*, hits close to home for this author. Most of the time, alliance agreements cannot be assigned or transferred to a third party without the written agreement of the other company. In May 2000, Cap Gemini Soggeti purchased the consulting unit of Ernst & Young LLP. At that time Ernst & Young LLP had an alliance agreement with i2 Technologies. As the i2 Global Alliance Partner for Ernst & Young LLP, I had to work with the lawyers from i2 Technologies, Ernst & Young LLP, and Cap Gemini Soggeti to have i2 Technologies agree to "assign" our global alliance agreement to Cap Gemini Ernst & Young by the purchase or transaction date. This was completed, and the Global alliance continued on with the new merged entity.

✧ The eighth item is *waiver.* The failure of either party to enforce the terms and conditions of any part of the agreement is usually not construed as a waiver of the future performance of the terms and conditions.

✧ The ninth item in the general provisions is *limitation on damages.* Frequently, parties to an alliance agreement limit or eliminate damages that entail loss of business, loss of profit, loss of data, or any other losses that are direct, indirect, or punitive. This limitation of liability provides the personnel of both companies relative freedom to operate with one another without constant concern for liability. There are exceptions, however, especially when alliance partners are working in highly sensitive environments that entail catastrophic consequences for mistakes, such as nuclear energy or off-shore oil exploration.

❖ The tenth item is *publicity and press releases*. For the most part, most alliance agreements call for the two parties to agree on publishing advertising or press releases only with the prior written approval of the other party. This is a critical item, especially in the world of the networked supply chain that entails multiple and sometimes competitive alliances.

12. Signatures

Every alliance agreement has to be signed to be effective. Signatures must be from individuals that have the specific authority to execute agreements on behalf of companies. Partners in law firms or consulting firms, corporate officers, vice presidents, and managing directors are a few titles of people that generally have authority to sign agreements. However, anyone with the vested authority by a company regardless of title can sign an alliance agreement. You should consult with your in-house counsel to determine who in your organization can sign an alliance agreement.

13. Attachments

Attachments to alliance agreements are usually reserved for specific, detailed procedures governing one or more of the items in the agreement. Examples of attachments are dispute resolution procedures, press release or publicity procedures, and software license procedures for use in demonstration (demos) or client pursuits. One recommendation is, when in doubt, be specific! In alliance agreements, it is better to be explicit than to try to suffer through an interpretation maze when a breach of the agreement is perceived.

Notes

1. www.Covisint.com, Creating a Global Marketplace, homepage, p. 1.
2. www.Covisint.com/ press release, "Covisint Receives FTC Antitrust Clearance," September 11, 2000, pp. 1–2.
3. www.Covisint.com/ press release, "Covisint Establishes Corporate Entity," December 11, 2000, p. 1.

CHAPTER THREE

3G Wireless Networks: The Future Is Now . . . or Is It?

There was excitement in Helsinki, one of the nicest cities in the world. It was summertime, when daylight lasts eighteen hours and the thoughts of winter have long faded away. The local residents were almost all outdoors, planning their holidays with their families and friends. They were using their mobile phones for talking with their friends, text messaging with vacation planners, and confirming schedules with secretaries. It was quite a scene for this visitor. In a backdrop of a city whose architecture has eloquently matched the old with the new, its people were operating with state-of-the-art communications for their everyday use.

In our meeting, we had representatives from over twelve countries from all over the world. The discussion had drifted to the compression of the lifecycles of mobile telephones. The representatives from a mobile manufacturer were outlining the functions and features of the latest mobile telephones, and comparing them with the mobile phones that everyone had in the meeting. The Finns had the Nokia 9210 Communicator, which was being advertised as the complete office in your pocket. The representatives from Asia-Pacific had the Nokia 8250. When the representatives of the mobile manufacturer looked to me, there were a few laughs in the room. I was the lone representative from the United States, and I had the oldest mobile telephone model. I had the Nokia 6150. (I did not want them to know that I had just upgraded from the Nokia 5160!) One of the representatives said, "Thank God for the Americans. When our mobile telephones get to the end of their lifecycles in EMEA or Japan, we just send them to the United States for the Americans to use as new technology."

Although there was a bit of dramatization in the statements, there was a lot of truth in them as well. Silicon Valley may be the overall technology center of the world. However, as far as mobile telephones and wireless networks are concerned, the world leadership in innovation is centered in and around Scandinavia.

The New Generation of Wireless Networks

In 1994, I took an ex-pat assignment in South America. I had responsibilities in two countries: Argentina and Brazil. In both countries, I was in the fortunate position to have a mobile telephone. Each mobile telephone was a Motorola unit, running on a first generation wireless technology.

The first generation (1G) wireless technology is comprised of analog systems that are designed for voice transfer (Exhibit 3-1). As such, the 1G wireless networks provide support for circuit-switched voice services. The most widely deployed analog systems are Advanced Mobile Phone System (AMPS) in North America, Asia/Pacific, Central and South America; Nordic Mobile Telephone (NMT) in Scandinavia; and Total Access Communications System (TACS) in the United Kingdom. Recently, Japan has adopted both Personal Digital Communications (PDC) and Personal Handyphone Systems (PHS). The PDC is a digital cellular standard that is unique to Japan. The PHS is a digitized

Exhibit 3-1. Definitions of wireless networks.

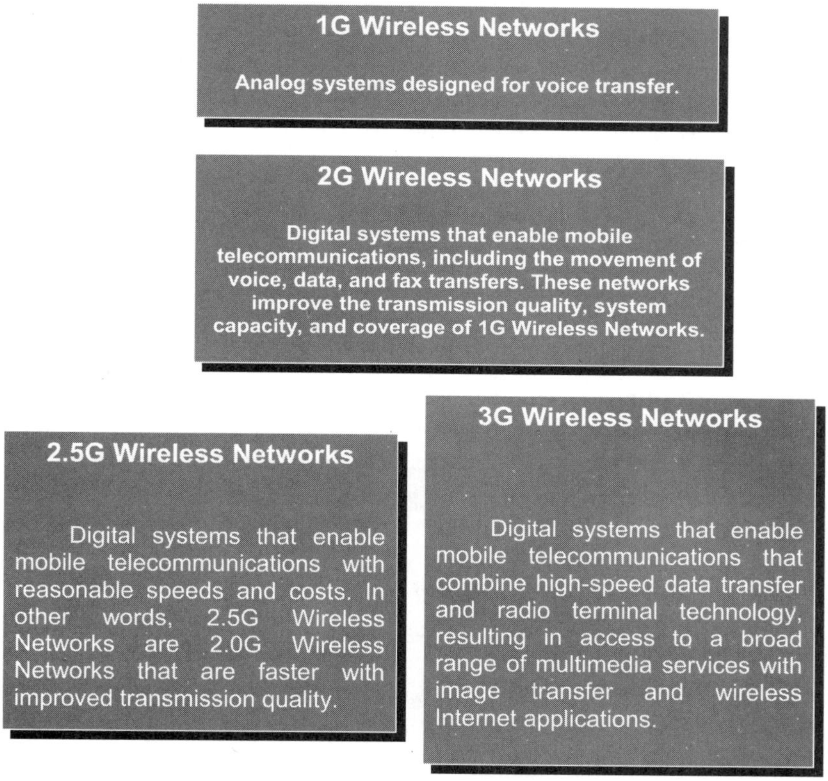

1G Wireless Networks

Analog systems designed for voice transfer.

2G Wireless Networks

Digital systems that enable mobile telecommunications, including the movement of voice, data, and fax transfers. These networks improve the transmission quality, system capacity, and coverage of 1G Wireless Networks.

3G Wireless Networks

Digital systems that enable mobile telecommunications that combine high-speed data transfer and radio terminal technology, resulting in access to a broad range of multimedia services with image transfer and wireless Internet applications.

2.5G Wireless Networks

Digital systems that enable mobile telecommunications with reasonable speeds and costs. In other words, 2.5G Wireless Networks are 2.0G Wireless Networks that are faster with improved transmission quality.

next generation of an analog-based cordless phone concept that enables outdoor uses of the phone and that is unique to Japan as well. The result is that most of Japan's mobile phones are now digital, evidence that the use of analog mobile phone systems is shrinking fast in the world today.[1]

The second-generation (2G) wireless technology involves digital systems that enable mobile telecommunications. This technology allows the movement of voice, data, and fax transfers. These networks improve the transmission quality, system capacity, and coverage of 1G Wireless Networks. The 2G wireless networks provide low-rate circuit-switched and packet-switched data services. The most widely deployed 2G mobile phone systems are Global System for Mobile Communications (GSM), IS-136 or Digital AMPS (DAMPS), IS-95 or cdmaOne, and PDC. GSM, IS-136, and PDC are time-division multiple access (TDMA) based systems, while IS-95 relies on code division multiple access (CDMA) as its air interface. GSM is the predominant standard in Europe, Is-95 and IS-136 are the standards in North, Central, and South America, and the Asia/Pacific region, and, as stated earlier, PDC is the standard in Japan.[2]

In the year 2001 we are in the 2G wireless technology environment. The 2G systems are still evolving, with new technologies like the High Speed Circuit Switched Data (HSCSD) and General Packet Radio Service (GPRS) being developed to allow greater data rates. Some industry analysts are trying to adopt a "2.5G" acronym for the time when wireless data becomes available at reasonable speeds and costs.

The European-based GSM system has 183 million mobile subscribers, followed by Japan-based PDC with 42 million, IS-95 with 32 million, and IS-136 with 24 million. Clearly, the largest number of 2G mobile subscribers, by far, are in Europe, with Japan and the United States far behind.[3]

If you are wondering why the United States is lagging behind Europe in advanced use of mobile networks and in number of subscribers, ask yourself a simple question: Have you ever used your mobile phone for anything but voice transfer or talking to someone? Many surveys have summarized that over 75 percent of mobile phone users in North America have used their mobile phones only for voice transfer. Since text messaging and fax transfer are already present with 2G wireless technologies, what then is holding the United States back? Perhaps it is the fact that our regular telephone service has always been superior to that of Europe and Asia. In Europe and Asia, mobile phone service was a way to leapfrog inferior telephone service in an expedited way. Whatever the reason, the prognosis for the near term is not much better. If we think that text messaging is a next step for the United States, let's take a look at what's around the corner.

3G Wireless Technology

Third generation (3G) wireless technology involves mobile telecommunications that combines high-speed data transfer and radio terminal technology. The creation of 3G wireless technology results in the ability to access a broad range of multimedia services with image transfer and wireless Internet applications. In other words, the common mobile phone user like myself will be able to access a broad range of multimedia services, such as video clips and high speed Internet access, with a mobile phone.

Imagine that you are the executive director of a major ski resort in Vail, Colorado. Your company has ski resorts all over the world, and the executive directors of the other resorts have been called to a worldwide videoconference to review the operations from a quality control standpoint. Your company thrives on standardization at the highest quality possible. The other executive directors on the videoconference are from resorts in the Alps, the Andes, and the Southern Alps in New Zealand. Now, imagine everyone on the videoconference moving together, for example, through the steps of a day in the life of a customer. The executive directors start with the resort check-in counter, move to the sleeping rooms, then proceed through the dining facilities, the buses to the ski lifts, the ski lifts themselves, the emergency rescue centers, the physical rehabilitation centers, and finally, the gift shops in the ski lodges. Now, imagine this videoconference being held on a real-time and fully interactive basis with all directors having access to the latest generation technology. (This assumes of course that the director from the U.S. can keep pace with his or her counterparts from around the world!) The possibilities with this technology are, in the words of my eighteen-year-old son, awesome!

The technology to enable the real-time sharing of images is being developed as this book is being published. In November 2000, Ericsson and Canon announced an alliance that involves the strategic collaboration around the transfer of digital images between cameras and mobile devices. In March 2001, Canon and Ericsson demonstrated how images taken on a Canon digital camera are transferred to an Ericsson mobile device using Bluetooth wireless technology. These images can then be viewed in the mobile phone display, sent as an e-mail attachment over the Internet, or sent as a message—all over the 3G wireless network and all from the mobile communications device. In other words, the technology to enable the executive directors at the ski directors to have a live videoconference (using images or pictures) is within a few years of being a reality.[4]

Let's take a look at another scenario, this time involving the area of learning. The majority of the top Master's in Business Administration (MBA) schools have some sort of "distant learning" capabilities either in place or under development. However, very few if any have "distant learning" programs under construction that are on-line, real-time, or that employ the combination of voice and video. Add to this scenario the concept of global teaching in an on-line, real-time, and mobile environment while employing voice and video, and there may be no schools on that list. (This is being written in mid-year 2001. By the time you read this, I hope that this list will be extensive and include our top MBA schools!)

The reach for the top professors in the top MBA programs with 3G wireless technologies can truly be global. Imagine a well-timed class that covers the corners of the world. For example, when a class is given in the early morning in the United States, it is early afternoon in Europe and late evening in the Far East. No matter what the schedule, it may not suit everyone, though students will turn out for a "live" course featuring a top professor with a state-of-the-art course and curriculum. Students will be able to take courses and interact with top professors without having to be physically present. For students wishing to attend a university in another country, this scenario eliminates the need for student visas. Professors can reach the best students without having to have them physically present on campus. In addition, professors can travel, consult, and participate on the lecture circuit and host their classes globally from a remote location. For both students and professors, the utilization of 3G wireless networks will clearly raise the bar of performance expectations for both. It will also provide the freedom of movement without sacrificing quality or time.

For those of you who are true technology buffs, here is some far-out news. The development of 3G wireless networks may be years away from completion. Despite this fact, there is on the horizon a fourth generation (4G) wireless network! Exhibit 3-2 presents the definition of a fourth generation wireless network.[5]

Whereas in this book I review the development of 3G wireless networks, and their impact on alliances, I will hold the reviews of 4G wireless networks for my next book!

3G Wireless Technology and Alliances

The global technologies and communications standards to support 3G wireless networks are complicated and evolving. The development of

Exhibit 3-2. 4G wireless networks.

> **4G Wireless Networks are expected to be based on orthogonal frequency division multiplexing (OFDM), which sends data over hundreds of parallel streams, increasing the available bandwidth. Fourth generation systems will also use technologies like adaptive processing (which helps clear up interference in transmission) and so-called smart antennas, which include a signal-processing capability to optimize their reception and radiation patterns.**

3G wireless networks represents a massive case study in how companies are coming together to form across-the-board alliances. There is a need for the wireless network providers, the software application developers, the network systems integrators, the Application Systems Providers (ASPs), the Internet Service Providers (ISPs), the wireless device manufacturers, content providers, and others to team together to provide total 3G solutions to the major telecom companies. The combinations of companies and people can run into the hundreds of thousands in terms of who is working with whom to provide the marketplace solutions. More than ever, companies must understand how to develop alliances as they come together to do business in this new, yet to be developed technology-based business.

As stated earlier, the development of a third generation of wireless networks is such an enormous and costly undertaking that major companies have to rely on alliances to enter the market. Let's take a look at the five types of alliances already announced, using the alliance framework introduced in Chapter One.

Sales Alliance

There are several sales alliances developing within the 3G wireless network marketplace. The large network owner-operators are frantically looking for ways to leverage the capacity on their soon-to-be-developed networks and to leverage the return on their massive investments. What is springing up are small "virtual network operators." These operators do not own 3G spectrum licenses, but resell 3G services on behalf of the large network owners. For example, U.K.–based Virgin Mobile and One2One have formed a sales alliance (see Exhibit 3-3). Virgin Mobile resells the services of One2One's network. Virgin Mobile and other virtual network operators are expected to surface in the United States in the next few years, extending the reach of the network owners through sales alliances.[6]

The use of network resellers is expected to grow as the costs to develop 3G wireless networks increase and the rollout timelines continue to slip. There is mounting pressure to start the cash flows from the initial investments into 3G networks.

These alliances are sales-based without joint development activities. They are only geographically based in the broadest of terms. There is no direct investment involved, nor is there an overriding reason to set up a separate, joint company. As such, virtual network operators are examples of sales alliances.

Exhibit 3-3. Sales alliance: Virgin Mobile and One2One.

Question	Type of Alliance				
	Sales	Solution	Geography	Investment	Joint Venture
Do you need an alliance? That is sales- and client-based?	Y	Y	Y	Y	Y
Is there the need for joint solution development?	N	Y	N	Y	Y
Is the need geographic-based?	N	N	Y	N	Y
Is there a necessity or a direct investment in the external company?	N	N	N	Y	Y
Is there an overriding reason to set up a separate company to acquire the needed products and services from the external provider?	N	N	N	N	Y

Solution-Specific Alliance

One of the hopes of 3G wireless network providers is to provide full-scale Internet access using mobile communication devices. These devices can range from the Nokia 9210 Communicator to the soon-to-be-released next generation of Palm Pilot communicators. The current generation of Net access applications are text-based and have limited access to Web sites.

America Online (AOL) and Nokia have announced a solution-specific alliance to develop and market a Netscape-branded version of a Nokia microbrowser based on Wireless Access Protocol (WAP), as illustrated in Exhibit 3-4. This solution-specific alliance allows AOL to extend its Netscape brand into the microbrowser/3G market, while allowing Nokia to provide a world-class Internet browser on its mobile communications devices. It is hoped that consumers will benefit by securing a replica of an HTML screen on their mobile communications devices. This replica will also allow consumers to adopt the use of 3G mobile devices at a faster rate, due to the similarity of Web-enabled screens between PCs and the mobile devices.[7]

The AOL and Nokia alliance is sales-based and involves joint solution development. Although each party will provide resources to the joint development effort, there was no direct investment made by ei-

Exhibit 3-4. Solution-specific alliance: America Online (AOL) and Nokia.

Question	Sales	Solution	Geography	Investment	Joint Venture
Do you need an alliance? That is sales- and client-based?	Y	Y	Y	Y	Y
Is there the need for joint solution development?	N	Y	N	Y	Y
Is the need geographic-based?	N	N	Y	N	Y
Is there a necessity or a direct investment in the external company?	N	N	N	Y	Y
Is there an overriding reason to set up a separate company to acquire the needed products and services from the external provider?	N	N	N	N	Y

ther company. There was no overriding necessity to set up a separate company, nor was the alliance necessarily geographically based. As such, the AOL alliance with Nokia is an example of a solution-specific alliance.

Geographic-Specific Alliance

When people think of the network side of the 3G wireless networks, they often think of Ericsson, Nokia, NTT DoCoMo, and Motorola. However, what these networks represent is a group of companies that come together under a master contractor like Ericsson or Nokia to provide turnkey implementations.

For example, Nokia has selected ABB, Bovis Lend Lease, MKI, and Wireless Facilities Inc. as its main partners for turnkey implementations of 3G wireless networks in Europe, the Middle East, and Africa (Exhibit 3-5). The main subcontractors supporting these partners include Skanska Telecom Networks, Flextronics Network Services, Boke und Walterfang GmbH, Pfleiderer AG, Landis Public Networks B.V., Electron Telecom B.V., Spie Trindel, ETS, SITE, eXI Telecoms, and MyCom. All of these companies have joined an alliance focused on providing turnkey implementations of 3G wireless networks specifically for the geographic areas identified above.[8]

Exhibit 3-5. Geographic-specific alliance: Nokia—Middle East, EMEA, and Africa.

| Question | Type of Alliance | | | | |
	Sales	Solution	Geography	Investment	Joint Venture
Do you need an alliance? That is sales- and client-based?	Y	Y	Y	Y	Y
Is there the need for joint solution development?	N	Y	N	Y	Y
Is the need geographic-based?	N	N	Y	N	Y
Is there a necessity or a direct investment in the external company?	N	N	N	Y	Y
Is there an overriding reason to set up a separate company to acquire the needed products and services from the external provider?	N	N	N	N	Y

These companies entered into an alliance that is sales-based. The solution was already designed, so there was no joint solution development necessary. This alliance is focused on specific geographic areas. Although each party will provide resources to the joint sales effort, there was no direct investment made by any of the companies. There was not an overriding necessity to set up a separate company. As such, this alliance led by Nokia is an example of a geographic-specific alliance.

Investment Alliance

The first network operator worldwide that is expected to operationalize a 3G wireless network is Japan's NTT DoCoMo. The two main driving forces behind NTT DoCoMo's swift movement into the market with 3G technologies are that their current network is virtually at capacity and that their spectrum in Japan was free![9]

However, another factor is at work to accelerate NTT DoCoMo's entry into the global marketplace. AT&T Wireless has announced an investment alliance with NTT DoCoMo (Exhibit 3-6). AT&T Wireless has invested $9.8 billion in NTT DoCoMo and its development of their mobile software platform I-Mode. This mobile software platform is the wireless standard in Japan. AT&T Wireless is planning a 3G wireless network that will leverage I-Mode within the United States. In the

Exhibit 3-6. Investment alliance: AT&T Wireless and NTT DoCoMo.

Question	Type of Alliance				
	Sales	Solution	Geography	Investment	Joint Venture
Do you need an alliance? That is sales- and client-based?	Y	Y	Y	Y	Y
Is there the need for joint solution development?	N	Y	N	Y	Y
Is the need geographic-based?	N	N	Y	N	Y
Is there a necessity or a direct investment in the external company?	N	N	N	Y	Y
Is there an overriding reason to set up a separate company to acquire the needed products and services from the external provider?	N	N	N	N	Y

short term, AT&T Wireless will leverage their investment to evolve from its 2G cellular Wide Area Network (WAN) to the 2.5G Edge Network.[10]

AT&T made an alliance that is sales-based and involves joint solution development. Due to the magnitude of the effort, a direct investment by AT&T Wireless was necessary. There was not an overriding necessity to set up a separate company, nor was the alliance necessarily geographically based. As such, the AT&T Wireless alliance with NTT DoCoMo is an investment alliance.

Joint Venture Alliance

As mentioned in the sales alliance section, there are several "virtual network operators" emerging in the marketplace. These operators do not own 3G spectrum licenses, but resell 3G services for the large network owners. Ericsson decided to create a joint venture with Apax Partners, selling 80 percent of its Enterprise direct sales and service operations to Apax for $480 million (Exhibit 3-7). Ericsson retained a 20 percent stake in the new joint venture, and will work with Apax Partners to develop network integration services for voice, data, and mobility products and services. The new company, which is called Enterprise Solutions, will focus primarily on Australia, Brazil, Germany, Italy, and the U.K. Enterprise Solutions also has offices in Argentina,

Exhibit 3-7. Joint venture alliance: Ericsson and Apax Partners.

Question	Type of Alliance				
	Sales	Solution	Geography	Investment	Joint Venture
Do you need an alliance? That is sales- and client-based?	Y	Y	Y	Y	Y
Is there the need for joint solution development?	N	Y	N	Y	Y
Is the need geographic-based?	N	N	Y	N	Y
Is there a necessity or a direct investment in the external company?	N	N	N	Y	Y
Is there an overriding reason to set up a separate company to acquire the needed products and services from the external provider?	N	N	N	N	Y

Belgium, Colombia, the Czech Republic, Hungary, Ireland, Mexico, Poland, Portugal, Russia, Slovakia, Switzerland, and Venezuela.[11]

This joint venture partnership between Ericsson and Apax Partners is sales-based and involves joint solution development. The new company is geographic-based, and involved a direct investment by Apax Partners.

There was also an overriding need for Ericsson to set up a separate company. In addition to the continuous need for capital (which most companies involved with 3G wireless networks have), insiders stated that Ericsson needed to focus on helping its clients to build 3G networks. The spin-off of Enterprise allowed Ericsson not only to focus primarily on building 3G networks, but to team up with a company that will focus on developing the needed systems and network integration services for Ericsson's network clients. As such, Enterprise Solutions is an example of a joint venture alliance between Ericsson and Apax Partners.

3G Wireless Technology and Alliances—Summary

These are exciting times for all of us. The 3G wireless network opportunities are huge for global and local companies. According to Nokia, worldwide mobile phone ownership should reach the 1 *billion* mark sometime during the first half of 2002. In addition, Nokia forecasts that the number of mobile Internet users will exceed traditional PC connections during the same time frame. No matter how you measure it, the development of 3G wireless networks is potentially enormous![12]

In addition, no one company can do it alone. Companies must come together and form alliances to develop and market the 3G wireless network solutions. It is a must for companies to understand the types of solutions and the right companies to partner with and form alliances. The Framework to Determine What Type of Alliance Is Needed will help companies determine how to proceed when the solutions and potential partners are identified.

Is Being behind EMEA and Asia-Pacific Good or Bad for the United States?

Several years ago I visited a new manufacturing plant site in the Southeast United States. In this new plant, the engineering department had always had the responsibility for the warehouse design and automa-tion. This did not make much sense to the company's supply chain guys, and, as it turned out, this would be the last plant for which the engineering department would have such responsibility.

This plant produced a product that had an inventory value of $6 a case. The shrinkage of a typical plant was less than 1 percent of total inventory produced. The inventory throughput rate from the time of manufacture to the time the product was loaded on the trailers was measured in hours! In addition, the plant was built to be the largest volume-producing plant within the company. The combination of high production volumes, high velocity, and low product value dic-tated the need for supply chain simplicity, low-cost supply chain de-signs, and speed!

What did the engineering department do? They installed a state-of-the-art automated storage and retrieval system (ASRS), complete with automated guided vehicles (AGVs). It was a fabulous *technology solution*. Unfortunately for the company, it was also slow and high-cost. The ASRS could not keep up with production volume, and the warehouse became the slowest moving component in the supply chain. The production lines were shut down due to the inability of the ware-house to keep up with the production volumes. In addition, the indus-trial engineers within the supply chain department figured out that the plant could lose 100 percent of the production volume to shrinkage and still not recover the incremental investment costs of the ASRS and AGVs versus a manual product inventory and material-handling process. The learning for the company was to avoid being enamored with technology and falling into the high-tech, high-cost trap.

The Telecom Debt Problem

The cost of developing 3G wireless networks is significant. The cost for telecom providers to bid and secure the needed wireless radio fre-quency spectrum to market 3G services to consumers is enormous. There is speculation that the massive debt being incurred by global telecom providers to secure the needed spectrum will lead to huge problems for many companies and countries.

In mid-2001, the debt incurred by global telecom companies is estimated at $650 billion! By contrast, the U.S. Government bailout of the savings and loan industry in the 1980s and early 1990s was approximately $150 billion. In addition to the failure of a quick materialization of the estimated revenues and profits from wireless, there is the rapid lifecycle of the equipment that renders these assets obsolete at a fast pace.[13]

Europe is right in the middle of this debt problem. The European 3G operators, which include Vodafone, France Telecom, Deutsche Telekom, British Telecom, the Netherlands Royal KPN NV, and Telefonica, have a total estimated debt of between $175 and $225 billion. Several of these companies have incurred cuts in their credit ratings, hampering their ability to attract the necessary investments to finish out the 3G wireless networks.[14] It is estimated that the European Telecommunications companies will have to spend an additional $100 million to get their 3G wireless networks operational.[15]

In the short term there will be winners and losers. British Telecom announced in May 2001 that it would sell its wireless investments in Japan and Spain to Vodafone in an attempt to pare down its debt. These investments were once considered strategic investments, designed to stimulate growth in regions thought to be prime for 3G wireless services. Instead, British Telecom is selling these assets to its wireless competitor, Vodafone, and proceeding with other plans to raise cash and reduce its debt further.[16]

Some experts predict that the global cost will exceed the current $1.3 trillion estimated by many to be the cost to fully develop and market 3G products and services. There is another problem facing the start of these cash flows. This problem is the mobile communications devices and their complexity.

The existing mobile communications devices in Europe are designed for 2G and are being developed for 2.5G wireless networks. As 3G wireless networks are developed, these mobile communications devices must be able to switch among 2G, 2.5G, and 3G networks, depending upon location and availability. The software and complexity for these devices are huge hurdles for the device manufacturers. Given the slowdown of the network completion due to the enormous debt burden of the network providers, the device manufacturers (Nokia, Motorola, Siemens, Ericsson, NEC, etc.) are being pressured to produce these "hybrid" devices that encompass multiple generations of wireless networks. In addition, some of these device manufacturers are also 3G Wireless network equipment providers. The pressure on the device manufacturers is no less severe than it is on the telecommunications companies.

The race to be the first company with 3G wireless phone services has also been delayed primarily due to the software complexities within the mobile devices. British Telecommunications PLC announced that it is delaying its plans to offer 3G wireless services on the Isle of Man in 2001 because of the dropping of calls when the user is mobile. BT Wireless is working with NEC Corporation to develop the software for the 3G mobile devices. NTT DoCoMo announced in April a delay in their 3G services offering to Japan. The fact that the two leading companies postponed their rollout another four to five months is not being well received by security analysts and users alike.[17]

What does this all mean? It means that the prospect for immediate revenues and cash flows from 3G wireless networks will be considerably delayed. Insiders in Europe are now telling me that it will be the end of 2003 or the beginning of 2004 before their services are available to the public with adequate coverage.

Huge debt loads, delays in network completion, complexities in device manufacturing, and restructurings by public companies all combine for an uncertain future for 3G wireless networks. Can things get any worse? They may, considering the result of supply and demand forces. With all of this, one must ask, what will the prices be for the 3G wireless products and services for the consumers?

Is the market really there for all companies to get a fair return on their investments? Let me go back to the first part of this chapter. The United States is behind in the adoption of 2G wireless solutions, which involves sending data over a wireless network. Will they be behind in the adoption of 3G products and services?

Another way to ask this question may be as follows: Will the United States accelerate their adoption of mobile technologies and embrace 3G products and services in the numbers needed to support these huge investments? Despite all the hype by Europe and Japan, the key to financial survival for many 3G alliance partners rests with the adoption of 3G products and services in significant numbers. To accomplish this, the telecommunications companies around the world need the U.S. market.

According to Craig Farrill, the managing director and chief technology officer at inOvate Communications Group, a venture capital firm and incubator, "The world view of the United States is that it's missed the boat. I don't think that view is fair or correct. The United States has more [frequency] bands, more operators, more technology, more venture capitalists, more investment, and lower penetration. I call that a good place to be."[18]

Perhaps Craig Farrill is correct. The adoption of 3G wireless technologies and their products and services in the United States will clearly rest with a positive cost/benefit analysis in their applications. There are two sides to this analysis—the benefits from its application, and the costs associated with the use of the technology. High business use adoption rates within the United States will occur only when the technologies enable the business processes of companies and contribute to reducing costs, increasing sales, accelerating free cash flow, improving fixed capital leverage, or lowering taxes. In addition, high personal-use adoption rates will occur only when the technologies enable the personal lifestyles of everyone above and beyond what people can enjoy from their PCs. The many players participating in the many alliances to bring 3G wireless technologies and their products and services to the U.S. market will have to prove their cost/benefit cases to both businesses and consumers. They must avoid having their products and services positioned as high-tech and high-cost. Otherwise, the adoption rate within the United States will continue to be very slow—for all the right reasons.

Sometimes, the market moves so fast that locking into a definitive agreement with other companies can potentially be a liability rather than an asset. How can companies get started, yet protect themselves from working with alliance partners until definitive agreements are reached? One answer is to construct a memorandum (memo) of intent, which will be described in detail at the end of this chapter.

The High-Tech, High-Cost Trap Revisited

Recently I had the pleasure to work with a global consumer products company. The company, which we will call GlobeTech, was reviewing a proposal from a 3G wireless content company to outfit their manufacturing equipment with 3G wireless terminals. These terminals would send statistical performance data from the equipment to the mobile devices of the equipment operator and the shift manager. The equipment operator would use the mobile devices to correct or modify the operating specifications of the equipment on an as needed basis, regardless of where he or she was in the plant. The demo was simple, using a variant of text messaging between a production machine and a mobile communication device.

GlobeTech's chief operating officer, a sharp businessman, reviewed the proposal and then asked the representative of the 3G wireless content company what Globetech's incremental costs and benefits would be. The costs could only be estimated, due to the uncertainty of how this technology would "fit" the production process. The benefits were also not clear, because GlobeTech already had sophisticated statistical process controls with their production equipment. The plants in his company had very few employees in the production process, and most of the processes were automated.

However, the chief operating officer, who was very opportunistic when it came to collective learning, asked the 3G wireless content company to perform an opportunity assessment on how this technology would benefit GlobeTech's production process. The result would have to be a very definitive cost/benefit analysis that was anchored in the business solution it was creating. He also demanded that this assessment be completed in four weeks, and assigned one of his top industrial engineers to the assessment.

After the meeting, he told me that he receives over fifty calls a week from technology providers wanting to demonstrate their products to him. Out of these fifty, he selects approximately five with whom to meet and whose products to research. This takes approximately one hour a day of his time, but it allows him to stay abreast of the new technologies in the marketplace. It also provides him an opportunity to use one of his plants to be a technology-based solution-creation incubator for the rest of the company. The message he wanted to send to all of his plants was to be aggressive on the innovation side, but avoid being enamored with technology and becoming high-tech, high-cost.

However, what the chief operating officer was doing was forcing the technology providers to develop the discipline to take their technologies and link them into creative solutions driving real business value. We will review this premise in greater detail in Chapter Four.

Summary

The upcoming 3G Wireless Networks promise to be a "big event" in the evolution of both mobile communications and technology. The investments are enormous, while the returns are at this point unknown. What is known is that this technology will be in operation in the 2002–2004 time frame, bringing with it many winners and many losers.

Alliances will play a key role in determining how the 3G wireless networks are brought to the marketplace and who the winners and losers will be in the telecommunications industry. The types of alliances are important to bring together the solutions necessary to realize the benefits of 3G wireless networks. The alliance agreement is necessary to establish a framework for the two parties to operate in the marketplace together. The memo of intent (MOI) is necessary to initiate the alliance in the face of some uncertainty. All three play critical roles for companies to get started.

There is a danger early on in alliances, especially technology alliances, to become enamored with technology and forget the value of applying the technology. It is important to avoid the high-tech, high-cost trap that many companies have fallen into in the previous ten to fifteen years.

What about companies trying to get started on getting a return on their 3G investments? In the face of device complexity, delays in network development, and consolidation due to enormous debt loads, the cash flows may be slow in materializing. The real winners may be the companies that restructure their debt early on, reposition their products and services, and emerge in a leaner, more competitive condition.

We have mentioned very little about the consumer, especially the corporate consumer. What should the corporate consumer do with this enticing yet uncertain technology? Consumers must focus on how companies might use 3G technologies to enable their business. In the next chapter, we will look at 3G wireless technologies within the construct of the Networked Value Chain to determine how an executive with a global telecommunications or mobile communications device company should approach tapping into the value streams of corporate users of 3G technologies.

How to Construct a Memo of Intent

The memo of intent (MOI) is a nonbinding yet important document for alliance parties to get started working together on a proposed business transaction. It has several parts, which are based on both business and legal terms.

First Paragraph

The first paragraph introduces the alliance parties by formal name, and includes the headquarters or principal place of business for each party. In addition, the first paragraph will contain the *effective date* of the memo of intent.

Background

After the first paragraph, there are usually a series of *background* items that frame out the business transaction that the parties are trying to achieve. For example, we mentioned earlier that America Online (AOL) and Nokia had announced an alliance to develop and market a Netscape-branded version of a Nokia microbrowser. In the *background* of the MOI, it would be stated that AOL is the owner of the Netscape HTML screen sets and all associated software. It would also identify Nokia as owning the mobile communications devices and all associated design documents. These items would be identified in attached schedules.

The background items would then include statements that AOL and Nokia intend to jointly develop a solution that would enhance AOL's Netscape HTML's screen sets and Nokia's mobile communications devices, jointly develop the processes and methods to create the solution, and then jointly promote and market the joint solution in the marketplace. These items set the stage for the MOI document. Let's review the major components of the MOI after the first paragraph and the background.

1. Purpose

The *purpose* is a brief but important paragraph. In the *purpose*, it is usually stated that discussions have taken place between potential alliance parties around the items in the *background*. In addition, it is stated that there is intent to finalize a definitive agreement in the future. Lastly, it is usually stated that the MOI is a nonbinding agreement, and that it only expresses a current intent by both parties.

2. Definitions

In *definitions,* capitalized terms have specific meanings. For example, "Netscape" or "Communicator" may have specific meanings to AOL and Nokia. It is in this section that these terms are identified with their specific meanings.

3. Joint Development

The *joint development* section covers at a high level the solution scope, the requirements definition for the joint solution development, and the build-out of the solution itself. As the market is moving so fast, there may be language included in the MOI that states that these items may be modified by notifying each other in writing.

Also included in this section is the identification of the responsible alliance party, and who leads what section of the joint solution development. It may include the number of people dedicated to the joint solution from both parties, what qualifications these people must have, and what roles the leaders will assume. The more specific the alliance parties can be here, the easier it will be to get started and finalize the definitive agreement.

4. Intellectual Property Rights

The *intellectual property rights* section in the MOI must follow (if present) any language that was agreed to in the alliance agreement. In this section, the parties agree to the ownership rights of the original materials identified in the *background,* and the ownership rights of the jointly developed solution as the original materials are modified. In addition, language may be needed for either party to license the other's knowledge or legally protected copyrighted or patented material as it is used in the joint solution. Usually, the knowledge, know-how, and concepts jointly developed in the joint solution development are co-owned by the alliance parties, unless otherwise specified.

5. Marketing

Regarding *marketing,* the alliance parties will agree to what type of marketing will be performed, the time period, and which party will be responsible for specific marketing activities. In the MOI, there may even be language specific to names and a number of dedicated resources to accomplish the specific marketing activities.

Perhaps the real value of *marketing* in the MOI rests with the internal and external communications regarding the execution of the MOI. These communications provide the catalyst for both alliance parties to come together around a joint solution, and to identify with each other in terms of alliance partners in a specific solution.

Other items to be covered are exclusivity, the approach to targeted accounts, and publicity. There may also be an agreement to establish a steering committee to monitor the progress of the MOI, the progress of the marketing of the joint solution, and the relationship of the parties as alliance partners.

6. Term and Project Costs

The *term* of an MOI may range from thirty days to six months, starting with the effective date in the first paragraph. The *term* is designed to provide a time frame for the alliance parties to begin working on the joint solution while negotiating the longer-term definitive agreement. Frequently there is language that extends the MOI by default or mutual agreement.

The *project costs* identify which company pays for what

resources and materials used in the joint solution effort. This section is important to avoid misunderstandings about such items as travel costs while alliance parties are working on game-changing marketplace solutions. An extension of the *project costs* is the establishment of a business plan. In this business plan, measurable solution development and sales targets are established, roles and responsibilities are defined, cost projections are estimated, and related activities are identified. For the MOI, there is usually a reasonable time period (thirty to sixty days) during which the two parties must complete the business plan.

7. Legal Issues

The *legal issues* include several items. Many MOIs are nonbinding, as stated in the *purpose* section of the MOI. The nonbinding language is restated in the *legal issues,* with emphasis that components of the MOI become binding only when incorporated into a definitive agreement. In addition, if the alliance parties exchange confidential information between the MOI and the definitive agreement, the two parties should execute a master nondisclosure agreement (NDA). (The NDA will be discussed in Chapter Four.) All materials exchanged would be subject to the terms of the NDA. In addition, language may be necessary to restrict the use of confidential material to a "need to have" basis in order to limit the exposure of this material to noninvolved employees of both companies.

The use of press releases is usually restricted in MOIs, which may allow them only with prior written approval by both parties. Occasionally, there are legal and legislative exceptions that override agreed-to restrictions in this area. Also covered in the *legal issues* are limitations of liability. Frequently, limitations of liability disallow claims by either party for any damages resulting from either the continuation or abandonment of negotiations. These damages include lost sales, lost profits, and injury to business reputation. They also include punitive or consequential damages. Usually excluded from these limits are infringements of intellectual property rights. The aggregate liability is usually capped at a level that has some significance, with limits ranging from $25,000 to $250,000.

The *legal issues* also cover the need for access rights, or the rights to use each other's materials before the definitive agreement is executed. For example, Nokia would have to secure access rights to use AOL's Netscape HTML screen if they were to use a modified version after the MOI and before the execution of the definitive agreement.

In addition, the governing law (country if global, state if within the U.S.) is identified for the MOI in this section. Also, many *legal issues* survive beyond the expiration of the MOI, such as the use of confidential information, and need to be identified as such.

At the end of the MOI, there is an authorized signature page. The MOI is only valid if authorized representatives (usually officers of the alliance companies) sign the MOI. Attached to the MOI are the addendums, mentioned earlier in the *background.*

Notes

1. www.fttp.netlab.ohio-state.edu/pub/jain/courses,cis788-99/ 3G_wireless/index.html, James J. Steinbugl, "Evolution toward Third Generation Wireless Networks," February 9, 2001, p. 2.
2. Ibid.
3. Ibid.
4. www.ericsson.se/press/20010323-0064.html, Ericsson Press Releases, "Ericsson Demonstrates Digital Image Transfer—from Camera to Mobile Phone, from User to User," March 23, 2001, p. 1.
5. www.layeronewireless.com/glossary.htm#d-f, Layerone Wireless Technology.
6. www.zdnet.com/mobilenews, Nancy Gohring, "Can U.S. Catch Up in Wireless?" *Interactive Week*, January 9, 2001, p. 3.
7. www.zdnet.com/mobilenews, Richard Shim and John Borland, "AOL, Nokia Team on Wireless Browser—Based on WAP," *ZDNet News*, January 18, 2001, p. 1.

8. www.wirelessdesignonline.com, "Nokia Meets the Need for Speed in 3G Network Deliveries," *M2 PRESSWIRE vis COMTEX,* March 8, 2001, p. 1.

9. www.zdnet.com/mobilenews, Nancy Gohring, "Can U.S. Catch Up," pp. 1–2.

10. www.zdnet.com/mobilenews, Jacqueline Emigh, "Where Should You Place Your Wireless Bets?" *Smart Partner,* December 13, 2000, pp. 1–2.

11. www.ericsson.se/press/20010308-0071.html, Ericsson Press Releases, "Ericsson Spins Off Its Enterprise Direct Sales Operations into Partnership with Apax Partners," March 8, 2001, p. 1.

12. www.nokia.com/Whatis3G, "Market Overview, Latest Figures," March 23, 2001, p. 1.

13. Gregory Zuckerman and Deborah Solomon, "Wrong Numbers: Telecom Debt Debacle Could Lead to Losses of Historic Proportions," *The Wall Street Journal,* May 11, 2001, pp. A1, A6.

14. "Pass the Painkillers," *The Economist,* May 5, 2001, p. 51.

15. Zuckerman and Solomon, "Wrong Numbers," pp. A1, A6.

16. Ibid.

17. Dan Roberts, "Launch 'Bug' Casts Doubt on 3G Mobile Phone Service," *The Financial Times,* May 15, 2001, p. 10.

18. www.zdnet.com/mobilenews, Nancy Gohring, "Can U.S. Catch Up", p. 1.

CHAPTER FOUR

Telecom Providers and 3G Wireless Device Manufacturers: A $1 Trillion Investment, yet Where's the Value?

It was very early one morning in April. The sky was still dark, about to enter the fifteen-to-twenty-minute time frame when the day explodes from darkness to light. The weather was very warm and humid in Singapore, with the dew dropping moisture from the leaves of the carefully planted foliage. As I was jogging down some of the safest streets in the world, I could not help but think of the meetings that were going to take place later in the day. This was the second day of a three-day conference, and already there was anxiety in the air.

Many of the world's largest telecommunications companies had come together to discuss the current state of their industry. It was not a pretty sight. Almost all of these companies had made huge investments in building the necessary infrastructure and securing the rights to the needed 3G wireless spectrums. The sheer debt load for many of them may cause the postponement of full 3G services for several years, and a few of the companies were even talking privately about bankruptcy, white knight joint ventures, or a bailout by their governments.

The discussions during the first day focused on addressing the intense need for the telecommunications companies to startup their 3G services as soon as possible to begin getting some return on their investment, despite full services still being years away. The attendees spent hours discussing ways to get 3G applications into the major trading blocs, and the more they searched for new applications as sources of revenues, the more flabbergasted I became. How did some of the best telecommunications companies in the world make these knee-bending investments in an emerging technology that may be years from providing a fair return on their investments? I knew it was important to be a player in the 3G wireless networks, but, I wondered, at what price?

The next morning, as the darkness gave way to light, my thoughts turned to the corporate or business consumer. Many companies had just begun to realize the value (or lack of value) that public eMarketplaces were producing for their enterprises. What was going to be their reaction to the sales onslaught about to hit their companies regarding the use of 3G wireless devices? Were they prepared to analyze the cost-benefits associated with these devices? Did these companies even know how to begin to assess how and where to incorporate these devices?

My thoughts were interrupted when I got back to my hotel, having finished my jog. There the bellman was just helping a lady into a taxi, having notified the taxi driver through text messaging from his mobile phone. The doorman at the hotel was sending a text message to the front desk that a wheelchair was needed for an incoming guest. The concierge was assisting a couple of businessmen with directions to their meeting, using his mobile phone to secure a route map for the guests. All three were going through their paces in their job while simultaneously talking on their mobile telephones. There clearly was a need for next-generation wireless devices. It was a matter of the fit into the work processes, and the price to value for their services.

Benefits of Mobile Commerce Services

As I witnessed at my Singapore hotel, there are benefits to using the mobile devices for commercial reasons. According to Durlacher, *Mo-*

bile Commerce Report 2000, and Cap Gemini Ernst & Young, there are distinct benefits with mobile commerce. The benefits derived from the use of 3G wireless networks are expected to parallel the benefits of mobile commerce. There are seven categories of benefits for mobile commerce services, and they are ubiquity, accessibility, security, convenience, localization, personalization, and instant Internet connectivity (Exhibit 4-1). Let's take a brief look at each one of these benefits.

✧ The *ubiquity* benefit is the ability of a mobile device to fulfill the need for real-time information and communication "anytime, anywhere." In many circumstances (e.g., new product development), this advantage can be significant.

✧ *Accessibility* is another benefit to many users. A mobile device user can be available twenty-four hours a day, seven days a week, and three hundred sixty-five days a year. In the not too distant future, users will be able to program their communication devices to limit their reachability to particular people or specific times.

✧ The *security* benefit involves a smart card in a mobile device that will authenticate the owner of the device. This provides a higher level of security in a fixed Internet environment, excluding the use of secured intranet sites.

✧ The *convenience* benefit refers to the small size, the portability of the device, and, in the not-too-distant future, significant data storage capabilities.

✧ The *localization* benefit is a critical one for many professions. It entails the ability to recognize where the user is physically located. From transportation to emergency rescue to law enforcement, this benefit can be broad and far-reaching.

✧ The *personalization* benefit enables users to tailor services to their specific needs. It also enables service providers to customize services based on stated or observed behavior.

✧ Lastly, the *instant Internet connectivity* benefit can be of major benefit for time-sensitive users and professions. Emergency rescue has a number of uses with this benefit that can result in saving lives.

Exhibit 4-1. Benefits of mobile services.

Unique Benefits of M-Commerce Services:

Ubiquity
- The advantage of a mobile device is its ability to fulfill the need for real-time information and communication "anytime, anywhere."

Accessibility
- A mobile user can be available irrespective of time and location. Users have the choice to limit their reach-ability to particular people or times

Security
- The smart card within mobile devices (SIM) provides authentication of the owner and provides a higher level of security than that which is available in a fixed Internet environment.

Convenience
- As well as being small, portable, and easy to use, mobile devices increasingly provide additional functions such as data storage.

Localization
- Mobile devices will soon be able to recognize where the user is physically located, enabling the offering of tailored and relevant information.

Personalization
- Personalization will enable services to be tailored to the particular needs of the customer as determined by their stated preferences or observed behavior.

Instant Internet Connectivity
- Unlike WAP, GPRS technology will enable easier and faster access to the web without the need for a connecting call.

Localization, Personalization, and Instant Internal Connectivity will drive future functionality.

CAP GEMINI
ERNST & YOUNG

Source: Durlacher, *Mobile Commerce Report*, 2000; Cap Gemini Ernst & Young analysis.

These seven benefits provide useful categories for users when performing their cost-benefit analysis for 3G wireless devices, 2G wireless devices, 2.5G wireless devices, and mobile commerce. However, for the business user, these benefits must be translated into a measurement of business value. In addition, the focus must start with the framework for business value and not with the technology device. Let's take a look at the use of a key framework to enable this translation from high-level benefit description to measurable business value.

The Networked Value Chain

The Networked Value Chain (Exhibit 4-2), which was introduced in October 2000 as the Networked *Supply* Chain (in the book *The Supply Chain Network @ Internet Speed*),[1] provides a framework for companies to incorporate process, technology, and people changes into a high-performing, technology-enabled supply chain.

As illustrated in Exhibit 4-2, on the top of the Networked Value Chain is the Executive Dashboard. This dashboard coordinates the

Exhibit 4-2. Networked Value Chain.

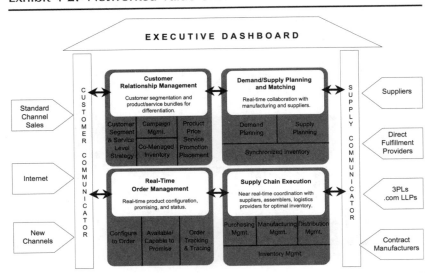

Source: Cap Gemini Ernst & Young.

supply chain strategy with the business strategy, and sets the stage for the four quadrants.

The first of the two quadrants on the left side is Customer Relationship Management. In this quadrant, companies focus on customer segmentation, service level strategies, and the four "P's" of merchandising—price, product, promotion, and placement.

The first of the two quadrants on the right side is Demand/Supply Planning and Matching. In this quadrant, companies focus on real-time collaboration with manufacturing and suppliers through demand planning, supply planning, and synchronized inventory.

The horizontal, left-to-right movement between the top two quadrants allows for the influencing of customer demand based on inventory visibility. This is the first value driver of the Networked Value Chain (Exhibit 4-3).

These two quadrants interface with the customers through the use of varying communication techniques. These techniques can be by telephone, by fax, by mail, by e-mail, by eProcurement portals, and by other methods, including EDI and in person. The customer touchpoints are critical to anchoring the supply chain. These two quadrants

Exhibit 4-3. Value Driver 1: influencing customer demand based on inventory visibility.

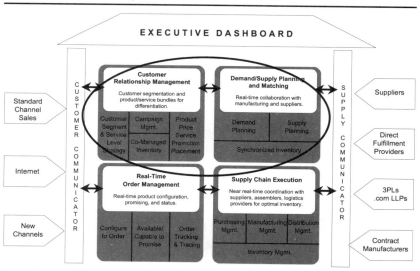

Source: Cap Gemini Ernst & Young.

also interface with suppliers using similar techniques. The use of networked technology is critical to enable speed and accuracy for companies and their suppliers in working with customers on an iterative basis. The objective is for the whole Networked Value Chain to get close to the customer to win their loyalty and trust. The outcome is to earn the opportunity to win market share and attain a more predictable understanding of actual customer demand.

The second of the two quadrants on the left side is Real-Time Order Management. Companies focus on real-time product configuration, promising, and status through configure-to-order, available and capable to promise, and order tracking and tracing.

The second of the two quadrants on the right side is Supply Chain Execution. In this quadrant, companies focus on near real-time coordination with suppliers, assemblers, and logistics providers for optimal inventory.

The horizontal, left-to-right movement between the bottom two quadrants allows for the coordinating of the Networked Value Chain to meet customer fulfillment. This is the second driver of the Networked Value Chain (Exhibit 4-4).

The bottom two quadrants in Exhibit 4-4 interface with the customers and suppliers using similar techniques to communicate. The customer touchpoints are critical to ensuring that the right product gets delivered to the right place at the right time. The supplier touchpoints are critical to enable collaborative planning, forecasting, and replenishment to achieve a "one number forecast" throughout the value chain. (A "one number forecast" refers to a common forecast that everyone in the supply chain agrees to share and use in their integrated supply chain planning and operations.) Together, these coordinated efforts rely on networked technology to achieve customer fulfillment.

3G Wireless Networks and the Networked Value Chain

In Chapter Three, we discussed the many alliances that are being formed to combine technologies to provide potential 3G solutions to the marketplace. We also discussed the enormous debt loads and the

Exhibit 4-4. Value Driver 2: coordinating the Networked Supply Chain to meet customer fulfillment.

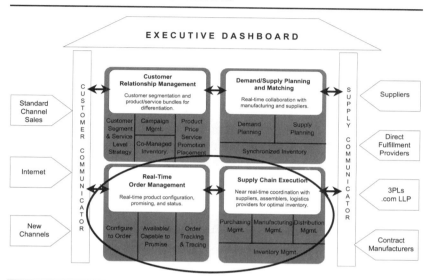

Source: Cap Gemini Ernst & Young.

need to generate cash flow as soon as possible. As a result, there is a tremendous amount of effort on the part of technologists and the telecommunications companies to create interest in the use of 3G wireless devices. There is even a big splash around the use of color on the device monitors to enhance the experience in playing video games. In my opinion, the telecommunications companies will not achieve a return on their 3G wireless investments through the marketing of these devices for playing games. They may not even reach a decent return at all by developing a solution, then looking for a problem to solve. Although the efforts to form alliances and develop technology solutions are necessary, they represent only one-half of the equation.

The participants in the entire 3G wireless networks extended enterprise supply chain must band together and focus on the application value side of the equation as well as the technology solution development. They must identify a need, and then develop a solution that includes the 3G wireless devices in the value streams of the Networked Value Chain.

This is the exact scenario that worries even the most ardent supporter of 3G wireless networks. The investments into the 3G spectrum rights were made at a time when euphoria over the new technology was at its peak. Grandiose predictions of cash flows resulted from even greater predictions of what the mobile communications device users would pay for these enhanced services. The major problem was that these predictions were made without any knowledge of the actual cost of developing a 3G network and of the complexity and cost of the multiple spectrum communications devices. Even more ominous is the fact that these predictions were made without any idea as to how these new products and services would add value to the users.

The Networked Value Chain offers a framework for determining how new products and services can tap into the value streams of users. Let's take a look at each quadrant of the Networked Value Chain, and how 3G wireless devices might tap into these value streams.

Customer Relationship Management

The customer is in need of a set of four tires for her 2000 Lincoln LS. She walks up to a tire dealership, enters the lobby, takes a number, and waits her turn for a sales agent. The tire dealership is equipped with an Internet-enabled desktop computer linked directly to the inventories at the dealership and at the warehouse, which allows the salesperson to interact with the customer, locate the proper available inventory, and commit the inventory to the customer. There was only one problem. There were two desktop computers, two salespersons, and ten customers in the lobby.

The woman in the above scenario takes out her mobile communications device and links directly into the dealer's customer service department. Through the tire company's data warehouse, she then uses a hard-coded link to go directly to the on-site dealer inventory to locate the exact tires she needs. Through the service department, she identifies the price, any promotions currently in place for the tires or the service, and the service times available. When the salesperson finally gets to the woman, she not only knows what she needs, but already has the tires located and committed to her.

Through an Internet-based mobile device, the tire company can work with customers on their time and at their convenience to configure the right order. The relationship with the customer is built on speed, accuracy, and convenience. These are the value drivers, and as such, the value streams that the telecommunications companies must tap. In addition, once the database is built that captures and includes customer preferences; the relationship can get very intimate. This can be accomplished in spite of the fact that the customer relationship is largely an electronic relationship.

Demand/Supply Planning and Matching

Everything seemed to work just right for the woman. Does it ever go as smoothly for you when you need tires for your car? The tire dealerships are inventorying fewer and fewer tires, so the chances of their having the exact tires for you in their inventory are relatively slim.

Let's revisit the woman's scenario. After she identifies the type of tires she needs from the company data warehouse, she then proceeds to the tire company inventory matching application. The system first looks for her tires at the dealer nearest her home or office, and then search for her tires in the warehouse. If neither that dealer nor the warehouse has her tires, the system searches other dealer inventories. If all inventory matching searches fail to identify the needed tires, the woman can then either substitute similar tires or order her tires direct from the tire manufacturer.

People like to have facts and be able to exercise their options. This woman has access to the inventory facts through having inventory visibility. She also has options. She can either substitute similar tires or order from the manufacturer. The possibility of a high pressure salesperson trying to substitute tires because the manager of the dealership wants to push a certain tire in stock is minimized by allowing the woman inventory visibility. The use of demand and supply matching with customer relationship management tools and techniques can build trust with a customer, which produces customer loyalty. It can also influence demand through inventory visibility.

What is the value of a 3G mobile communication device to this woman? The value is mobility. If the right processes and systems were in place, she could accomplish the above from her desktop unit in her home or at her office. However, she can use the 3G mobile device from anywhere. This can free up her time to multi-task in her professional and personal worlds.

Real-Time Order Management

The owner of the Lincoln LS has now been able to identify the right tires for her car and to locate the needed tires within the tire company's warehouse inventory. She now has two options. She can either continue to wait for the tire salesperson, or she can use the tire company's real-time order management system.

Through the use of her 3G mobile communications device, she can move from the inventory visibility and demand/supply matching application to the service order application. The woman chooses the dealership of her choice, and selects the service appointment scheduling option. She keys in the code for the tires she has selected and the preferred service date and time. The system either confirms her appointment, or prompts the woman to select another appointment due to constraints in delivery time or service. The woman can select to have the digital image of the appointment sent to her home office fax or her e-mail address so that she can record the appointment in her calendar.

Supply Chain Execution

Unbeknownst to the woman, there is a final step in this process. The warehouse, the manufacturer, the transportation or third-party logistics company, and the dealership all need to be in collaboration to execute the woman's order. The warehouse must have real-time, up-to-date inventory records. They must also know their own shipping constraints to respond to customer orders, and have these constraints accurately reflected in the on-line real-time order management system. The manufacturer must also know their own response times to either manufacture the tires to the woman's order, or to manufacture the tires to replenish the inventory depleted by the woman's order. The transportation or third party logistics provider must know their response times and have them hard-coded in a matrix supporting the real-time order management system.

In addition, the real-time order management system must be able to link all the value chain participants with the right movement documents, the right financial transfer documents, and the right information. If any part of the value chain fails, the woman will show up for her new tires and be extremely disappointed. She will be at best an unhappy customer, and at worst a lost customer. Therefore, the "networked" part of the Networked Value Chain must be operational to meet customer fulfillment.

In the real world, a major tire company like Goodyear may have tens of thousands of customers in a given day and week. The complexity of inventory management, manufacturing to match supply with actual and anticipated demand, customer relationship management, and supply chain execution can be enormous. It is critical for all Networked Value Chain participants to have accurate information and to share their planning, forecasting, and replenishment data. The Networked Value Chain must function as one entity if the value of 3G mobile devices is to be maximized.

This point brings up the challenge facing the major telecommunications companies with 3G wireless mobile devices. At least in the United States, the value of these devices will be measured in terms of the incremental value they can provide above and beyond current systems and current cellular telephones. This presents a two-part challenge to the telecommunications companies. The first challenge is to identify and quantify the value of the "mobile" part of the mobile communications device. Will the woman in the above scenario value the mobile device to identify her tires, order the tires, and schedule the service? She may if she is a working mom with limited time but ample disposable income. She may not if she is a stay-at-home mom with ample time but limited disposable income.

The second challenge is the solution itself. The mobile devices may allow freedom to multitask and allow greater access for many people. However, are companies prepared with the right solutions and applications to maximize the advantages of the 3G mobile devices? Let's go back to Chapter Three. Are the universities prepared to structure courses that involve sending digitized images when communicating with mobile students? Are companies prepared to host teleconferences that are mobile, while sending digitized images back and forth? What happens to data capturing? What about the reuse of knowledge objects? What about disciplined, standardized processes?

Seeking the Right Alliance Partners

The critical success factor for telecommunications companies may be to work with each industry sector, identify and quantify the value of

3G wireless devices, and formulate value-based solutions for the industry with the right alliance partners that embrace the 3G wireless devices. This is a daunting task, but a necessary one to differentiate 3G wireless devices.

Sales Alliance

There are numerous industries that rely on dealer or retail networks to sell a vast array of products and services. Tires, cars, auto parts, electronics, home improvement materials, landscaping, food, and numerous other products are sold through dealers and retail outlets. The telecommunications companies can identify one industry group with a major company that has an existing system—such as tires—and develop a sales alliance with the major company and perhaps the industry association. With a sales alliance, the key is to tap into an existing system to drive greater sales—for the company with the system as well as for the major telecommunications company and the mobile device manufacturer.

Solution-Specific Alliance

Very few companies have real-time order management systems that are complete with networked customer fulfillment capabilities. Perhaps the telecommunications companies can pick one or two key industries that rely on dealers or retailers for product sales and service and identify a "beta" client. The telecommunications company and the mobile device company can enter into a solution-specific alliance with the beta client to develop an industrywide real-time order management system that connects to customer fulfillment and utilizes mobile devices. The beta company benefits by having access to an innovative solution ahead of its competitors. The telecommunications company and the mobile wireless device manufacturer benefit by creating a solution that is dependent on mobile devices.

An example of a solution-specific device may be the development of a disease-recognition solution that incorporates the digitized, color images of lab cultures and communicates them to doctors around the world for analysis. Imagine how the Centers for Disease Control could use these digitized color images sent by their workers from locations in Central America, Africa, Asia, or any other part of the world. The accuracy of their work, matched with the ability to communicate with the CDC labs on a real-time basis with enhanced data, would dramatically improve their productivity and their results.

Geographic-Specific Alliance

There are some industries that have transcended the limits of geography and that are truly global. The investment banking and securities trading industries do business twenty-four hours a day, seven days a week, and 365 days a year. However, what about the ski industry we discussed in Chapter Three? Although people can (and some try to) ski year around, the ski resorts and supporting companies usually operate only during the winter months. Some ski resorts do open up in the summer for hiking and fly-fishing, while they focus on off-season maintenance and repair of their ski facilities.

Telecommunications companies and mobile device manufacturers can develop an alliance with major ski resorts and their associated communities to develop a real-time, personalized reservation and vacation planning system. This system could identify lodging, transportation, ski lift tickets, supplies, dinner options, and alternative entertainment options that are indigenous to the area. It could "commit to promise," matching the customer demand to their supply. The customer could configure their vacation from anywhere, while the service providers could commit-to-promise on all vacation details.

The difference between this solution and the use of a travel agent is the geographic-based "travel solution" focused on the customer that is integrated into the service providers. The current travel systems are event-based, with the most advanced integrated solution matching airline reservations with cruises. In addition, travel agents are "sold-to" by service providers to "push" their services. This real-time solution would give the option to the customer to select what they wanted, with the assurance that the providers would commit-to-promise as well.

Investment Alliance

In the consumer products and retail industries, major retailers are aggressively rolling out *scan-based trading* (SBT), which is the process by which consumer products companies are paid when (and if) their products sell in retail outlets. The proof of a "sale" is the scanner detail generated at the cash register.

Wal-Mart and Home Depot are among several retailers that are rolling out SBT with their store-door delivery suppliers. The process to manufacture, ship, and stack the store shelves must be very defined and disciplined. However, the missing link is the discipline around the store set or store shelf "plan-o-gram" that positions the consumer-product company's products on the store shelf of the retailer.

The plan-o-gram positions the company's products for maximum throughput and profitability. It is the responsibility of the store-door delivery salesperson to ensure that the plan-o-gram is replenished exactly as needed by the consumer-product company and demanded by the negotiations agreement with the retailer. It is even more critical with SBT, where the responsibility to document the shipment of product to the retailer and the placement of inventory on the store shelves rests with the store-door delivery company—and not with the retailer.

The use of 3G mobile devices to capture the images of the store shelf plan-o-gram can be a major enabler of SBT. The digitized images with date and time stamps can provide proof of placement of inventory on a retailer's store shelf. It can also have a secondary benefit of quality assurance though the supervision of direct-store-delivery personnel.

However, the investment to replace the handheld DSD computers with 3G mobile devices can be daunting. Despite the benefits of digitized images of store sets, the upgrade investment from handheld computers to 3G wireless devices can be inhibited by the thin profit margins in the grocery industry.

This scenario—an emerging solution driven by mega-retailers where the significant up-front investment serves as a major inhibitor—offers a solid opportunity for telecommunications companies and mobile device manufacturers to create investment alliances. For example, a major SBT supplier such as Frito Lay could join forces with a major telecommunications company like Southwestern Bell Corporation (SBC) and a major mobile 3G wireless device manufacturer like Nokia. Nokia and SBC could "invest" in 3G wireless devices for Frito Lay that would mirror the functionality of handheld computers and utilize the benefits of digitized images with voice transfer.

Frito Lay wins by gaining first-to-market access to the next generation of store-door delivery mobile devices at cost or a dramatically reduced cost. SBC and Nokia win by using an industry leader like Frito Lay to develop the de facto standard of mobile communications devices for all DSD companies participating in SBT programs.

Joint Venture Alliance

The above investment alliance may need an additional alliance partner. Fujitsu is a major manufacturer of existing handheld computers used by many direct store delivery suppliers. These handheld computers capture replenishment data and connect to host computers to track inventory movement. They can even produce an invoice for the retailer (nonscan-based trading) for the inventory replenished on the shelves.

There is an opportunity for SBC Corporation and Nokia to enter into a joint venture with Fujitsu to evolve and manufacture handheld computers that are 3G wireless enabled. This joint venture will allow for the physical separation of the 3G wireless enabled handhelds from the traditional Fujitsu handheld computer division and the separation of the 3G wireless handhelds from the mobile communications devices division of Nokia.

The advantage of a joint venture is the alignment of focus and financial incentives through a separate physical entity. This separate physical entity will allow for a joint team to penetrate a key industry sector, driving a growth in 3G wireless services that is solution-based.

In April 2001, Ericsson Inc. and Sony Corporation announced their intent to form Sony Ericsson, a joint venture to design, produce, develop, and market current and 3G mobile communication devices. This joint venture was announced as a 50-50 joint venture, with Ericsson's CEO becoming chairman and the head of Sony's handset division becoming the CEO of the joint venture.[2]

Ericsson had been struggling with operating losses, attributed to its global handset division and its investments in 3G technologies. Ericsson's market position in handset sales dropped to number 4 during the first quarter of 2001, falling behind Nokia, Motorola, and Siemens AG.[3] The joint venture will allow Ericsson to maximize leverage of its first-rate networks division, while leveraging Sony's design and marketing core competencies. It also allows Ericsson to stem the tide of its operating losses in its handset division, while staying connected through the joint venture to this all-important segment. The joint venture also allows Sony to expand its access to the mobile communications device market at a time when 3G wireless networks are about to be rolled out in Japan.

The use of alliances to combine core competencies can be timely and rewarding. However, the creation of solutions with multiple companies within these alliances can pose a daunting challenge, even for the most adept organizations. Let's take a look at a process to guide the creation of solutions with multiple, diverse organizations.

Scan, Focus, and Act

The use of a framework is critical to guide the collective thought processes and create innovative solutions. This framework needs to be able to harness divergent and convergent thinking in a way to forge action steps that have the consensus buy-in of all participants. Let's look at one framework that embraces the concept of divergence, convergence, and consensus around next steps. This framework involves three parts: scan, focus, and act.

Scan

In the beginning of the first step, the ground rules for the process need to be established. These ground rules should include one person speaking at a time, mutual respect for all people, and sticking to the task within each step. After the ground rules are established, the multiple companies must embark on the Scan step.

During the Scan step, the participants work on divergent thinking around a loosely defined objective. Divergent thinking involves brainstorming, where all ideas are good ideas. These ideas must be captured (preferably electronically, but flip charts will do fine as a traditional substitute). The facilitator must be strong, and not allow the "qualification" of ideas in the Scan step. This step is designed for participants to do a creative "brain dump." Premature qualification or judgment on ideas will not only kill potentially good ideas, but also will inhibit the surfacing of ideas from people who would choose not to have their ideas challenged or choose to avoid embarrassment.

The facilitator should let the brainstorming or divergent thinking go as far as the production of ideas will allow. When the ideas slow considerably and the energy diminishes, the facilitator should take the action to close this step. The Scan step can be mentally exhausting, and can also be challenging for execution-minded executives. The facilitator must allow for a proper break immediately after the Scan step.

The facilitator should also consider inviting selected subject matter experts into the Scan step. Divergent thinking relies on the use of creative thinking, or "out of the box" thinking, as some people prefer. This type of thinking is not common. You may know of people that excel in this area, in which case their use can help augment the free-thinking capability of the group and enhance the output of the entire process.

Focus

During the break after the Scan step, the facilitator and his or her team need to collate the brainstorming ideas. These ideas should be grouped in a loose confederation that supports the overall objective. For example, if Frito Lay, SBC Corporation, Nokia, and Fujitsu were participating on the store door delivery/scan-based-trading 3G mobile device, the groupings could include plan-o-gram images (before and after replenishment), store sets with associated product facings, replenishment data capturing, and reconciliation models that tie to scanner data. There even could be a "competitor activity" section to provide the Networked Value Chain participants with competitive activity on a real-time basis with image transfers.

After the proper mental and physical break, it is time to let loose the execution-minded executives. In each grouping, the group will have the opportunity to "converge" their thinking around the validity and application of the ideas. This is the time where off-the-wall ideas are either thrown out or become the next Windows 2000 or Post-it Notes product.

Some leading companies use technology to "neutralize" forceful or aggressive senior executives. One company in particular has desktop computers hooked right into a master computer and overhead screen. All the brainstorming or divergent ideas under a group heading are placed for comment to the large group. The comments are then sent to the master computer anonymously, and are displayed for all to see, followed by an open discussion on the comments. This works especially well when there is a very strong, overbearing boss who does not like open discussion on ideas other than his own.

The ideas are then grouped into "definitely consider," "maybe consider," and "do not consider for this objective." The facilitator must guard against jumping straight into solutions, or "Act." The end result of the Focus or Converging step must be a list of "definitely consider" ideas under group headings that support the overall objective. Formulating solutions before finishing the Focus step will preempt the value of all solutions.

In the Focus step, the creative, freethinking subject matter experts should still participate. Their ideas should not be subject to elimination by narrow-minded executives who may or may not understand a creative idea if it hit them in the face. There must be a balance, albeit a delicate one, that the facilitator must strive to achieve.

Act

The team is now ready to take the "definitely consider" ideas under each group heading and craft an innovative solution supporting the overall objective. This solution should have a scope, a description of how the solution would work (process and high-level activities), and an anticipated time line for the solution.

Each solution should then have a responsible person who would "own" the solution development. In addition, the people who are designated to support the responsible person in terms of approvals, resources, or other tasks should be identified as committed participants. There should also be a solution steering committee made up of senior representatives from each participating company. A schedule of steering committee review dates mapped to the solution development time line and milestones should be completed and distributed. One Fortune 100 company has their executives sign the summary document that results from an Act step. This summary document is then blown up, laminated, and distributed for display in the lobbies of the offices. The chief executive officer wants the responsible executives to walk past these laminated summary documents every day and be physically reminded of their commitments.

The Scan, Focus, and Act process is a powerful framework that helps enable the creative crafting of unique, game-changing solutions among alliance partners. There is one item missing from the above framework, which is, how do you get people from different companies to come together and discuss their thoughts in a creative but protected environment? What will guard against having one company shop the creative ideas to the highest bidding competitor? One way is to have the participating companies sign a nondisclosure agreement (NDA) before starting the Scan, Focus, and Act process. The section at the end of this chapter walks you through the process of how to construct an NDA.

Summary

The telecommunications companies and the 3G wireless device manufacturers have a huge financial challenge to address. They must find innovative ways to differentiate 3G wireless devices in the marketplace. To accomplish this, they must tap into the value streams of specific industry sectors, and develop solutions that require the use of 3G wireless networks and 3G wireless devices.

The Networked Value Chain provides a solid framework for telecommunications companies and mobile device manufacturers to use to tap into the value streams of industry sectors. It also provides a solid framework for them to use to establish the needed alliances to achieve the penetration of the value streams.

Alliances are critical to create innovative solutions and to make operational the solutions in the marketplace with the needed speed. Alliance partners bring expertise and capabilities to jump-start needed solutions. The key is to understand how to work with alliance partners to maximize the leverage of combined capabilities and result in a win for all parties.

How to Construct a Nondisclosure Agreement

A nondisclosure agreement is a legal document that identifies confidential information and the expected behavior of the participating parties in relation to coming into contact with this information. Two or multiple parties may sign this document, depending upon the need and the situation. Let's look at a potential NDA that would cover the joint venture discussions between Frito Lay, SBC, Nokia, and Fujitsu.

The introduction of the Nondisclosure Agreement usually contains four to five paragraphs. The first paragraph identifies the participating parties by formal name, and establishes the effective date for the NDA. The second paragraph identifies what company owns what material, and identifies that the participating parties desire to explore a joint solution that utilizes the mentioned material and is implemented through jointly developed processes, methods, or other resources. The third paragraph introduces the fact that the participating parties wish to disclose certain information deemed confidential and proprietary to each other. The fourth paragraph describes the purpose of disclosing the proprietary information (e.g., ". . . the purpose of the disclosures of proprietary information is to facilitate solution discussions between the multiple parties to achieve a joint venture around a joint solution or to disband without a joint solution . . .").

In support of the objectives stated in the introduction, most nondisclosure agreements cover eight or more frequently cited items.

1. The first item describes how "confidential information" is deemed confidential. For example, confidential information can be in written form and marked "confidential," in oral form and identified as "confidential" when spoken, or—in the absence of written and oral form—any information that a reasonable party would deem to be confidential and nonpublic in nature. Some NDAs list specific examples of confidential information, such as customer lists, specific software technology, trade secrets, ideas, concepts, designs, flow charts, drawings, diagrams, or other intellectual property. In some cases, NDAs even cover the results of the use of confidential information in joint solution settings.

2. The second item identifies that each party is receiving the information in confidence. It also specifies that each party agree not to copy, disclose, or publish the confidential information other than to those connected individuals that must per-

form their duties to support the identified solution. This item also demands that the connected parties become bound by the NDA. In addition, this item will restrict the use of the confidential information by each party to the solution or joint venture being discussed.

3. The third item identifies the part of confidential information that is excluded from the NDA obligations. This includes information that was in the public domain when the participating parties received it, information that entered into the public domain through means other than what was controlled by the participating parties, and information already in the possession of the participating parties when it was introduced during the joint solution or joint venture discussions.

It also includes information developed or received by employees of the participating companies independent of the solution or joint venture discussions, information disclosed and approved for released with permission, and information required to be disclosed by law or government authority. Sometimes, the NDA will outline a process that requires the receiving party to notify the owner of the confidential information of the legal requirement, which provides adequate time for the owner to try and obtain a protective order for that information.

4. The fourth item specifies that the parties either have acquired the right or interest to the confidential information through their efforts with the solution development or the joint venture, or have acquired no right or interest to the confidential information.

5. The fifth item specifies that all originals and any copies of confidential information remain the property of the originating party. In this item, the parties may be required only to produce reproductions of confidential information in its original form with the proper copyright or confidential markings. In addition, the parties may also be required to return all confidential documents or certify their destruction after use.

6. The sixth item specifies that the obligations of the parties cannot be assigned, sold, or transferred to an outside party. It also identifies the state or country that will govern the NDA.

This item can also specify that any changes to the NDA must be made through an amendment signed by all parties.

7. The seventh item covers the notification of one party to the other parties that subsequent communications are no longer confidential. It also covers the method by which this notification can be communicated (e.g., mail, in person, e-mail, etc.).

8. The eighth item covers the term of the NDA (e.g., three years from the effective date, or termination at any time in writing by either party). In addition, this item may identify the term of the confidential information that could eclipse the term of the NDA.

The ninth and subsequent items may cover items beyond the previous eight. This could include protective measures when the parties come together in joint solution development (e.g., no laptop computers used in and out of the meeting rooms). It could also include noncompete clauses for specific participants and nonsolicitation and/or nonhiring of personnel by parties to the NDA.

The NDA is then completed and executed by officers or authorized personnel for each participating party. The signatures, printed names, and dates of signatures complete the execution of the NDA. All personnel with each party then fall under the NDA. As my son says, the parties are now "good to go!"

The NDA is a document that can stand up in a court of law if confidential information is compromised. By having a signed NDA, companies like Frito Lay, SBC Company, Nokia, and Fujitsu can come together for the purpose of developing a joint solution and discuss confidential information with a feeling of legal protection. Without the NDA, companies may be reluctant to share key information, which considerably diminishes the potential for developing a game-changing solution. The items identified above should be considered as a sample of or a template for constructing an NDA. Anyone developing an NDA should always work with legal counsel to construct the right NDA for the right situation.

Notes

1. Fred A. Kuglin and Barbara A. Rosenbaum, *The Supply Chain Network @ Internet Speed* (New York: AMACOM, 2001).
2. "Ericsson, Sony Plan 50-50 Joint Venture," *Dallas Morning News* from *The Wall Street Journal*, April 24, 2001, p. 4D.
3. Almar Latour and Edward Harris, "Ericsson Loss Puts Its Board in Crisis Mode," *The Wall Street Journal*, April 23, 2001, pp. A15, A16.

CHAPTER FIVE

Mission Impossible? From Intense Competitor to Alliance Partner!

The autumn morning was crystal clear, with a high blue sky and a gentle southern breeze. As I walked across the tarmac of Edwards Air Force Base, my pulse quickened when I approached my assignment for the day. Today, I was to be the chief test pilot for the new F-22 Raptor.

The F-22 Raptor is being developed by the U.S. Air Force to replace the current F-15 fighter jets. The increasing sophistication and the threat of hostile air forces with integrated air defense systems have combined to create the need for a next-generation fighter. The new F-22 will have a balance of speed and range, enhanced offensive and defensive avionics, and low observability, or stealth. Its design will also emphasize reliability and maintainability of systems.[1]

Ringing in my ears were the words of my commanding officer, as he quoted the F-22 press guide. "The F-22 provides a first-look, first-shot, first-kill capability through the use of stealth technology and advanced sensors. The F-22 also requires a shorter takeoff and landing distances, as compared to current frontline fighters. F-22 pilots will be able to engage the enemy over its own territory and support long-range air-to-ground assets such as the F-15E. The F-22 also brings its own precision ground attack capability to the battlefield."[2]

Just as I was about to climb into the cockpit, I was awakened by the American Airlines pilot and his welcoming announcement on our flight to Los Angeles. The last words in my dream were my commanding officer saying, "Don't crash my new test fighter . . . do you know how much they are worth . . . payroll deduction won't even cover the loss of the tires . . ."

It is obvious I had been dreaming. The reason I had this dream was the person sitting next to me on the plane. As I boarded my flight to Los Angeles, I took my seat on one of American Airlines' Boeing 757. As a Partner/VP with a major consulting firm, I am very cautious as to when and where I work on my personal computer (both the days and nights have 1,000 eyes—or more!). Which is why I asked the gentleman sitting next to me what he did for a living. He told me he was a design engineer for a major defense and aerospace company (Lockheed Martin Aeronautics Company) that built fighter planes. This brief introduction had apparently led to my dream.

Our conversation on the plane evolved into a discussion on the process to bid, design, build, and manufacture fighter planes. Besides my heightened fascination with the process, there were five main learnings that surfaced from this discussion.

1. The process to bid, design, build, and manufacture fighter planes can take 20 to 30 years!
2. The process to bid on these huge fighter plane contracts is time-consuming, extremely high-cost, and politically sensitive.
3. Original concepts and specifications evolve over time.
4. Competitive bidders can and in some cases must be cooperative alliance partners in the design and build phases of the process.
5. There is an incredibly high demand for people who know

when and how to compete, and then know when and how to cooperate with competitors.

The U.S. Air Force is building the F-22 with an alliance among Lockheed Martin, Boeing, and Pratt & Whitney. It is managed by the F-22 System Program Office, which is part of the Aeronautical Systems Center at Wright-Patterson Air Force Base in Ohio. The F-22 is slated to be operational in 2005.[3]

The F-22 and Alliance Partnerships

This is all very interesting, but you may wonder what all of this has to do with alliances? The answer is a lot! The five learnings listed above all point to the need to compete with your eventual partners over a protracted period of time. This industry provides an acid test for relationship-building and alliance skills built around a single program and which may span entire careers.

In addition, there were hard feelings and a lack of a true alliance partnership among the competitors who teamed to win the F-22 design. These competitors spent several years putting their heart and soul into competing for the F-22 award. It was very difficult for them to embrace their competitors as alliance partners virtually overnight. Perhaps a process to connect with the different personality or social styles of the key people involved would have facilitated a tighter alliance partnership among the competitors.

In this chapter, we will review the different personality social styles and how connecting with them can facilitate the process for competitors becoming alliance partners. But first, let's take a look at the F-22 lifecycle and the F-22 design evolution and see how fierce competitors became reluctant but eventual alliance partners in this critical program.

The F-22 Lifecycle

The formal origins of the F-22 can be traced back to its predecessor, the Advanced Tactical Fighter (ATF) program. The U.S. Air Force

Aeronautical Systems Division (ASD) released a request for information for concepts for an advanced tactical fighter in 1981. However, the term "advanced tactical fighter" already appeared in a general operational requirements document issued to contractors in 1972, which pertained to a new air-to-ground fighter to complement the then new F-15 fighter.[4]

The time span from the original concept (1972) to operational status (2005) is thirty-three years. This is unbelievable! Even using the formal origin date of the F-22 of 1981, the time span is twenty-four years. I was nineteen years old and a sophomore in college in 1972. It is possible that many of you weren't even born yet!

What is amazing is the numbers of companies that competed for the contracts to design, build, and manufacture the F-22 during these years. What is even more amazing is how these companies had to transition from "competitor" to "alliance partner" along the way.

The F-22 Design Evolution

In the mid to late 1970s, studies for new fighter airplanes shifted from the ASD to the U.S.A.F. Flight Dynamics Lab (now called Air Vehicles Directorate of the AF Research Laboratory, or simply the Lab). In essence, the ASD supported aircraft development programs while the Lab pursued technologies related to military aircraft.

From 1975 to 1980, the Lab sponsored four R&D contracts that would have direct input into the F-22 Design proposals. These four contracts were as follows:

1. 1975: "Advanced Technology Ground Attack Fighter" (General Dynamics and McDonnell Douglas)
2. 1975–1980: "Air-to-Surface Technology Study" (six companies)
3. 1980: "Tactical Fighter Technology Alternatives" for future air to ground fighters (Boeing and Grumman)
4. 1980: "1995 Fighter Technology" (General Dynamics and McDonnell Douglas)

In the early 1970s, Lockheed performed some of the first studies for a "Super Stealth" air-to-ground attack airplane for the U.S. Navy, according to Bart Osborne, program manager for Lockheed's Tactical Systems in 1972. (Bart was also Chief Engineer of the Demonstration/ Validation phase of the ATF Program in the mid 1980s.) On the surface, it appears that the Lockheed work on "super stealth" went dormant while the company pursued the F-117 program. ("Stealth" in military terms means the ability to detect the enemy before he detects you!)

However, Stephen Justice, one of Lockheed's design engineers on the F-22, places this in perspective:

> I wouldn't say that Lockheed's work on Stealth was dormant during this time frame. In the pursuit of the stealth fighter program, Lockheed focused its efforts in applying lessons learned from the true first generation of stealth aircraft, the A-12/SR-71/D-21 Blackbird family, to the next generation of observables reduction. Most external sources ignore the Blackbird family as the first generation of stealth and consider the Have Blue/F-117 to be the first generation. However, the insiders know differently. Lockheed's significant efforts to mature the technologies for a stealth fighter disappeared behind a curtain by design, only to be revealed by the first public disclosure of the F-117 by the USAF in 1989.

Boeing studied a wide range of air-to-ground fighters in the 1970s, ranging from supersonic to subsonic designs. General Dynamics studied a wide range of advanced fighter concepts and modifications to existing fighters (F-16, F-15, and F-111). The advanced concepts included a conventional aircraft (Plain Jane), a supersonic stealth configuration, a small inexpensive fighter (Bushwhacker), a large fighter (Missileer), and a highly stealthy all-wing fighter (Sneaky Pete).

These and other studies were focused on identifying the most promising design concepts and enabling technologies for the next generation fighter.

Preeminent Characteristics for Achieving Air Superiority

The "1995 Fighter Technology" study completed by General Dynamics and McDonnell Douglass in 1980 identified three critical characteristics for achieving air superiority. The preeminent characteristic was identified as "stealth." The other two critical characteristics identified were "speed" and "maneuverability."

Stealth

According to Bill Moran, Deputy Director of the F-22 Program in Ft. Worth (and formerly the General Dynamics Program Manager for analyses for flight dynamics), stealth characteristics have long been regarded as the preeminent characteristic by fighter pilots. He identifies the "Red Baron Study," a real-time U.S. Air Force analysis of combat in Vietnam, that showed that over 50 percent of the aircrews shot down and over 80 percent of those fired upon were unaware of their attackers. Available data support similar experiences in World War II and Korea. People close to the F-22 design team have told me that the first attempt to use radar-absorbing materials was by Germany in the 1940s. Both General Dynamics and Lockheed explored stealth technology in the 1970s and researched ways to avoid the detection of flat surfaces on radar. Some of this early work found its way into the F-117 Nighthawk, and set the stage for the use of stealth technology in the F-22.

Speed

Speed was the second of the three critical characteristics for an air superiority fighter. The ability both to outrun an opponent and to fly long distances in the shortest time possible was the driving force behind the F-22 Flight Dynamics Lab work. This work produced studies that focused on an aircraft that would have supercruise and supersonic flight capabilities without using an afterburner. (The afterburner is a source of infrared energy, and as such would work against the stealth objectives for the F-22.) Early work in this area showed up in the B-58 Hustler and F-16 variants. However, any mil-power supersonic capability the F-16 had had been merely residual and only existed in a "clean" configuration (no external weapons). Even then, the achievable Mach number would be something like 1.02. The F-22 was designed to achieve a supercruise mach number of at least 1.4 with weapons (albeit shielded in internal weapons bays).

Maneuverability

Maneuverability was the third of the three critical characteristics for an air superiority fighter. Fighter pilots use maneuverability primarily for defensive tactics. There are four common measures of merit for maneuverability.

- ✧ *Sustained g Capability:* The ability to turn hard without losing airspeed and altitude
- ✧ *Instantaneous g:* The ability to turn the nose of the aircraft without regard to the effect on speed
- ✧ *Specific Excess Power:* A measure of an aircraft's potential to climb, accelerate, or turn at any flight condition
- ✧ *Transonic Acceleration Time:* For example, the time needed to go from Mach 0.8 to Mach 1.2

When comparing two fighter jets using these characteristics, one can assess which fighter will have the tactical advantage in a maneuvering engagement. As such, fighter pilots want good maneuverability everywhere, increasing their tactical effectiveness.

Other Characteristics

Other characteristics were reviewed but judged to be less critical than stealth, speed, and maneuverability. These characteristics involved the operating of aircraft from battle-damaged runways and included short takeoff and landing (STOL), short takeoff and vertical landing (STOVL), and vertical takeoff and landing (VTOL). The cost of designing this capability into the ATF far outstripped the desirability of this characteristic. The takeoff and landing distances governing this characteristic were lengthened during the demonstration/validation phase of the program to mitigate the extra weight and cost of the program.

The Challenge

The integration of stealth, speed, and maneuverability became the challenge for the ATF program. The complexity was enormous. A stealth aircraft necessitates a large, internal weapons bay. This internal weapons bay increases the cross-section of the aircraft, which works against the super-cruise or speed characteristic. Maneuverability increases the size of the wings and tails, which in turn demands larger engines. Larger engines work against the stealth characteristic. The experts say that the complexity list goes on and on. The demand for expertise in each critical characteristic was extremely high.

Steve Justice said it best:

> As a chief engineer on an airplane program, I knew that I had the right balance across the disciplines when each of the lead personnel had the same size tears in their eyes. No single discipline can win, although some may be pushed to the background, and there are repeated examples of this in military aircraft. In the case of the F-117, aerodynamic efficiency was the most obviously compromised area. While it cannot be totally ignored, in the case of the F-117, it was better to just burn more fuel and retain the low observables characteristics than increase the aero efficiency to get the necessary range-payload performance. The biggest hits to aero efficiency came from the highly swept wings and faceted shape, both of which were overcome with improvements to stealth technology for the F-22.

The 1981 ATF Request for Information

The requirements for the 1981 Advanced Technical Fighter RFI released by the U.S. Air Force ASD were as follows:

- ✧ Air-to-ground fighter
- ✧ Fly Mach 2.5 at high to medium altitudes
- ✧ Carry standoff weapons designed to destroy tanks and other ground targets

Nine airframe companies and three engine manufacturers responded to the RFI. Lockheed and Boeing submitted responses that took a supersonic approach and favored air-to-ground missions. The General Dynamics response favored a couple of concepts developed in

1976–1978. One was the Model 21, and the other a next-generation "Sneaky Pete." Because of its classification, the real drawings of the next generation of "Sneaky Pete" could not be submitted. Bizarre as it is to the nonmilitary person (like me), these real drawings became the starting point for all flying wing (tailless) studies explored in the next phase of the ATF program!

Four Generic Fighter Designs

The ASD categorized the aircraft designs submitted and investigated by the responding companies into four groups. The ASD labeled these groups as follows:

- ✧ N for numbers or aircraft to be bought cheaply and in high numbers
- ✧ SDM for supersonic dash and maneuver, emphasizing speed and maneuverability
- ✧ SLO for subsonic low observables, based on a flying wing design
- ✧ HI for high-Mach/high-altitude, representing a large missileer

The mission analyses on these four generic aircraft designs favored the SLO, or flying wing design. The SDM that emphasized speed and maneuverability came in second, with the N and HI not rating well.

The Years 1981 to 1985

When the RFI results were released in late 1981, the ATF program gained momentum. In late 1981, the Tactical Air Command issued a "mission element need statement" and a corresponding "statement of need." The latter document described threats, theatres of operation, and capabilities needed to accomplish the mission identified in the "statement of need." The "statement of need" was provided to the responding companies in mid-1982 for their comments. These steps formally made the ATF the replacement for the F-15. The ATF System Program Office was formed at Wright Patterson AFB in 1983.

In May 1983, a request for proposal (RFP) was issued for the ATF engine. General Electric (engine F120) and Pratt & Whitney (engine

F119) were awarded contracts to build and test competing engine designs. During this same time period, an RFP was issued for a concept definition investigation for the ATF. Seven aircraft companies (Boeing, General Dynamics, Grumman, Lockheed, McDonnell Douglas, Northrop, and Rockwell) responded and prepared proposals to be submitted mid-June 1983.

At the end of June (and a two-week delay), the ASD asked the seven companies to add an addendum to describe their stealth-related skills and experience. This was highly unusual, since most if not all of the stealth work was classified at that time.

Each of the seven companies that bid on the concept definition investigation phase was awarded contracts worth approximately $1 million. This work was performed from September 1984 to May 1985. The work submitted by the seven companies would lead to the demonstration/validation phase. The Air Force issued the requests for proposals for the demonstration/validation phase in September 1985, with a December 1985 deadline for responses. The intent of the Air Force was to award four winning companies $100 million contracts for the demonstration/validation phase.

Up until the time that the Air Force issued their request for proposals in September 1985, Lockheed's performance had lagged behind its competitors. During 1985, Lockheed set out to make a "curved stealth aircraft" to improve its performance in speed and maneuverability. This revamped approach and Lockheed's stealth experience worked to their advantage.

Boeing's concept was a larger aircraft than Lockheed's or General Dynamics. They designed the airplane around the weapons bay. The company's design appeared to be well developed. In addition, the company had extensive experience in integrating avionics and a significant production capability.

The General Dynamics concept was a semi-tailless approach that did well in maneuverability and supersonic cruise. It did not do well in the stealth characteristic. It did, however, achieve a high state of detailed design. This detail design included preliminary structural designs with locations for manufacturing breaks to allow for the aircraft to be divided among several partners. General Dynamics also had extensive fighter design, manufacturing experience, and rapid prototyping with its F-16.

Late in 1985 there was an amended request to increase the importance of the stealth characteristic. Lockheed made no changes, while Boeing made some minor changes to their design. General Dynamics had to reevaluate its design, settling on the twin tails design.

The MR-006: From Competitor to Alliance Partner

The Air Force made a significant amendment to the RFP for the demonstration/validation phase when they added prototyping. Each responding company was required to build two prototypes. One prototype was to be with the General Electric F-120 engine, and the other prototype was to be with the Pratt & Whitney F-119 engine.

The Air Force then added a modification request MR-006 to the RFP. In addition to the flying prototypes requested above, the Air Force changed the winning company scenario from four $100 million winners to two $700 million contract award winners. The addition to the proposal described how companies would design, build, and test these two flying prototypes. A ground-based avionics test lab was required, while a flying avionics test-bed was optional.

Then, in late 1985, the Air Force did the unthinkable. After years of intense competition and fierce fighting for positioning with the Air Force on the ATF program, the companies received a letter from the Air Force encouraging teaming.

(Think about how you would respond if you were asked by your largest customer to immediately team with your fiercest competitor!)

Boeing, General Dynamics, and Lockheed signed a teaming agreement in June 1986. Each proposal response was sent in "blind," and the winning company would be the "prime contractor." Northrop and McDonnell Douglass announced their teaming agreement in August 1986. Grumman and Rockwell did not team.

In October 1986, five years after the initial RFI, the Air Force announced that Lockheed and Northrop were the top two contenders. Not surprising, the two companies that did not team were nonwinners. The stage was set between the two alliances to compete against each other for the final right to design, build, and produce the ATF.

The Road from Competitor to Alliance Partner

The ATF, or F-22 Raptor as it is now called, was and is a huge program. Each company invested hundreds of millions or more in research into the critical characteristics of the new fighter. The intent of the Air Force was to utilize a way to keep as much as possible of the talent behind the research and knowledge developed over the years as part of the on-going program. With only one winner out of the seven competing companies, the talent pool would have been seriously depleted. Through teaming, the Air Force was able to keep the talent of three of the seven competing companies as part of the ongoing program.

However, the real challenge was about to begin. How do you retrain intense competitors to become alliance partners literally overnight? The answer is not blowing in the wind. It is rooted in understanding the basic personality types of people, and how these personality types interact with other personality types and job-related stimuli. The following example showcases how the use of personality typing helped Frito Lay knock down traditional functional barriers and connect people throughout their networked supply chain.

Real World Example: Frito Lay, Charlie Cotton, and the Networked Supply Chain

During my years at Frito Lay, I had the pleasure of working for Charlie Cotton. Charlie was vice president of logistics and area vice president of manufacturing, among other positions, during his tenure with Frito Lay. In the early 1980, Charlie began a journey to pull together multiple vertical supply chain functions and create a horizontal supply chain. The end customer anchored this horizontal supply chain. His vision was to have all networked supply chain partners working together to provide the finished Frito Lay products to the final customer. This required people working with people from different companies, different training, and different performance measurements and incentives.

Charlie recruited strategic-thinking managers to work within his vision to transform the functional supply world of Frito Lay into a networked supply chain. He also recognized one major inhibitor to his transformation process, which was that the Frito-Lay managers were functionally trained and execution-focused, and as such they relied on the command-and-control approach to working with people. Charlie also knew that his managers used this approach when they dealt with outside suppliers and transport providers. It was as if his managers were competing with their suppliers and transport providers in a continuous win-lose environment. Charlie knew that this approach would not work very well in his plan to migrate from a functional, competitive environment to an extended-enterprise networked supply chain.

There were three major components to Charlie's people plan. The first was to recruit the strategic-thinking managers, as stated above. The second component was to rotate people between functions as functions were rolled into the supply chain operations group. The third one was the most effective, and for the time, the most innovative component to his plan. Charlie had key managers in his organization become "people leaders." These key managers worked with Stephen R. Covey and his workshop on "Seven Basic Habits of Highly Effective People." (Remember, this was in the mid-1980s, before Covey's book was published in 1989![5]) Charlie complemented the Covey training with personality or social styles training. All of us key leaders became Covey-ized and personality-typing trained.

Charlie promoted two types of personality/social styles profile programs with his key leaders. For an overall perspective, he promoted the Myers-Briggs profile, using the Keirsey Temperament Sorter Test.[6] From a networked supply chain effectiveness standpoint, Charlie promoted the Wilson Learning Center Social Styles Profile.[7]

Migrating people from a functional, internal environment to a networked supply chain environment was a significant challenge. Charlie began his journey with a traffic and transportation of finished goods organization. He then added order entry (from manufacturing), warehousing (from manufacturing), inbound raw material transportation (from purchasing), inbound procurement callouts and master contract balancing (from purchasing), sales distribution operations (from sales), vend and food service order entry, customer service and delivery (from channel sales), production schedule-need sheet preparation (from manufacturing), and systems application development for operations (from the IT organization). Charlie knew that his key leaders would begin working with vend and food service customers, potato farmers, cellophane manufacturing agents, railroad operations and service personnel, produce brokers, technology providers, seasoning manufacturing agents, and many more external partners as he evolved Frito Lay into a networked supply chain. The command-and-control training to drive execution within the four walls of Frito Lay would have to migrate to an influencing management style as the key leaders worked with people outside of Frito Lay.

According to Charlie, for us to be effective in migrating to an influencing management style, we first had to understand who we were and what style we were born with. The understanding of who we were was addressed through the Covey "Private Victory," which is a summary of his first three habits.[8] The understanding of the personality or social style profile we were born with was addressed through the Keirsey Temperament Sorter Profile and the Wilson Learning Center Social Styles Profile. The next step, understanding the personality types of others and knowing how to connect and influence others, was addressed using the Keirsey Temperament Sorter.

The Keirsey Temperament Sorter Profile

The Keirsey Temperament Sorter is an outstanding program. The following brief overview is designed to showcase the need to understand how personality types will interact differently in any given situation. I recommend that you read *Please Understand Me II*,[9] take the Keirsey Temperament Sorter Profile test, and thus tap thoroughly into the complete value of understanding personality types, including your own.

David Keirsey originally published the Keirsey Temperament Sorter in the book *Please Understand Me.*[6] The main point underlying the Keirsey Temperament Sorter is that people are different from each other, with the underlying premise that the differences are probably good. The Keirsey Temperament Sorter utilizes the Myers Briggs letters to identify descriptive words for personalities. These letters or descriptions are in alternative pairs. People fall into one category or another, with varying degrees or emphasis. These alternative pairs of letters are as follows:

E = Extroverted	or	I = Introverted
S = Sensory	or	N = Intuitive
T = Thinking	or	F = Feeling
J = Judging	or	P = Perceiving

After completing the Keirsey Temperament Sorter questionnaire, a person will fall into one of four broad categories. These categories are SPs, SJs, NFs, and NTs. The SPs are "Artisans," the SJs are "Guardians," the NFs are "Idealists," and the NTs are "Rationals." There are actually four personality types within each of those four groups.[10]

The Keirsey Temperament Sorter is a wonderful program for identifying your personality type, understanding your tendencies, and understanding the other fifteen personality types. Once you have achieved an understanding, you can apply this knowledge to understanding personalities within business environments and scenarios. Let's take a look at different personality tendencies and how these tendencies could have been applied to the F-22 Raptor program.

Outgoing or Reserved

In the major personality typing programs, there is an identification of whether people are outgoing or reserved. Keirsey identified outgoing personalities as "extroverted," and reserved personalities as "introverted." My daughter is the classic extrovert, and can talk to almost anyone in any situation. She will walk up to a group of people, listen to the subject of the conversation, and away she goes. My son, on the other hand, is slightly introverted. When he is in a group of people whom he does not know very well or knows only slightly, he will primarily listen and will speak only when spoken to. He prefers small groups as opposed to large groups and prefers to be around people he knows well in familiar surroundings. When he gets home from school, he will need to have an hour to recharge his batteries before getting involved in another social setting. My daughter gets home, only to pick up the phone or get on her e-mail to converse with her friends.

Sensing or Intuitive

Again using my children as examples, my son is a sensing personality. He is very hesitant to get into new situations, and will have to personally touch and feel something new before he gets comfortable with the situation. In fact, he almost has a crisis dealing with new experiences (new job, new role in school) until he is forced to go through the experience for the first time. After he goes through the new experience for the first time, the crisis is over, and he is at ease with the new situation. (He has worn out his parents though during the process!)

My daughter, on the other hand, is naturally intuitive. She can evaluate a situation, rely on her intuition, formulate how she should interact with the situation, and proceed with confidence. If she experiences anything different than anticipated, she quickly adjusts her intuition "map" and continues on. This allows my daughter to enter new situations with heightened anticipation and an intuitive mental road map to guide her as she experiences the new situation.

Thinking and Feeling

My son and daughter are close on this one. My son is between a thinker and a feeler. He wants to major in philosophy, and is focused on helping other people through the pursuit of "The Truth" (Aristotle and St. Ignatius would be pleased by his love of their philosophies!). He is active in civic and community service projects. However, he picks the projects based upon his scrutiny of their value to society and their "fit" in his social order mental model.

My daughter just focuses on helping people. She loves working with people to collectively work together and help others. For my daughter, the helping of others does not have to fit a mental, social order model that is based on "truth." She only desires the group interaction and the result of other people benefiting from her time and actions.

At work I did a quick mapping of my counseling family in "Thinking" or "Feeling." I used a scenario that involved a little league baseball team. In my scenario, I told the group that there were twenty-four children on the little league team. In addition, I told my counseling family that there was money only for eighteen children to attend a summer baseball camp 200 miles away. I then asked the counseling family members to separate themselves into two groups. The first group was to come up with a formula to select what eighteen children should go to the summer camp. The second group was to address alternatives to the baseball camp.

What occurred was fascinating. The group that separated itself to address which eighteen would be selected to go to the summer camp developed elaborate formulas to make their selections. These formulas ranged from athletic performance to fund-raising performance to a general lottery. This group, because of the directive given to them, attracted the "Thinkers" in the counseling family.

The group that was challenged to come up with alternatives had a totally different result. They made a blanket decision that if the team went to the summer camp, no child was to be excluded for any reason. After this decision, they then proceeded to look at fund-raising alternatives to raise the funds from a level supporting eighteen children to the level needed for the entire team. They also designed a wide array of support that included the parents, the community, and the summer camp itself. This group, because of the directive given to them, attracted the "Feelers" in the counseling family.

The end result was a polarization of the two groups. The same result occurs in the business world with real business scenarios.

Judging or Perceiving

Once again, my children are opposites with this personality pair. My son is disciplined in making scheduled judgments. He is factual, routinized, and primarily unimpulsive. My daughter is always open to probing for options. She has limited use for routinized, disciplined theories and wants to enjoy life. My son will carefully pick what foreign country to visit. My daughter will measure her success in terms of the number of new stamps in her passport.

In summary, then, my children tend to be very different personality types. I have observed them looking at the same situations in life and reach very different decisions on how to proceed.

In many respects, the same is true in the business world. People react to the same situations in vastly different ways. Let's take a look at Charlie Cotton's vision, and how this training helped Charlie in his pursuit for supply chain excellence.

Charlie's Vision

People have different personality types. What Charlie Cotton saw was the value in people understanding what personality type they were, recognizing what personality type the person they were interfacing with had, and understanding how to "connect" or communicate with the other person.

For instance, when I was an Area Networked Supply Chain Manager, and I had to interface with an extroverted marketing manager of a large grocery chain, I would focus on the traits of an "extroverted" personality style. I am an "extrovert" as well, so I would have to discipline myself to "listen" and allow the extroverted marketing manager to talk.

When I interfaced with a "Feeling" potato farmer, I would have to discipline myself to "tap into" my relationship with the farmer. An example of this was to have dinner with the farmer, drink a beer or two, and even tour his potato field. The same held true for when I interfaced with the "Thinking" design engineers of cellophane manufacturers and the "Thinking/Judging" production managers in the manufacturing department. By focusing on my personality style and the style of the person with whom I was communicating, I was able to effectively "connect" with people through the traits that supported their social style.

Charlie's approach helped Frito Lay build a world-class networked supply chain. It also provided a pathway for people influencing others when they must work together to produce a common good or service. The approach of using social styles can have a powerful impact on getting competitors to work as partners. Let's visit this scenario as it could have been applied with the F-22 program.

The F-22 Program and Personality Types

Earlier we saw that the process to bid, design, build, and manufacture fighter planes like the F-22 could take twenty to thirty years. This process is time-consuming, extremely costly, and politically sensitive. Original concepts and specifications evolve over time. In every step, real people are involved. These people have different levels of involvement with the program as well as different views of how the program should evolve to be successful.

When, at the encouragement of the U.S. Air Force, Lockheed, General Dynamics, and Boeing agreed to team on the F-22 program, the winning company was to be the lead or prime contractor, with the other two companies becoming subcontractors to the winner.

The challenge was twofold. The first was the challenge of perception. Exhibit 5-1 is the artist's rendition of the Lockheed-Boeing-General Dynamics YF-22 (or F-22) and the Northrup-McDonnell Douglas YF-23. These U.S. Air Force fighters, designed to the same set of speci-

Exhibit 5-1. YF-22 and YF-23 Demonstrators.

Lockheed-Boeing-General Dynamics YF-22
and Northrop-McDonnell Douglas YF-23
USAF Museum Photo Archives

fications and design requirements, look very different in this exhibit. Now, take a look at Exhibit 5-2. The artist's rendition of the Navy's Joint Strike Fighter Demonstrators shows a second time how different teams created different fighters from the same set of requirements. How can different teams with such different views ever come together overnight and function as a joint team?

The second issue was how competitors could become partners overnight. When Lockheed won the bid for the F-22, this meant that General Dynamics and Boeing became subcontractors to Lockheed. After years of intense competition, the companies became partners overnight.

There was very little time for the members of the competitive teams to immerse themselves in the spirit of alliance partnership. Within three days of the announcement, Boeing and General Dynamics managers and technical teams were in Lockheed's facility in Burbank, California, to attend a win party and begin the "open kimono" (technology disclosure) sessions. How did the announcement affect the members of the winning team from Lockheed and the losing

Exhibit 5-2. Joint Strike Fighter Demonstrators.

Lockheed Martin X-35

Boeing X-32

Source: U.S. Navy.

teams? For this let's again hear from Stephen Justice from Lockheed, who was a design engineer on the winning team.

> The Ft. Worth plant was owned by General Dynamics at the time, and they lost the ATF down-select. Kevin was the lead designer for their effort. With the teaming agreement wording and the announcement that Lockheed had won, it meant that Kevin had to overcome the emotional impact of the competitive defeat, immediately uproot his personal life, and help bring the best of the best together from the General Dynamics design team in Texas to the Lockheed team in California. This was not easy for him. Like most people, Kevin was proud of his effort, and his initiation into the Lockheed effort only cemented the idea that he had a better design team. In my personal opinion, in some ways his perspective was right and in other areas it was wrong. Kevin still feels some of the pain of the loss. *I still feel the pain of lost programs that occurred many years ago.* We are human and invest a big chunk of our heart, soul, and personal time into the machines we design—they are a part of us, and it hurts when someone calls our kid ugly. The bottom line is that the Lockheed-General Dynamics-Boeing team had the best answer, regardless of how painful or pleasant the journey was.

Whoa! Stephen's comments shed a real inside look at what happens to people when competitors become alliance partners. Real people have real feelings, real families, and real pride in their work. One wave of a magic wand telling people that they are now alliance partners instead of competitors does not necessarily solve the people issues that surface when different teams merge into one unit. In Kevin's case, he had to uproot his family, move halfway across the country, and join a competitor's team with a different view of the objective of the program.

There is another dimension to the people side of the teaming challenge. Different people see the same situation from different perspectives. Let's look again at Exhibit 5-1. Here are the two different designs of the F-22 that the two primary competitive teams came up with based on the USAF specifications. If you look hard, the two designs are very different. Since the two groups of design teams were all highly qualified and trained to do the design work, how then did they come up with such different designs from the same specifications? The answer is that different people have different perspectives on the same situation in life.

What Would Have Helped?

There are winners and losers in all facets of life. In this case, two losing teams actually became part of a winning alliance partnership. It appeared that the alliance partnership was on site within days of the announcement, working together on the next steps of the program. It also appeared that Lockheed had stronger internal efforts than perhaps General Dynamics and Boeing to sensitize their emerging, high-potential employees to the many issues of managing complex, cooperative programs.

Let's go back to Stephen Justice, and take another inside look at what Lockheed did try to do to blend the competitors together in one team.

> Despite the fact that we were in competition with a team that, without question, launched into the development of the winning member's design, the Lockheed team spent several months going through a massive configuration search to make sure that no good idea that was brought to the table was shoved underneath it. Man, was that ever painful. I still wince thinking about those days. That effort put all three concepts back on the candidate list, and variants of them grew the list to a total of *seven*—each of them getting an equal investigation into technical and cost merits. The bottom line was that in order to establish a multicompany team that had ownership in the design, the combined team almost had to start over. The good part was that the design, while based on the original Lockheed concept, had many elements of the other guys' designs and engineering lessons-learned embedded in it. It was a better airplane than any of the individual efforts, by far.

The contract and investment was split 34/33/33, with the winner (Lockheed) having the 34 percent share. The single rationale for this, and I think that it was a good one, was that there needed to be a *clear* leader when it came time for making tough decisions. The airplane business doesn't provide singular solutions—there are multiple solutions to the same problem or requirements. That means that some decisions cannot be based on data alone because the data cannot point to a clear single deciding factor. Even though this arrangement was agreed to, tensions periodically increased among the company teams when "their" solution wasn't chosen. In my opinion, General Dynamics (now Lockheed Martin Aeronautics–Ft. Worth), Boeing, Northrop, Grumman, Rockwell, and McDonnell Douglas, to this day, still feel that they should have won the ATF competition.

According to Stephen Justice, there appeared to be the right effort by Lockheed to anchor the newly formed team around a common, blended design. The structure of the contract also called for the winner (Lockheed) to be the clear leader to make the tough decisions when needed. The result was positive from a design standpoint—a better airplane than any of the original individual efforts.

However, there still exists the people issue. The fact that program decisions could introduce divisiveness within the overall team, and that many losing companies still feel that they should have won the ATF competition, both point to the intense pride that people had in their work. It also points to the lack of a true, joint ownership feeling in the newly formed team. Perhaps more attention should have been given to culture blending and how people from three different companies would begin working together in one cohesive group. The Lockheed, General Dynamics, and Boeing senior executives could have crafted a multidimensional communication program, as their competitive F-22 teams became alliance partners that leveraged the internal work that Lockheed was doing with its high-potential employees. This multidimensional communication program, designed around personality types, would have helped connect the message that they were all winners with the F-22 program. It could also have been used to facilitate two-way communications among the new team members to enable a teamwork environment beyond the blending of ideas and perspectives around the ATF design.

For example, one group would have wanted clear objectives with an identification of the new organization and its leaders. They would also have wanted options in the new organization. Another group would have wanted the recognition of being winners even in losing, with attention being given to them in a very public manner. A third group would have wanted an explanation as to why the new team was the best solution, despite the bid being awarded to Lockheed. They would have wanted approval for their past work and their new position in the alliance partnership. And still another group would have wanted a measure of respect for their past work, despite being on the losing end of the winning team. They would have wanted evidence to support the decision (maybe not possible) and input on how to move forward to solve the problem of building the F-22.

It is entirely possible that the joint Lockheed, General Dynamics, and Boeing team was overloaded with one or two specific groups of personality types, given the intensity of the engineers on the teams. Perhaps it would have been beneficial to include some nontechnical project leads that had more diverse personality types to balance the team. Having more people without an engineering background may have reduced some of the internal competition, while at the same time the addition of more extroverted personalities may have potentially enhanced the communications within the team.

There was also an added pressure on these team members. Because of the nature of their work, they could not discuss their work outside their program areas. If the team was made up of all highly competitive, introverted engineers, then how and with whom could they discuss their issues, frustrations, and problems? In addition, when these Defense engineers were taught to be secretive for years, how do you legislate that they are to be outgoing with competitors on a joint team? Add to this the shrinking Defense budget and intense bottom-line pressure on Defense firms, and you can add communications walls among competitors as thick as the old Berlin Wall.

Breaking down these communications walls is a difficult task for any alliance, let alone one with these special considerations. This is all the more reason that the senior executives should have identified the people constraints and established the right team and culture blending to enable the joint team beyond the joint design efforts. Perhaps the only way to accomplish this was a separate joint venture alliance with its own identity. With a separate joint venture, everyone ends up with one single identity—and an external common enemy with which to be competitive.

Despite the competitive problems among the joint Lockheed, General Dynamics, and Boeing teams, the F-22 is shaping up to be an outstanding success story in the chapter of the national defense of the United States. At the time of the teaming agreement and the award of the F-22 contract, few if any companies were practicing what Charlie Cotton was initiating at Frito Lay or Lockheed was doing with its high-potential personnel. Even today, very few companies, public or private, actually take the time to develop a multidimensional communication program for alliance partners to effectively work together. The need to do so actually increases significantly when competitors become alliance partners. For those companies that take the time, the reward is having their people embrace the new partnership and letting go of their old ways and beliefs. Whether it is working in a Frito Lay Networked Supply Chain and letting go of a command-and-control, one-style-fits-all approach or working in a Lockheed/General Dynamics/Boeing alliance partnership, embracing the new partnership, and letting go of their former positions as competitors, the value of connecting with people during change can be huge.

Another recommendation for companies migrating from competitor to partner is to utilize the Alliance Agreement for behavior guidance. For example, how powerful would it be if competitors that are working together in Covisint or the F-22 program place in their alliance agreements the requirement for everyone to take the Keirsey Temperament Sorter test and discuss the results in a new extended team? Or how powerful would it be for the competitors to be required to attend a Covey three-day workshop on "The 7 Habits of Highly Effective People"? Or both? The expectations for achieving performance goals are set by the executives. Why not have the executives give the competing teams the tools to rapidly migrate to a high-performing partnership as people begin working with people?

Summary

Alliances between companies involve people. Too many alliances are announced and become "empty press releases." Companies need to recognize the value of training their people to connect with other people through the recognition of personality types. The transition from controlling to influencing the behavior of other people just doesn't happen with a telephone call or a press release. It takes an investment of time to recognize the social styles of your alliance partner and customize your message and approach to connect to others through their personality types. The end result will be a desire for people to work with you beyond the reason of *having to* work with you. This may be the difference of an average alliance partnership and a highly successful alliance partnership.

Notes

1. "F-22 Raptor," Codeonemagazine.com, F-22 articles, Lockheed Martin Aeronautics Company, January 8, 2001, p. 1.
2. Ibid.
3. "F-22 Raptor to Undergo Tests," Codeonemagazine.com, F-22 press releases, November 3, 2000, p. 2.
4. "F-22 Design Evolution," Codeonemagazine.com, April 1998, p. 1.
5. Stephen R. Covey, *The 7 Habits of Highly Effective People: Restoring the Character Ethic* (New York: Simon and Schuster, 1989).
6. David Keirsey and Marilyn Bates, *Please Understand Me: Character and Temperament Types* (Del Mar, Calif.: Prometheus Book Company, 1984).
7. *Social Styles Summary* (Eden Prairie, Minn.: Wilson Learning Corporation, 1986).
8. Stephen R. Covey, *The 7 Habits of Highly Effective People*, pp. 63–182.
9. David Keirsey, *Please Understand Me II: Temperament, Character and Intelligence* (Del Mar, Calif.: Prometheus Nemesis Book Company, 1998).
10. Ibid., pp. 11–3.

CHAPTER SIX

Transportation: Win-Win Must Mean Profit-Profit

Like Father, Like Son

On a recent Saturday afternoon, my eighteen-year-old son and I were returning to our home from a visit to a major Less-Than-Truckload (LTL) trucking company. My son Karl had arisen early on this Saturday morning in order to visit the trucking company to apply for casual or part-time work on the freight docks. This dock work involves loading and unloading trailers. The LTL freight companies look for big, strong, and young men and women to fill in for vacationing regular dockworkers in the summer. When I was Karl's age, I had the good fortune to be introduced to casual dock work. In a way, I was helping my son retrace some of my steps as he reached his eighteenth birthday.

The terminal manager of this freight terminal took us on a tour of his facility. We visited the over-the-road driver room and tractor yard, the tractor and trailer maintenance facility, the city dispatch office for city pickups and deliveries, and the freight docks. The terminal manager was spending a lot of time with the young men explaining the operation and the economics of productivity as measured by his company. Karl seemed fascinated by the entire visit.

Little did he (or I, for that matter) realize that we would be spending the whole afternoon talking about the economics of LTL, truckload, and intermodal shipments. We would also be discussing the economics behind innovations in productivity that led to alliances between railroads and truckload carriers. The economics of alliances are essential, and must be tracked and measured for alliances to be successful. Let's take a look at the financial considerations behind the unlikely alliances that have occurred between traditionally fierce rivals.

LTL Trucking Company Cost Components

Before we left the terminal, my son asked me to explain the economics of LTL transportation to him. I began my answer by telling him that there are whole departments at universities like Penn State, Ohio State, Indiana, Tennessee, and several others dedicated to teaching and researching his question. However, like any dad and consultant, I jumped right into my answer after qualifying the magnitude of his question.

There are three basic groups of costs for an LTL trucking company.

✦ The first group is *terminal costs*. Terminal costs include the cost to pick up shipments, handle the shipments at the origin freight terminal, handle the shipments at a cross-dock or break bulk terminal, and handle the shipment at a destination terminal. It also includes local sales costs. Some companies split out the terminal handling costs from the city pickup and delivery costs. The terminal costs are approximately 37 percent of an LTL trucking company's total costs.

✦ The second group of costs for the LTL carrier is *linehaul* or *over-the-road costs*. These costs involve the drivers, tractors, trailers, operating costs like fuel, and associated repair and maintenance costs necessary to move the trailers from one destination to another. Linehaul or over-the-road costs are approximately 55 percent of an LTL trucking company's total costs.

✧ The third group of costs is *administrative costs.* This includes corporate overhead, cashiers to bill customers and collect receivables, over-short-and-damage (OS&D) personnel to complete wayward shipments and reconcile problem shipments, marketing, national account sales, and terminal routing personnel. Usually, when a cost does not fit the first two groups, it falls into the third group. Administrative costs represent approximately 8 percent of an LTL trucking company's total costs (Exhibit 6-1).

Exhibit 6-1. LTL Freight Company: cost components.

Terminal Costs = 37% of Total Costs
  Pickup and Delivery
  Terminal Freight Handling
  City Dispatch
  Local Sales
  Other

Linehaul (Over-the-Road) = 55% of Total Costs
  Equipment
  Driver Wages
  Maintenance and Repair
  Fuel
  Other

Administrative/Overhead = 8% of Total Costs
  Corporate
  Cashiering/Accounts Receivable
  Accounts Payable/Other CFO functions
  OS&D/Claims
  Purchasing
  Marketing
  National Account Sales
  Other

Source: Annual reports from multiple trucking companies.

For LTL trucking companies, it is easy to identify the over-the-road cost component as the largest cost component of the P&L. As I was discussing productivity and cost control with Karl, the subject of the LTL relay network surfaced. I told him that what goes around must come around. If the Roadway Express road domicile of Adelanto, California, sends a 53-foot trailer with a road driver to Oakland, then the driver must return with a 53-foot trailer in order to keep the trailer pools of each domicile intact. In addition, I began to discuss the economics of the over-the-road relay and tonnage balances.

On the trip from Adelanto to Oakland, the driver will drive ten hours and then sleep for eight hours. As such, Oakland has eighteen hours from the time of dispatch to come up with a loaded trailer for the return trip to Adelanto. If they fail to come up with a load, the driver must return home with an empty 53-foot trailer. As I told Karl, the more loaded miles, the better, and that he should think of every shipment in terms of dollars, not pounds. When a trailer returns empty, the revenue dollars on the trailer are zero. As such, the return trip is pure cost to the LTL trucking company. Exhibit 6-2 is an LTL Relay System Network map of Roadway Express, showing Adelanto, Phoenix, and their connectivity to Oakland.

Our conversation also led to a discussion about rates. In a deregulated environment (the trucking industry was economically deregulated through the Motor Carrier Act of 1980) the rates on shipments are subject to negotiations among shippers, consignees, and carriers. I went on to tell my son that LTL trucking companies really have to know their costs and the tonnage balances in each shipping lane to determine what rates they need to charge their customers. The trucking companies must also look for innovative ways to reduce costs and improve service to differentiate themselves from their competition.

As I was discussing how companies differentiated their services to their customers, we passed a railroad hump yard or rail car switching station. This is where the railroad mixes and matches the railcars and puts together their 80- or 120-car trains. The railcars are pushed up a little hill or "hump" and let go down the rail. There is a switchman that guides the railcar onto the right track to connect to its proper train.

Karl's eyes lit up as he asked why there were so many J.B. Hunt trailers and containers on the railcars. Our discussion was about to

Exhibit 6-2. Roadway Express map of LTL relay system: California–Arizona.

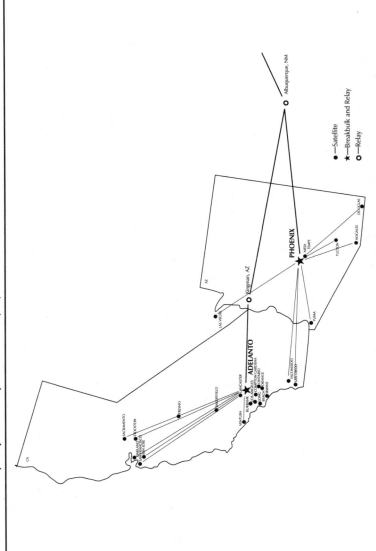

Source: Roadway Express, Inc.

evolve from LTL trucking to truckload carriers and intermodal transportation.

Truckload Carrier Cost Model

The cost structure of a longhaul truckload carrier is different from that of an LTL trucking company. The major components of the costs are pickup and delivery, linehaul, and administrative (Exhibit 6-3). Pickup and delivery costs are approximately 15 percent of a truckload carrier's total costs. Linehaul or over-the-road costs are approximately 77 percent of the total costs, while overhead represents 8 percent of the total costs. There are no terminal charges for truckload shipments, because they are not unloaded until they reach their final destination.

The reason for the number of J. B. Hunt trailers and containers on the rail flatcars was purely cost-related. I used the example of a

Exhibit 6-3. Truckload carrier: cost components.

Pickup and Delivery = 15% of Total Costs
    Pickup
    Delivery
    Other

Linehaul (Over-the-Road) = 77% of Total Costs
    Equipment
    Driver Wages
    Maintenance and Repair
    Fuel
    Other

Administrative/Overhead = 8% of Total Costs
    Corporate
    Cashiering/Accounts Receivable
    Accounts Payable/Other CFO functions
    OS&D/Claims
    Purchasing
    Sales and Marketing
    Other

Source: Annual reports from multiple trucking companies.

truckload shipment from Atlanta to Los Angeles, with a one-way distance of approximately 2,200 miles. The truckload rate per mile is $1.47 plus a 7½ percent fuel surcharge.[1] The total sale for the truckload carrier is $3,477. The pickup and the delivery for this shipment will cost the carrier approximately $522. The administrative cost is 8 percent, or $278. The linehaul or running cost per mile is approximately $0.90, or $1,980. Thus, on the surface, it appears that the truckload carrier has made a gross profit of $697 on this load from Atlanta to Los Angeles.

One-Way Cost Model

Revenue		$3,477.00
Minus P&D	522.00	
Minus Admin	278.00	
Minus Linehaul	1,980.00	
Cost Total	$2,780.00	
Gross Profit		$ 697.00

I then walked Karl through the issue of tonnage or load balance. If the truckload trucking company had to deadhead (go empty) from Los Angeles to Dallas to pick up a load of freight, then the profit on the load to Los Angeles from Atlanta would be in essence wiped out. The return to Dallas is 1,400 miles. With a linehaul cost of $0.90 per mile, the cost is $1,260. The company returns to Dallas 50 percent of the time, so the average cost of the return deadhead to be considered in the fronthaul rate negotiations is $630. As such, the rate of $1.47 plus the surcharge per mile is virtually break-even.

Cost Model with Load Balance Factored in

Revenue		$3,477.00
Minus P&D	522.00	
Minus Admin	278.00	
Minus Linehaul to L.A.	1,980.00	
Minus Deadhead to Dallas	630.00	
Cost Total	$3,410.00	
Gross Profit		$ 67.00

The above cost models used approximate cost percentages secured from multiple sources in the industry. Actual company cost percentages will vary. However, these examples do show that the linehaul or over-the-road cost component is very critical to manage at 77 percent of total costs, that tonnage balances are critical to profitability, and that overall profitability for truckload companies is very low. These are the reasons why the intermodal innovation of double-stacked containers had such a profound impact on truckload carriers.

APL, J.B. Hunt, and Intermodal Innovation

American President Lines

In 1984, the American President Lines (APL) railroad created a breakthrough solution for the transportation industry. The APL succeeded in developing "stacktrain" technology, an innovation that doubled train capacity by stacking containers two high on specially designed railcars. This "stacktrain" technology, combined with the establishment of the necessary clearances to double-stack containers on rail flatcars, provided an industry-changing solution to the marketplace. This work involved raising bridge levels, redesigning flatcars that transported containers, and reworking track to ensure the proper clearances. The net result was that the linehaul or point-to-point costs for the two containers were almost the same as the costs for shipping one container. This produced big savings for shippers. It also had a devastating effect on longhaul truckload (TL) trucking companies. Let's take a look at a pro-forma cost model for the same truckload shipment discussed earlier but shipped as a double-stacked container.

The truckload/container shipment from Atlanta to Los Angeles has a container rate per mile of $0.77 plus a $3^3/4$ percent fuel surcharge.[2] The total sale for the truckload carrier is $1,757.53. The pickup and delivery for this shipment will cost the carrier approximately $522. The administrative cost is 8 percent, or $140.60. The linehaul cost is estimated by several railroads at $.015 per ton-mile, or $660 (1.5 cents times 20 tons times 2,200 miles.)

Double-Stacked Container Cost Model with Load Balance Factored In

Revenue		$1,757.53
Minus P&D	522.00	
Minus Admin	140.60	
Minus Linehaul to L.A.	660.00	
Minus Deadhead to Dallas	330.00	
Cost Total	$1,652.60	
Gross Profit		$ 104.93

Not only could the railroad make a profit at $.77 per mile per load, but they were now in an excellent position to severely undercut the longhaul truckload carriers' rate of $1.47 per mile. This was not an advantageous position for truckload carriers. The APL intermodal innovation of double-stacked containers changed the rules of the game for shippers, truckload carriers, and railroads virtually overnight.[2]

The J. B. Hunt Response

J. B. Hunt reacted to this change with as much foresight as APL. They set out to cede the longhaul market to the railroads, and concentrated on regional pickup and delivery to "feed" the railroads with double-stacked containers of freight. This in essence was a transformation of their company. It also meant that they were becoming alliance partners with the railroads, who have traditionally been the trucking companies' archenemies.

There were three areas where J. B. Hunt and the railroads had to work closely together. The first was the J. B. Hunt equipment mix. The second was their joint ability to track and trace shipments. The third was their ability to structure pickup, delivery, and joint linehaul networks to determine what predictable service they could provide to their joint customers and how both transportation companies could make money with this new innovation.

The Alliance-Driven Transformation

Equipment Mix
The first area that J. B. Hunt addressed to transform their basic longhaul trucking company into an intermodal company was their equipment mix. In early 2001, J. B. Hunt had over 22,000 stackable

containers (as opposed to 13,000 trailers for over-the-road trailers) for use in their intermodal operations. Clearly they have transformed their equipment mix from a predominately over-the-road company mix of trailers to an intermodal company mix of containers.[4]

Tracking and Tracing

The second area addressed by J. B. Hunt was their information technology systems and their ability to track and trace shipments across the truck/rail/truck intermodal boundaries. J. B. Hunt has developed integrated railroad electronic information systems for real-time load status updating. Their use of information technology has earned them the *Computerworld* Premier 100 award for being one of the 100 most effective users of Internet technologies. In addition, *Information Week* has identified J. B. Hunt as one of the top 100 technology innovators in the market.[5]

Regional Feeds

The third area was the physical network transformation. J. B. Hunt now focuses on the regional "feeds" into the railroad hubs. A regional feed is defined as a pickup and delivery of a container load of freight from within 600 miles of the railroad hub or rail intermodal site. (There is a rule of thumb that trucking executives and the American Association of Railroads use when discussing railroad competitiveness with truckload trucking companies, which is that at less than 500 miles, truckload carriers are cheaper; at from 500 to 700 miles, the competitiveness is in a gray area; and at over 700 miles, the intermodal solution is cheaper. It is no surprise that J. B. Hunt selected 600 miles for its regional feed radius!)

In essence, J. B. Hunt replaced the old drayage companies that used to take containers to and from destinations within a couple of hundred of miles from the railroad hub. This was a big change for the railroad. I remember when I was with Frito Lay shipping intermodal loads of commodities, and relying on drayage companies to pick up and deliver loads from and to the railroad. In my experience, the drayage company was the bottom of the food chain for trucking companies. Railroads were always trying to find the lowest-cost drayage company to pick up and deliver containers. Many drayage companies operated solely within a commercial zone around a major city, and were exempted from federal safety regulations. Many drayage compa-

nies were not only low-cost, but low-service and low-safety. The reliability of drayage companies was poor at best.

What are the results of J. B. Hunt's efforts? In 1989, J. B. Hunt
initiated its transformational intermodal program with the Santa Fe
Railway. At that time, they averaged twenty container loads a month.
In early 2001, J. B. Hunt had alliance partnerships with eight North
American railroads. These railroads are Burlington Northern Santa Fe
(BNSF,) Norfolk Southern, CSX, Kansas City Southern, Union Pacific
(UP,) Illinois Central, Canadian National, and the Florida East Coast
railroads. J. B. Hunt now averages 50,000 container loads a month. In
addition, J. B. Hunt has supervisory personnel at rail intermodal facili-
ties, while their railroad alliance partners have personnel at J. B. Hunt's
corporate offices to focus on service efficiencies.[6]

The Financial Connection of the Intermodal Alliances

The financial benefit of an alliance must be a two-way street. Let's take
a look at how the railroads and J. B. Hunt have benefited from their
alliances.

J. B. Hunt's financial strategy included the expansion of the drayage zone around the rail hubs to 600 miles. This move allowed the
railroad to expand their "regional freight feed" from at most 200 miles
to 600 miles. With the railroad operating in a derived demand environment, this tonnage and container unit addition for the railroads was
significant (Exhibit 6-4).

The move to expand the drayage zone of 200 miles to a regional
feed of 600 miles also helped J. B. Hunt adapt to the intermodal environment from a position of profitability. Trucking companies are
asset-intensive. They must leverage their fixed-asset base. It is common
knowledge among transportation companies that their assets have
wheels and are "born to run." Insiders tell me that they must average
3,000 miles a week for a single tractor and 5,000 miles for a team
tractor in order to make money. A new single tractor may cost $60,000
to $75,000. Assuming a company runs the tractor 1 million miles in its
lifetime, this translates into a purchase cost of from 6 cents to 7.5 cents
per mile.

Exhibit 6-4. U.S. intermodal traffic: 1980–1998.

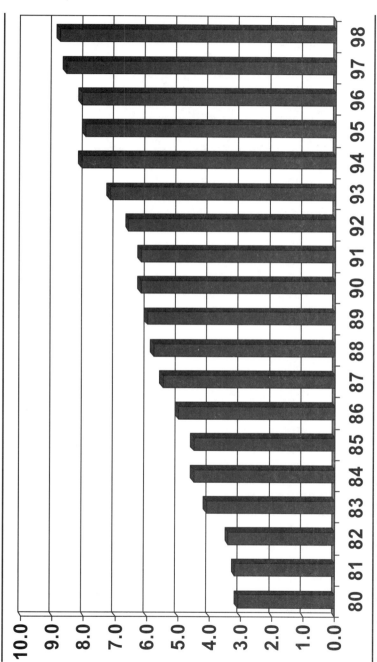

Source: American Association of Railroads.

Now, the actual depreciation cost will include depreciation sched-ules over the allowable number of accounting years, as well as the capitalization of such major maintenance items as in-frame overhauls. There will also be a residual or salvage value that will remain, say 10 percent of the purchase price. However, the direction of the analysis is the same. What would happen if J. B. Hunt only utilized its tractors for 1,000 miles a week instead of 3,000 miles a week? The purchase cost of the tractor just increased to 18 cents to 22.5 cents per mile. The impact on profitability would be devastating, given that the profit margins in the industry run in the single digits. This would have been the scenario if J. B. Hunt had taken over only the drayage activities for the railroads and had not expanded the radius of the pickups and deliveries. J. B. Hunt had to change the scenario in order to address the double-stack container threat, transform itself to an intermodal company, and stay profitable.

Another problem for J. B. Hunt to deal with was the over-the-road driver shortage and the factors driving this shortage. Truck driv-ing is a very difficult profession. Over-the-road truck drivers may aver-age 2,000 to 3,000 miles per week, often driving at night and sleeping during the day. They spend many days and nights away from their homes, returning to their loved ones only once a week, and often only once every other week. Their diets are made up of truckstop food and vending machine items. Except for the occasional loading and unload-ing of trailers, they get very little exercise. In addition, they have to deal with the incredible stress of driving 80,000 pounds down the road in all kinds of weather conditions, not to mention the drunks and road rage drivers that infest our highways.

Because the economy has been relatively good throughout the 1990s and into the early 2000s, many drivers have opted to find other professions. The available pool of drug-free, alcohol-free workers will-ing to handle the high stress and physically degrading lifestyle of a truck driver has therefore dwindled in recent years. By instituting the regional feeder concept with railroads, J. B. Hunt improved conditions for its drivers by changing a longhaul system into a regional system. These over-the-road drivers can drive up to 550 plus miles in ten run-ning hours before they have to take a Department of Transportation (D.O.T.) mandated safety break of eight hours. This means that drivers can make a pickup, take the shipment to the rail hub, and be home the same night or at least the following night. The ability of having their drivers home three to four nights a week has made a big difference in driver turnover and driver morale.

The regional feed also allowed J. B. Hunt to pick up a minimum of five loads a week for each tractor. The more loads and "loaded miles," the greater the fixed asset leverage and the more profitable their asset-intensive operations have become.

The J. B. Hunt transformation from a longhaul trucking company to an intermodal company is a solid success story. It was triggered by a significant innovation by their old enemy, the railroad. Its success is now in part due to the alliance partnerships that J. B. Hunt has with railroads and the financial win-win approach that they have with these alliances. Let's now take a look at other alliances in the transportation and logistics industries.

Other Types of Alliances

Sales Alliance

Kent International Freight Services Ltd. is an international freight-forwarding company based in Swanscombe, Kent, in the United Kingdom. Since 1990, the company has specialized in freight forwarding to and from Eastern Europe, including Russia, Ukraine, the Baltic States, Belarus, Kazakhstan, Uzbekistan, Turkmenistan, Azerbaijan, Poland, and Moldova. Kent International Freight Services utilizes a network of transportation and warehousing companies to provide door-to-door service to its customers. In addition, Kent provides other value-add services, such as packing, insurance, customs clearance, and export documentation. A freight-forwarding company is a great example of a company that enters into a series of sales alliances to provide its door-to-door services.[7]

Solution-Specific Alliance

Schneider National Inc. is North America's largest truckload or over-the-road hauler of freight. In April 2001, Schneider named QUAL-COMM Wireless Business Solutions, a division of QUALCOMM Incorporated, as its provider of choice for trailer tracking solutions. Schneider worked with QUALCOMM in 1990 to adopt the Omni-

TRACS® system, which at the time set the standard for excellence in mobile communications in the transportation industry.

According to Scott Arves, Schneider's chief operating officer, "While we're still in a development and testing mode, we're very pleased with what we've seen, and we will continue to work toward a solution that will set the standard for asset tracking management." Chris Wolfe, senior vice president and general manager of QUAL-COMM Wireless Business Solutions, said, "Schneider's input has proven to be an invaluable contribution to the success of our transportation products and services."[8]

The solution involves the placement of wireless communications and sensor technologies in each trailer, which will detect when the trailer is connected or disconnected from a tractor and whether it is loaded or empty, and which will use Global Positioning Satellite (GPS) technology determine its position. (Just imagine the possibilities with 3G wireless communicators and truck drivers!)

Geographic-Specific Alliance

Caltex Australia and TNT Australia announced in May 2001 an alliance to provide a dynamic logistics and fulfillment solution for Australia. Caltex is a major refiner and marketer of petroleum products in Australia. It is also in convenience retailing. TNT is a global provider of mail, express, and logistics services. People who buy goods online can use the Caltex Pick Up Point service and TNT transportation services. The customer identifies the Caltex Pick Up Point, purchases the goods online, and TNT then delivers to that point (most likely a convenience store or retail outlet). Customers can then pick up the goods at their convenience and pay for the goods at the time of pickup. This is a great example of a geographics-specific alliance in the transportation and logistics industries.[9]

Investment Alliance

The Danzas Group selected NextLinx Corporation for its landed cost and compliance solutions pilot project. This pilot is designed to support the logistics and procurement processes of the Industrial Brance de Organizacion Techint, an Italo-Argentine multinational group that specializes in steel products. NextLinx's Trade Engines will support the quoting phase of the procurement process, using the transportation costs provided by Danzas. Techint will then be able to compare competitive bids on a global and landed cost basis. An insider from Argentina told me that there is an investment alliance among Danzas, NextLinx, and Techint. Techint plans to provide this procurement solution to the rest of the Techint group and potentially the external marketplace.[10]

Joint Venture Alliance

In November 2000, Ryder System, Inc., and Toyota Tsusho America, Inc., formed TTR Logistics. TTR Logistics is a joint venture that will focus on transportation and logistics opportunities with Toyota and other Japanese automotive industry companies operating in North America. The joint venture will initially focus on the logistics supporting Toyota and the suppliers supporting Toyota. In the future, the joint venture will include global transportation management, distribution management, and supply chain logistics and design. "This joint venture combines Ryder's logistics management, integrated technology capabilities, and extensive experience managing customers' transportation and logistics networks throughout North America with Toyota Tsusho's Japanese network, industry relationships, and expertise in cross-dock and warehousing operations," said Tom Jones, senior vice president of Ryder's Global Automotive Group.[11]

Five Types of Alliances Summary

From the sales alliance in the U.K., to the solution-specific alliance in North America, the geographic-specific alliance in Australia, the investment alliance in Argentina, and the joint venture in Japan and North America, alliances in the transportation and logistics industries are thriving. The name of the game is not just to do alliances, but also to create financial benefits for clients and alliance partners. Frequently, it takes a major change or transformation to provide combined solutions with alliance partners. Let's take a look at another company that is on the front end of their transformation through alliance partnerships.

Hays Fourth Party Solutions

The global third party logistics (3pl) field is very crowded. It is focused on reducing costs in logistics tasks (such as transportation, warehousing, and sorting), kitting, or subassembly. Because the 3pl field is focused on doing like activities for less cost, their margins are small and their people are focused on tactical execution. There is a low amount of value-add in the traditional 3pl suite of services.

Hays Fourth Party Solutions (Hays) is a European-based company that has recently embarked on a transformation program of its own. This transformation program is designed to migrate their company from a 3pl to a fourth-party-solution company. The transformation process involves moving their company from a tactical execution company focusing on reducing costs to a strategic company focused on value-based solutions.

Hays has entered into an alliance partnership with i2 Technologies to transform their suite of services beyond reducing costs. These services include supply chain design, end-to-end fulfillment, dynamic optimization, end-to-end management, and change management. As such, Hays now works with i2 Technologies, their customers, and their service providers to provide to their customers extended supply chain planning and advisory services, the latest end-to-end fulfillment technologies, and the brick and mortar tactical execution to make it happen. The move into supply chain consulting, together with their alliance partnership with i2 Technologies to access the latest supply chain technologies, will allow Hays to "move up the food chain" and enter into value-based contracts with their customers.[12]

The Hays transformation program has just begun. We are all anxiously awaiting signs of success. Many 3pls have tried unsuccessfully to break out of the low-margin trap of purely reducing costs and move to higher-margin strategic value-add services. It takes a complete remaking of the company and upgrading of the management skill sets. It also takes strong alliance partnerships that can provide an immediate stair-step difference in services to be offered to customers.

The financial win-win in alliance partnerships don't just happen, they are created with careful thought and effort. They result from a sound alliance agreement, supported by a strong business plan between the alliance partners. At the end of this chapter there is a section that presents a detailed look at how an alliance business plan can be established.

Compensation Strategies with Alliances

In the section on "How to Construct an Alliance Business Plan," you will read about how a bonus plan crafted for alliance partners successfully resulted in driving sales for the alliance partners. It should come as no surprise that companies get the performance that they measure and incent. When constructing a business plan with an alliance partner, performance measurements and compensation strategies must be considered and included where possible.

For sales alliances, the performance measurements are relatively straightforward. The sales of each other's products and services should be carefully tracked. The alliance personnel supporting the sales alliance should have a portion of their compensation tied to the sales of the alliance partner's products and services. For the very serious alliances, the funding for these cross-alliance sales bonuses should come from the alliance partner benefiting from the sales.

The compensation program for solution-specific alliances should be twofold. The performance incentives should focus on the joint solution development time lines and deliverables. Bonuses should be paid on meeting time lines with quality deliverables. This is important, because without joint solution development, the alliance salesmen would not have anything to sell! Also, sales bonuses should be paid to alliance salesmen for joint solution sales.

The compensation strategies for geographic-specific alliances should be almost identical to the compensation strategies of the sales alliance. There are two major items to be incorporated in the geographic-specific alliance compensation structure. The first item is the obvious one. The sales being compensated must be specific to a geographic region. The second involves the differences of the types of compensation in different regions around the world. For example, in high-tax countries like Germany and Australia, sales bonuses may be paid in the form of company-paid automobiles, gasoline or petrol, housing, and other noncash items that represent value to the alliance salesperson.

For investment alliances, the compensation strategies should be multifaceted. The investment into an alliance partner should be tracked and measured like any other investment. If this investment is in equity, then the return on investment (ROI) should be measured on the appreciation (or lack of appreciation) of the equity. Sales bonuses should be crafted similarly to what was discussed with other types of alliances. If the investment alliance includes joint solution development, then the performance measurements of meeting time lines with quality deliverables discussed in solution-specific alliances should also be incorporated.

Joint venture alliances sound complex, but they are actually relatively straightforward from a compensation standpoint. Joint ventures have their own set of books from sales and profit and loss standpoints. The alliance people should be compensated based upon the performance of the joint venture and their own individual performance and contributions. The alliance partners must make every effort to craft a separate and distinct compensation and incentive program for the joint venture employees to avoid suboptimal behavior on behalf of either alliance partner.

People will be motivated by how their performance is measured and how they are compensated. Companies that enter into alliance agreements must recognize that their employees are entering into a unique and different operating environment. This operating environment relies on influencing the behavior of others. In this operating environment, people from different companies come to the alliance with different performance expectations and different compensation structures armed with the challenge of producing common results.

It makes good business sense for the executives from each alliance partner to recognize this different operating environment and the challenge for alliance team members to produce common results. It makes even better sense for these same executives to align the compensation programs of the alliance partners around the expected common results. Otherwise, there will always be the tendency for alliance team members to perform according to how they are incented and be suboptimal in their behavior within the alliance.

Summary

Alliances must be win-win financially in order for them to be justified. There are too many "empty press releases" of alliance partnerships that avoid the simple premise of how both partners will make money from the alliance. It takes hard work on both sides to make an alliance successful. It may even take a major transformation of a company, as we saw with J. B. Hunt and Hays. The linkage of an alliance business plan to the overall alliance agreement provides the necessary framework to address how both parties can make money. It will also avoid having the alliance partnership dissolve and end up in the graveyard for good ideas without follow-up execution.

My son did get a little bored during our Saturday review of transportation. I know from experience that he will not have the time to get bored working on the freight docks!

How to Construct an Alliance Business Plan

The alliance business plan should be done on an annual basis, and support the overall alliance agreement (as outlined in Chapter Two). There are six major sections to an alliance business plan. These sections are as follows:

1. The types of work to be performed by both parties to the alliance.
2. The revenue targets that each alliance partner commits to achieve in the given fiscal year.
3. The dedication of personnel to support the achievement of the agreed-to revenue targets.
4. The cross training of personnel needed to achieve the revenue targets.
5. The marketing or advertising efforts needed to support the types of work needed to drive the revenue targets.
6. Any other items necessary to achieve the business plan goals.

Each of these sections will now be discussed in detail.

✧ *Section 1.* The types of work to be performed by both parties may be a subset of the activities described in the overall alliance agreement. It could also be the complete set of activities described in the alliance agreement. Either way, these activities

---

should extend from the alliance agreement and not conflict with it. Frequently, this section identifies those specific activities that each alliance partner will focus on for the specific fiscal year of the business plan.

This section is one of the most important sections in the annual business plan. The work to be performed by both parties should revolve around the agreed-to joint solutions and action plans that the two alliance partners plan and agree to for the upcoming fiscal year.

The joint solutions that the two partners agree to are important for many reasons. At the top of the list is the connectivity between the joint solutions and the rest of the six sections of the business plan. If the business plan is to be a "bottoms-up" plan (or a plan that all levels of the two companies plan for and agree to), then the plan must be rooted in specific ways that the objectives can be attained.

A few years ago I was invited to participate in an alliance discussion between a Brazilian company and a German company. It was late November, and we were at a resort in the city of Recife in Brazil. The Brazilians were anxious to have their summer arrive, not for the weather (Recife is very close to the Equator and enjoys relatively hot weather year round), but for the opportunity to enjoy their holidays with their children. The Germans were enjoying the weather, but were extremely anxious about the discussions about their alliance.

When we finally worked our way beyond the introductions and into the alliance discussions, it became evident that the original alliance discussions and alliance agreement missed a major supporting section. The sales and revenue expectations of the alliance were discussed at length, but the corresponding activities to drive the realization of these sales and revenues were never discussed between the two companies and completed as an alliance team. As such, there was a huge disconnect between the expectations on both sides as to how the sales and revenue expectations were to be achieved. These two companies spent the better part of their meeting identifying and agreeing on the activities to drive the sales and revenues expected from the alliance. The problem was that the partners were three months into the alliance, and the executives were expecting results. This meeting was designed to review results and short-term activities to accelerate the sales pipeline. Instead, this meeting turned into a planning meeting because Section 1 had never been jointly completed.

✧ *Section 2.* The revenue targets must be specific. They must also be commitments. In cases like the arrangement the railroads had with J. B. Hunt, the revenue commitments might be "tonnage commitments" to take the supply-and-demand pricing variable out of the commitment. Either way, the establishment of specific goals for both alliance partners serves as a cross-company incentive to maximize the financial benefit for each partner.

Three years ago, I was working with a friend who owns her own company. She had an alliance with a large, multinational company that liked her differentiated products and services. If David were a woman and married Goliath, it would parallel this alliance.

In late December, I was having dinner with my friend and discussing her company and the type of year she was finishing. Her comments really shocked me. She stated that she had a record year, but she was very disappointed in her "Goliath" alliance. She stated that her alliance partner had used her differentiated products and services to gain access to a number of other companies. (For example, in the past few years, many small companies have developed specialized Internet products that assist companies in developing their Intranets and enabling Web-connected sales channels. Although these products may have small sales volumes, they provide a door for larger hardware and software companies to attract new clients and sell their products and services around the specialized products.) The "Goliath" salespersons then used this access to sell their traditional or nonalliance solutions. When we discussed her frustrations with the alliance relationship, she became aware that her alliance partner could not help it. Their objectives and incentives were hardcoded to their traditional solutions. There had been no attempt to incorporate the goals of my friend's company into the objectives and incentives of the "Goliath" salespersons, who had used the differentiated products and services as a "Trojan Horse" to sell the products and services on which their incentives and compensation were based.

The lesson learned in this example is to build the proper

objectives into the incentive plan for both alliance partner personnel. This cross-company incentive, when properly crafted, will help maximize the financial benefit for each alliance partner. Without this cross-company incentive, alliance partners will realize what they incent their people to attain. Unfortunately for my friend, the short-term return from the alliance was a negative return on her investment. Unfortunately for the "Goliath" alliance partner, the longer-term return from the alliance will be zero. My friend gave written notice to her partner and terminated the alliance agreement. Unfortunately for both, the potential value of the alliance relationship was significant but not realized because of the lack of joint planning of goals, objectives, and incentives.

✧ *Section 3.* The dedication of personnel is necessary to support the types of work identified in Section 1. There should be a strong link between the types of work to be performed by parties, the revenue commitments (or other measurable, financially connected items, like tonnage in transportation), and the dedication of personnel to make it happen. Do not leave this part uncovered! Too many times, alliances are created with the understanding that people will do the alliance-related work in their night job. This does not work well at all!

On a humorous note, a couple of years ago I was working with a client from the Asia-Pacific region of the world. This client had entered into numerous alliances, and was going through an alliance performance review process. One by one, the alliances were reviewed. Included in this review were the results from each alliance, the joint activities between the alliance partners, and the personnel driving the activities.

By the third alliance review, I noticed that a couple of the same names were appearing next to competing alliance activities. By the time that the fifth alliance was reviewed, there were no new names being identified with the alliance activities. In all there were seven alliances reviewed, with the same names appearing with multiple alliances. The trouble was that many of these alliance partners were competitors with one another.

I happened to know that the market share that my client had with two of these alliance partners was fourth or fifth among all competitors. The lack of dedicated resources significantly hurt their alliance penetration through a lack of client sales coverage. Perhaps what hurt them the most was the marketplace recognition that their alliance people were working with multiple competitors. Even with the existence of a nondisclosure agreement (NDA), the alliance partner personnel were reluctant to embrace the client personnel for fear that they would be divulging information that would leak back to their competitors. The dedication of personnel to support the joint activities, goals, and objectives is critical to the attainment of the expected results from alliance relationships.

During the evening dinner, I had a chance to meet some of the alliance managers. One of the alliance managers had a reversible hat, with the name of one alliance on one side and that of another alliance on the other side! He said that one of his toughest tasks was to remember what alliance he was working with at what time. The hat was humorous, but the scenario was actually quite serious and somewhat sad. The lack of commitment to alliances will certainly contribute to a lack of long-term relationships and results.

✦ *Section 4.* Alliances involve working with partners in other companies with complementary but different products and services. For example, J. B. Hunt personnel have to work extensively with railroad operations in their new intermodal world. The Hays Fourth Party Solutions personnel will have to learn extended supply chain consulting and state-of-the-art supply chain technologies. As such, the cross-training of personnel to do the alliance work is absolutely critical to the success of the business plan. The training specifications must be spelled out, with the costs, availability, and even methods described in detail.

There was a large supply chain project that an Argentine company and a French company jointly sold to a major automotive original equipment manufacturer (OEM). The French company was to handle the administrative logistics from the clearance of customs through the movement from customs to the final destination. The Argentine company was to handle the physical movement of the goods and the sequencing of the products to the assembly line at the destination plant. Together, these two companies created an alliance that was supposed to provide for the seamless movement of goods and information into and out of South American countries. The OEM in this case was to provide the assembly sequencing information and all other extraordinary information that would adjust or impact the assembly schedule.

Problems arose when the Argentine personnel were not trained in the process and systems of the French company. The Argentine personnel had no knowledge of how and when the products were clearing customs, and as such did not incorporate this information into their logistics scheduling process. The products would sit for days after clearing customs, while the automotive OEM altered their production schedules due to the late deliveries of the expected products. The cross-training of the dedicated personnel in the services of their alliance partner would have alleviated the disconnects in this situation.

The cross-training of personnel would also have averted an embarrassing situation. The French company had the customs clearance documents in both electronic and paper formats. These two formats included three languages—French, Spanish, and English. The embarrassing situation arose when the service was initiated in Brazil, since the official language of Brazil is Portuguese! If alliance partners are to be incented on each other's success, then they must understand each other's products and services being offered to the marketplace and be sensitive to potential missteps in the integrated process flows.

✧ *Section 5.* There are alliance partnerships that require marketing and advertising to support the achievement of the business plan goals. The marketing programs should be spelled out in specific terms, with the responsibilities identified for each partner. Advertising commitments can be specified by type of advertising. In many cases, the advertising component can be described in terms of cash commitments.

There was one company that funded the marketing and advertising program of its alliance partner, but ceded the marketing efforts to junior personnel. The marketing and advertising budgets were slammed together, only to be managed as a cost item to be cut and reallocated to other causes. As such, no marketing and advertising was accomplished. This action not only defeated the purpose of the marketing and advertising budgets, but also created ill will among the alliance partner personnel. The lesson learned here is that alliance commitments must be honored, and must be treated in a different light from normal day-to-day business activities.

❖ *Section 6.* The other category of the alliance business plan is the catchall category. For example, some alliance partners will include a provision in the business plan that the variable compensation or bonus payouts to those dedicated individuals in the alliance will be dependent on the achievement of the business plan. This sometimes includes the achievement of the alliance partner's revenue goals as well as their own company's revenue goals. Other alliance partners have specified weekly, monthly, quarterly, and/or annual performance measurement reporting mechanisms and meetings to track and monitor progress toward achievement of the business plan goals.

One company I know continuously struggled with the performance of their alliances. One year, they instituted a bonus plan that included a component that tied directly to their alliance partner's targets. The performance of this one alliance took off like a rocket. The cross-incentives between alliance partners brought the two alliance partners closer together and resulted in a tight working relationship between the two teams. At times, outsiders did not know which alliance manager worked for which company.

Business Plan Summary

The above six steps are the basics of an alliance business plan. Alliance partners must be careful to make sure that the business plan "connects" to both the alliance agreement and the financial win-win for both parties. My advice is to make the alliance business plan simple, yet specific in nature. It also must be measurable, and link to the performance-based rewards system for both alliance partners.

Notes

1. J. B. Hunt Spot Quote Rate from Rate Desk (1-501-820-7143), Mr. Kevin Parkinson, March 9, 2001.
2. Ibid.
3. www.APL.com/html/APL_history_html/timeline:1950-present, year 1984.
4. www.jbhunt.com/Intermodal, J. B. Hunt Intermodal, p. 1.
5. www.jbhunt.com/Aboutjbhunt, J. B. Hunt Awards, p. 1.
6. www.jbhunt.com/Intermodal, J. B. Hunt Intermodal, p. 1.
7. www.kentinternational.co.uk, Home page, p. 1.
8. www.schneider.com/welcome/in_the_news/articles, p. 1.
9. www.tntauto.com.au/index_news/html, pp. 1, 2.
10. www.aeilogistics.com, p. 1.
11. www.businesswire.com/webbox/bw/12000/203252300.html, *Ryder System Forms Automotive Logistics Joint Venture with Toyota Tsusho*, p. 1.
12. "Hays Fourth Party Solutions," Hays, The Business Services Group, Marketing Brochure, 2001.

CHAPTER SEVEN

Health Care: Alliances and a Healthy Supply Chain

It was January 4th, and the college football championship game was under way. The patriarch of the family was enjoying the game when the chest pains started. This was not a foreign feeling, because he had two previous open-heart bypass surgeries after heart attacks. He took some nitroglycerin and called his cardiologist. Before long, he was being transported to the hospital emergency room.

The hospital emergency room doctor had been in contact with both the ambulance paramedics and the cardiologist, and had already made the necessary arrangements to send him to the cardiac intensive care unit. Efforts were made immediately to stabilize him and begin the journey of evaluating what was wrong and what course of medical action was necessary and possible.

This patient would eventually have an angiogram, which would indicate the need for another bypass and a valve replacement. Because he was 85 years old, the operation would be high-risk. However, with the lower half of his heart plugged due to a malfunctioning valve and only one remaining bypass vein working from the previous surgery, the patient's chances were better with the high-risk surgery than with just going home in his current position.

From the cardiac intensive care unit, this man would be taken to the cardiac care unit to stabilize and prepare for surgery. After surgery in the operating room (OR), he would be returned to the cardiac surgery intensive care unit for recovery. He would then make a stop on the pulmonary floor to be weaned off the ventilator, and then go to the rehabilitation unit for physical and occupational therapy.

The journey for this heart patient passed through six major units in the hospital. He would be in the hospital for over 120 days because of complications with his respiratory system and pneumonia. Yet as complicated as his journey was, the journey for his medical supplies and medical devices was even more complicated. Let's take a look at how some of the medical supplies and devices arrived at the right place and the right time for him to use during his hospital stay.

Hospital Procurement and Supply Chain Management

The heart valve for this patient was ordered from the valve manufacturer directly by the heart surgeon team. (I have a laugh when I see "valve manufacturer," since the valve actually was a pig's valve!) The order instructed the manufacturer to ship the valve climate-controlled direct to the storage center in the OR.

The sutures were sent to the OR from the materials distribution center in the hospital. The purchasing department ordered the sutures from the wholesaler/distributor, who in turn ordered the sutures from the manufacturer. The materials distribution center would also send the sutures to every floor inventory closet or cart on an as-needed basis.

The pulmonary doctors ordered the anesthesia drugs directly from the manufacturers. These drugs would then be delivered through the in-house pharmacy directly to the OR storage center. Sometimes these drugs would be delivered through the materials distribution center to the OR.

The ventilator machines were ordered directly from the manufacturer by the hospital purchasing department, with approval by the pulmonary department. These ventilator machines would be delivered directly to the hospital by the manufacturer. There was also an inventory of ventilator machines at the wholesaler distributor, allowing for delivery to the hospital if the manufacturer could not fill the order. The parts for these machines were delivered by the wholesaler distributor, and inventoried by materials distribution.

Follow the Bouncing Ball . . .

In the hospital being described, nurses and doctors on each floor have the authority to order the necessary medical supplies and devices. They also have the option to order from their material distribution department, through their purchasing department, through their pharmacy department, or directly from the manufacturer. If you add in the wholesaler/distributor, the order-to-delivery supply chain paths within the hospital are almost too numerous to count. Did I mention that this hospital is part of a large health care group with over 100 hospitals and medical facilities?

Also, there is the delivery-to-cash part of the order-to-cash cycle. The challenge to connect the order and the delivery to the exchange of cash in an environment that allows for multiple order points and multiple supply points for the same materials is significant. Add on top of this the need to connect over 100 hospitals with similar environments, and the challenge becomes huge. However, the challenge to provide the same service with the same medical materials and devices at a dramatically reduced cost becomes huge as well.

The Adaptive Health Care e-Supply Chain: Guiding Principles

For health care providers, the supply chain represents between 20 percent and 30 percent of the typical total operating expenses. With almost 28 percent of supply chain expenses related to administration, overhead, and logistics, the opportunities to reduce costs and improve service are significant.[1] However, there must be an effort to transform the health care supply chain to an Adaptive Health Care e-Supply Chain (Exhibit 7-1) to align the objectives of buyers and sellers and realize the opportunity to reduce costs and improve service.

The Adaptive Health Care e-Supply Chain involves a community of supply chain partners and capabilities pulled together or "powered by" the Networked Value Chain. At the heart of the Adaptive Health Care e-Supply Chain is the reliance on alliances to pull the extended capabilities together in one value stream.

Exhibit 7-1. The health care e-supply chain: powered by the Networked Value Chain.

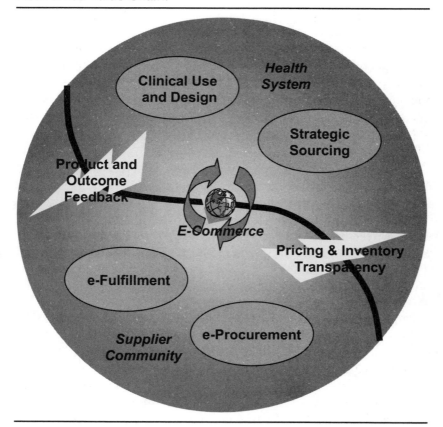

The Adaptive Health Care e-Supply Chain is based on four primary guiding principles (Exhibit 7-2). Let's take a look at these four primary guiding principles and how they anchor opportunity realization for health care providers.

Guiding Principle #1: Assume Accountability

The health care providers that are serious about improving service and reducing costs must also be serious about understanding their role and presence within an extended enterprise. The health care provider is just one major participant in the health care networked value chain. As such, to improve service and reduce total costs, there must be an alignment of objectives within the health care networked value chain. This alignment must include all companies that provide goods and services to and through the health care providers.

Alignment of networked value chain participants must be supported by accountability. This accountability needs to be matrixed, with accountability to their own company and accountability to the extended enterprise anchored by the ultimate customer. In hospitals and medical facilities, the service accountability must be primary, with joint ownership occurring between the care providers (doctors and nurses) and the supply chain executive working directly with hospital administrators.

The only way for this transformation to succeed is to have board-level sponsorship. There must also be a supply chain executive who has purchasing and logistics skills as well as leadership skills to influence the behavior of disparate groups. Last but not least, there must be patient service and budgetary responsibilities for the networked supply chain activities and costs to break the trap of the cost-plus pricing we discussed earlier.

The balancing act between patient care and cost management is a delicate one. The limits on Medicare and insurance company reimbursements dictate the need for strong cost control. The quality of health care must never be compromised by artificially limiting care for patients. However, there is an in-between area that can produce positive cost-control results while maintaining or improving service levels. It takes a supply chain executive with strong leadership skills, strong influencing skills, the ability to forge strong alliances, and accountability for service and cost performance to achieve that balance.

Exhibit 7-2. Guiding principles for the health care e-supply chain.

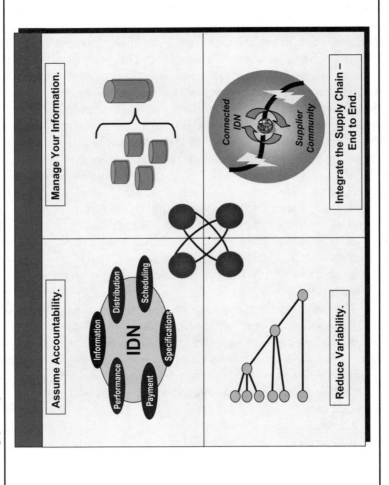

Guiding Principle #2: Manage Your Information

Health care providers must be able to have access to their own supply chain data, and convert this data into information, knowledge, and wisdom. In the Adaptive Health Care e-Supply Chain, this data may come from multiple alliance partners and multiple sources within the health care system. The purpose of the data and information is to utilize it to drive decision-support activities that focus on improving service levels and reducing costs. These decision-support activities rely on Content management to enable supplier relationship management capabilities through strategic sourcing programs.

Content management requires the creation and maintenance of a global e-based catalog that integrates product and supplier data into a single, searchable structure. There are four steps to convert product data into a single set of comparable and useful information.

⟡ *Step 1*: Aggregation integrates data from multiple suppliers into a single catalog.

⟡ *Step 2*: Normalization presents the data with a uniform nomenclature.

⟡ *Step 3*: Rationalization applies a structured order format for all descriptions.

⟡ *Step 4*: Classification provides a logical organization of detailed information about products that can be used to input and maintain the data within the system.

A simple example for latex gloves demonstrates the utility of this process.

Within the health care industry, the development of a content management system is made more complex by the need to incorporate clinical data (e.g. outcomes data, procedural guidelines, clinical usage patterns) with standard procurement information (e.g. pricing, availability, substitute products). In many health care supply chains, the health care product and service suppliers have the clinical data, whereas the wholesaler/distributors and maybe the hospital administrators have the standard procurement information. The patient care providers (doctors and nurses) just want the right product at the right

Vendor	Original Description	Normalized, Rationalized Description
Safeskin	Gloves Latex Exam Str Pwd Free	Gloves Exam Latex Sterile Powder Free
J&J	Ltx Exam Glv Ster Pow Fr	Gloves Exam Latex Sterile Powder Free
Owens & Minors	Exam Ltx Sterile PF Gl	Gloves Exam Latex Sterile Powder Free

Source: Lydon Neumann, CGE&Y Health Care Supply Chain Leader.

time. The integration of clinical information with standard procurement information contributes to improved service and reduced costs through improved clinical outcomes from appropriate product choices and more effective supply utilization.

Guiding Principle #3: Reduce Variability

The product variability within a health care provider frequently arises from individual product preferences on the part of the physicians and nurses. It also occurs when there is an absence of a strong Content program that provides the proper e-based catalogs that help standardize product and use descriptions for the physicians, nurses, administrators, and anyone else authorized to do the procurement.

The service variability occurs when there is an absence of both a strong supply chain process and effective alliances that integrate the Adaptive Health Care e-Supply Chain. Reducing variability requires a comprehensive, systematic approach to managing product differentiation while executing within a disciplined, adaptive supply chain enabled by technology.

The scenario involving the 85-year-old heart patient is a solid example of high variability. The variability in the number of authorized personnel to procure a seemingly endless list of products and services from a number of sources contributes to confusion. It also contributes to a significant number of excess inventories at each supply point to ensure the availability of the products if and when the products are ordered from each supply point. Standardizing the product and use descriptions of the medical supplies and devices, reducing the number of alternative items per product, and formalizing the procurement process with stated authority, responsibility, and accountability will contribute to reduced variability.

Guiding Principle #4: Integrate and Adapt the Supply Chain End-to-End

Many other industries are rapidly utilizing technology and alliances to integrate and adapt their supply chains. In the automotive industry, Toyota is recognized as the market leader with their five-day order-to-ship program. This program pulls all of their suppliers and alliance partners together electronically to dynamically reoptimize the supply chain as automobile orders are received through the Internet. Wal-Mart is leading the "pay-for-scan" or scan-based trading effort in the consumer products and retail industries. This effort requires the payment to direct-store-delivery suppliers if and when their products are sold in a Wal-Mart store. Suppliers must have strong inventory tracking and inventory visibility processes and technology to know what products were delivered to what Wal-Mart stores. This allows suppliers to match deliveries with scan data and perform inventory reconciliations on an online, real-time basis. In both cases, the supply chains are integrated and required to adapt to marketplace demand.

Similar opportunities exist for health care providers. The Adaptive Health Care e-Supply Chain embraces the concept of designing an end-to-end Networked Supply Chain that brings together the manufacturers, the wholesale-distributors, and the internal hospital departments into a disciplined supply chain process. This end-to-end Networked Supply Chain must be anchored by the hospital, the end user of the products and services, and the provider of cash to the entire supply chain. In addition, there must be the enabling technologies supporting the electronic linking of everyone in the supply chain. Last but not least, there must be the presence of the alliance agreements with supply chain partners that align objectives and govern performance-based investments and rewards.

Guiding Principles Summary

Assuming accountability, managing information, reducing variability, and integrating and adapting the supply chain end-to-end are all critical to rapidly improving service and reducing costs for health care providers. These four guiding principles must be present and pervasive throughout the Adaptive Health Care e-Supply Chain to enable the necessary activities to drive the needed results in service and cost reduction.

Recently I worked with a large health care provider that had a history of total physician choice when it came to ordering medical supplies, equipment, and pharmaceutical drugs. They also operated at a loss for a particular quarter, and decided to research how they might reduce costs without impacting patient care or laying off people.

Through the use of Content catalogues, the hospital administrators were able to work with the physicians and nurses to reduce the number of approved options for thousands of line items. For example, there was a dramatic reduction in the number of approved hip replacement kits once the physicians understood the clinical outcomes of the options presented to them. The physicians still controlled what hip replacement kits they could order. However, the reduction of the number of options allowed the health care procurement office to consolidate ordering volumes with approved suppliers. The added numbers also allowed the hospital administrators to work with the suppliers to improve on-time delivery service while reducing inventories.

The strength of the above scenario was the establishment of a board-approved procurement program that relied on physician participation, strong Content, and supplier/alliance relationships. The "physician choice" premise was maintained by engaging the physicians to understand and approve the options regarding the number and type of hip replacement kits. The administration of the procurement program became the responsibility of the supply chain executives. Each hospital had a supply chain manager that had a matrix reporting relationship. These supply chain managers reported to the hospital administrators and to the central supply chain executive for cost performance. Everyone reported to the hospital operating committee (primarily made up of physicians) for patient service performance. The hospital operating committee reported to the board of directors for patient service performance and cost control. The result was a dramatic increase in order fill rate to over 99 percent and a cost reduction of 11 percent.

Alliances are also extremely important for health care providers and suppliers to successfully form an Adaptive Health Care e-Supply Chain and achieve results similar to those stated above. Let's take a look at Content and Strategic Sourcing, and how the proper use of alliances can produce significant value to all supply chain participants.

Content and Strategic Sourcing

Content

The management of Content within an Adaptive Health Care e-Supply Chain is a significant challenge. The manufacturers have information related to the production of the medical supplies and devices. Their research and government approval departments will (or should) have some clinical use data. The wholesalers/distributors will have movement data, while the health care providers will have a mix of data depending upon point of procurement, material receiving and handling, and point of use.

Chances are that all participants in the supply chain will have disparate systems. This means that product descriptions will probably differ from system to system, requiring rationalization and normalization. Product descriptions need to include common units of measure and an agreed-to classification structure. There is also the challenge concerning the quality of the product descriptions and the timeliness of the updating of the needed information.

The participants in the Health Care Adaptive e-Supply Chain must agree on a standard way to describe, measure, and classify medical supplies and devices. They must also agree on the information technology that is needed to support the use of this standardized information and the processes that are needed to keep the information current.

Despite significant cost-benefit scenarios for most health care providers, their ability to create their own Content eCatalogues is limited. The limitations are generally related to time or speed-to-value, catalogue expertise, systems integration expertise, and end-to-end supply chain process expertise. Health care providers are and should be focused on patient care, just like Toyota is focused on designing, assembling, and selling automobiles and Wal-Mart buying and reselling general merchandise to the general public.

As such, alliances are invaluable in the creation of the processes and technology to support a strong Content program for health care providers. For example, i2 Technologies (through its Aspect Development acquisition in 2000) offers a first-rate global eCatalogue that standardizes and integrates product data from all sources into a single data repository. This single data repository allows for a quick search by physicians, nurses, and hospital administrators to compare and contrast product performance, product prices, and any other needed service and cost information. Health care providers can either buy the eCatalogue software from i2, enter into a joint development alliance for reselling to others, enter into a solution-specific alliance, or even establish a joint venture alliance with i2.

These alliances could also be accomplished with a consulting and information technology firm like Cap Gemini Ernst & Young to utilize supply chain process and systems integration expertise, while accessing the eCatalogue of i2 through an alliance with or purchase from i2. Either way, the Health Care providers generally do not have the expertise to map out their supply chain processes, create their own eCatalogue technology, standardize and cleanse the data from multiple sources, or integrate the eCatalogue into the systems of all supply chain partners. They can, however, access them faster and perhaps cheaper through alliances or acquisition from companies who are experts.

Strategic Sourcing Process

Many purchasing departments have a standard process and set of procedures to work with suppliers. The people who work in these purchasing departments work hard to make sure that all suppliers are treated equally. The problem is that the medical supplies and devices that the health care provider uses vary greatly.

The Five-Step Strategic Sourcing Framework (Exhibit 7-3) incorporates the Guiding Principles and encompasses the value of Content. For the health care provider, this framework can provide significant returns or provide the foundation for the Adaptive Health Care e-Supply Chain. The steps in the Strategic Sourcing Five-Step Framework are:

1. Opportunity assessment
2. Commodity profile
3. Strategic direction

Exhibit 7-3. Strategic sourcing five-step methodology.

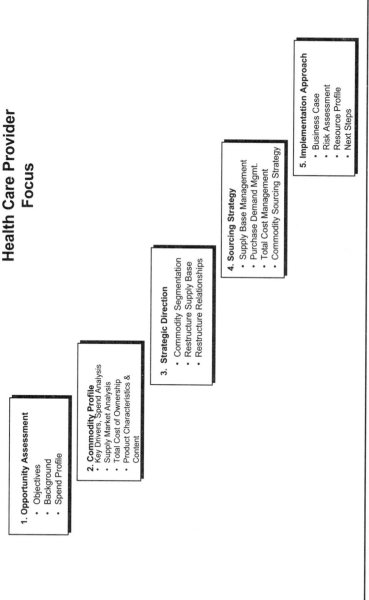

Health Care Provider Focus

1. Opportunity Assessment
- Objectives
- Background
- Spend Profile

2. Commodity Profile
- Key Drivers, Spend Analysis
- Supply Market Analysis
- Total Cost of Ownership
- Product Characteristics & Content

3. Strategic Direction
- Commodity Segmentation
- Restructure Supply Base
- Restructure Relationships

4. Sourcing Strategy
- Supply Base Management
- Purchase Demand Mgmt.
- Total Cost Management
- Commodity Sourcing Strategy

5. Implementation Approach
- Business Case
- Risk Assessment
- Resource Profile
- Next Steps

Source: Cap Gemini Ernst & Young.

4. Sourcing strategy
5. Implementation approach

✧ *Step 1, Opportunity Assessment* (Exhibit 7-4), sets the stage for Steps 2 to 5 to be completed. It is critical to perform the opportunity assessment properly in order to maximize the benefit of the strategic sourcing process. The first task is to establish the *objectives* of the Strategic Sourcing effort. These objectives should be broad statements that the health care provider wanted to achieve through this process. The next task is to do a *spend profile* for each commodity group. This spend profile should be done by hospital, division, or business unit. In addition, this spend profile should include indirect materials (e.g., cleaning solvents), direct materials (e.g., medical supplies and devices), capital expenditures (hospital facility, equipment expenditures), and services (janitorial, landscaping, parking, contractors, etc.). The commodities in the spend profile should then be grouped by same or similar suppliers, same or similar procurement processes, and same or similar product specifications.

The next task should be to identify each commodity profile group by purchase volume, price, product specifications, the procurement process, and other constraints such as government regulations or customer requirements. This information should come from the health care provider's "Databases and Content Catalogues." *It should also be provided by and/or validated by key alliances and best practices in health care and sourcing.* The commodity profile groups should then be ranked by total dollar "spend," the cost-to-total-cost percentage, and by intangibles, such as customer perception, product differentiation, and the impact on the operation of a sourcing failure. (In health care, the cost of sourcing failure can be measured in lost human lives.)

The next task should be the identification of *Quick Hits* to realize fast savings. In addition, a *high-level pro-forma savings potential* should be completed utilizing the highest ranked purchased commodities. *Inhibitors and Enablers* should then be identified to determine the feasibility of the realization of the savings. Using this information, the *Strategic Sourcing Plan* can then be completed. This plan includes the profiled commodities, the commodity segmentation and the appropriate alliance relationships, the sourcing strategy, and the implementation plan.

Alliances are critical to this step. An alliance partner in the health

Exhibit 7-4. Step 1: Opportunity assessment.

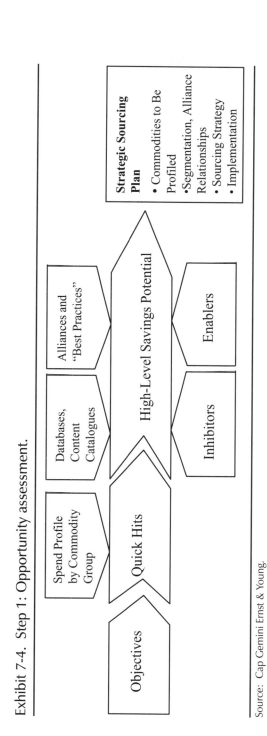

Source: Cap Gemini Ernst & Young.

care provider industry can be a wholesaler/distributor, a major consulting firm, or even a major technology company. The outside, objective opinion on the *Quick Hits* and the *High Level Savings Potential* can be an immense help in validating the benefits to be derived as well as the Implementation Approach to achieve these benefits. The consulting firm and the technology company may have deep strategic sourcing experience, and can augment the health care provider in this area if their experience is not as strong as needed.

❖ *Step 2, Commodity Profile* (Exhibit 7-5), takes the initial work in the Opportunity Assessment step to a deeper level. The *Spend Analysis* uses the four categories (direct materials, indirect materials, CapEx, and services), and segments "spend" by hospital group, by medical facility, by supplier, and by product or medical device. The *Spend Analysis* should also include historical spend data and future spend trends.

The *Product Characteristics* include functional, design, and quality specifications, content standardization of specifications, the level of customization and standardization for each product or commodity (e.g., left-handed hip replacement kits), specification ownership by commodity group, consumption or volume levels, physician choice options, and product segmentation. As discussed in Content, these product characteristics are critical to be able to standardize specifications and formalize procurement process disciplines within the health care provider organizations.

The *Total Cost of Ownership* task includes internal ownership costs (e.g., inventory carrying costs, risk of obsolescence) and external ownership costs (e.g., inventory build-up by the supplier due to inconsistent ordering and variable ordering disciplines by the health care provider). Many leading health care providers will build a Total Acquisition Cost (TAC) model to support the identification of total cost components.

The *Key Drivers* include the supplier cost performance, the supplier service/patient care performance, and the product economic levers. These key drivers should be built into a scorecard for future supplier performance measurement. For example, the service/patient care performance of the supplier for the heart valve for the 85-year-old patient should carry considerably more weight than the supplier cost performance. The reverse is true for the sutures for this patient.

Exhibit 7-5. Step 2: commodity profile.

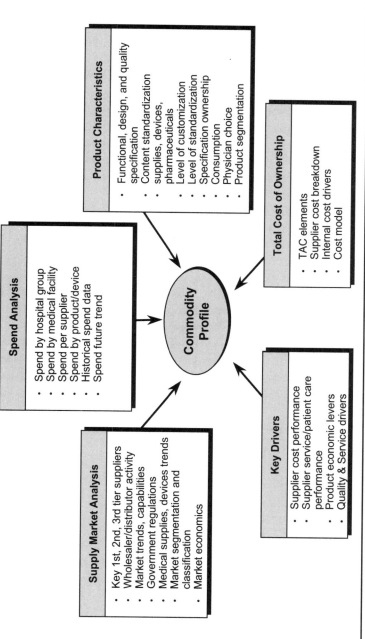

The *Supply Market Analysis* is an important task. The number of suppliers by commodity group should be identified. In addition, the ability of the health care provider to substitute products by commodity group should be measured. The market should also be measured on the ease of entry (or lack thereof) for new suppliers. The health care provider should then assess its buying strength versus the suppliers' selling strength for each commodity group. For example, with sutures the health care provider should leverage its buying power and take the proverbial "big hammer" approach to supply and service. Concerning heart valves, the health care provider should find a differentiator to work with the limited number of heart valve suppliers.

The *Commodity Profile Process* (Exhibit 7-6) pulls these tasks together in a repeatable process. It begins with reviewing the Assessment Hypothesis and Objectives, and leads into the analysis of the Product/Commodity Characteristics. From this point, the analyzing Current and Future Spend, building Total Acquisition Cost Model, analyzing Supply Market, and modeling Supplier Cost and Performance drivers are performed concurrently and collaboratively. This work is then pulled together to generate Commodity Group Profiles and to generate Commodity Group Opportunities.

Included in the commodity group opportunities must be an early assessment of the approach to be taken with suppliers. The assessment should consider whether or not purchase volume consolidation, purchasing process improvements, price, geographic sourcing capabilities, product specifications, or supplier relationship changes are in order. Step 3 will cover this in more detail, but an early assessment should be done at the end of this process.

❖ *Step 3, Strategic Direction* (Exhibit 7-7), maps the commodity groups against the estimated business impact and supply market challenge. It also incorporates the current and future spend by commodity groups to ensure that the right long-term sourcing strategies will be implemented. The result is a quadrant that identifies four distinct supplier sourcing approaches for the health care provider to use; based upon which quadrant the commodity groups are placed.

The low-business-impact, low-supply-market-complexity commodity groups fall into the *Routine* quadrant. The Sourcing Strategy in that quadrant should focus on simplifying and streamlining the acquisition process, reducing the number of suppliers and simplifying

Exhibit 7-6. Step 2 (continued): commodity profile process.

Develop Commodity Profile

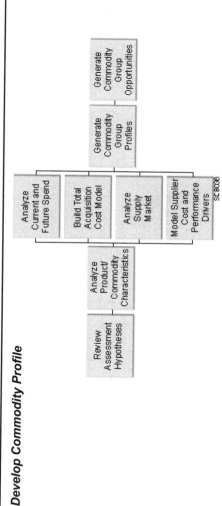

SCB036

- A robust commodity profile is key to developing and implementing an effective sourcing strategy.

- Work in this stage begins with analysis of product and commodity characteristics to determine the functional requirements, specification issues, and relevant technology trends for the commodity family.

- Detailed analysis of spend history and projections is obtained.

- Cost driver analysis and a TAC (Total Acquisition Cost) model is developed, where appropriate, and a supply market analysis is conducted.

- The level of detail in this stage is used to confirm (or refute) identified opportunities from the assessment, and to provide the factual basis for strategy development.

Source: Cap Gemini Ernst & Young.

Exhibit 7-7. Step 3: strategic direction.

Map commodity groups against the estimated business impact and the supply market challenge.

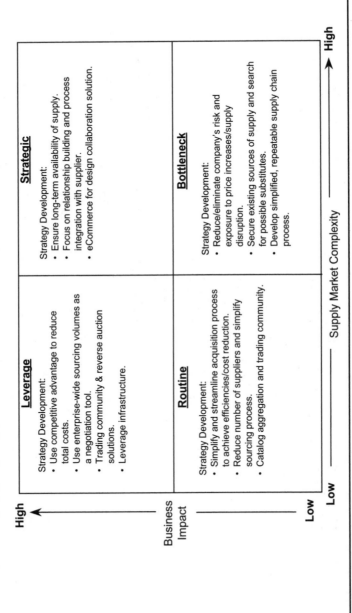

Source: Cap Gemini Ernst & Young.

the sourcing process (volume concentration and price), and catalog aggregation and use of trading communities (e.g., indirect procurement portals). Once again, common sutures fall into this quadrant.

The high-business-impact, low-supply-market-complexity commodity groups fall into the *Leverage* quadrant. The Sourcing Strategy in this quadrant should focus on the health care provider using its competitive advantage to reduce total costs. It should also focus on using total sourcing volumes as a negotiation tool, using trading communities and reverse auction solutions, and leveraging one's infrastructure. A solid example of this is a health care provider that specializes in open heart surgery and is a teaching hospital group. Its specialization, concentration, infrastructure, and influence within the buyer community allow it to have leverage with suppliers of open-heart–specific commodity groups.

The low-business-impact, high-supply-market-complexity commodity groups fall into the *Bottleneck* quadrant. In this quadrant, the Sourcing Strategy should focus on reducing and/or eliminating the health care provider's risk and exposure to price increases and/or supply disruptions. Securing existing sources of supply while searching for possible supply substitutes is one key approach. Another is to develop a simplified, repeatable supply chain process that minimizes the possibility of supply disruption. Ventilators and respirators are examples of a Bottleneck commodity group. There are limited numbers of suppliers, and the supply chain process can be cumbersome for the health care providers to order and receive them in a timely, predictable manner.

The high-business-impact, high-supply-market-complexity commodity groups fall into the *Strategic* quadrant. The Sourcing Strategy in this quadrant should focus on ensuring the long-term availability of supply through relationship-building and process integration with suppliers. In this quadrant, there are a limited number of suppliers for very specialized commodity groups. Specialized anesthesia drugs and left-handed hip replacement kits are examples of commodity groups that fall into this quadrant.

Once the health care provider segments and maps the commodity groups into the four quadrants, the first pass should be taken to restructure the supply base and supplier relationships. For example, greater control should be given to each local hospital or medical facility for the purchasing of the Routine commodity groups. The health care provider should establish the framework (e.g., indirect materials procurement portal) for the local hospitals to use. However, care should be taken not to overmanage these low-business-impact, low-supply-complexity commodity groups. The reverse should occur with the Strategic commodity groups.

✧ *Step 4, Commodity Sourcing Strategy* (Exhibit 7-8), involves the development of the commodity group sourcing strategy. This sourcing strategy provides the blueprint for how a commodity group is managed. In this step, Supply Chain Imperatives such as planning and scheduling, inventory management, order-to-delivery demands, and lead-time requirements are identified and documented. The Supplier Contract Type is identified as well, which includes length of time, terms and conditions, cost targets, and performance targets. The Supply Base Profile is completed, which includes the size, structure location, and levels of spend. In a major way, the previous work in Content is pulled into the Sourcing Strategy though the identification of Content Imperatives.

Alliances play a critical role in whether the health care provider will be successful in Strategic Sourcing. The types of alliances (see Chapter One), along with the roles, responsibilities, and operational interfaces, must be identified in this step. Alliance partners can range from Content providers, strategic sourcing specialists, technology providers, to outsourcing partners.

Included in Step 4 are the risk assessment, benefit analysis with the associated timing of the benefits, and migration plans. These three items serve as the foundation for the Sourcing Strategy blueprint.

To ready the strategic sourcing blueprint for implementation, the health care provider should incorporate opportunities from three key dimensions. These three key dimensions are: Supply Base Management, Purchase Demand Management, and Total Cost Management (Exhibit 7-9).

In *Supply Base Management*, the focus should be placed on restructuring relationships, increasing competition, and restructuring the supply base. Restructuring relationships should include contract consolidation, entering into alliances for supplier development of critical, high-business-impact/high-supply-market-complexity commodity groups, and extending contracts into long-term agreements. Increasing competition should include bid-based renegotiation, price/perfor-

Exhibit 7-8. Step 4: commodity sourcing strategy.

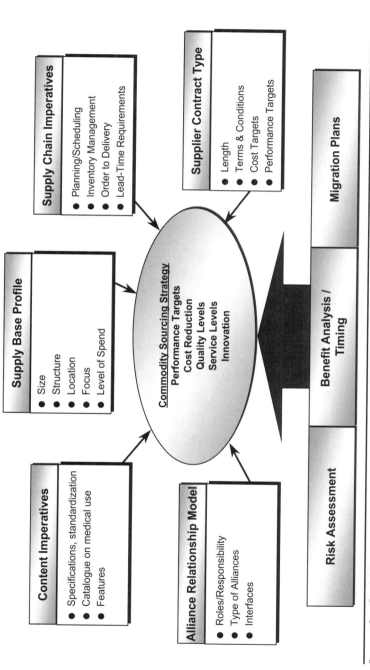

Content Imperatives
- Specifications, standardization
- Catalogue on medical use
- Features

Supply Base Profile
- Size
- Structure
- Location
- Focus
- Level of Spend

Supply Chain Imperatives
- Planning/Scheduling
- Inventory Management
- Order to Delivery
- Lead-Time Requirements

Commodity Sourcing Strategy
Performance Targets
Cost Reduction
Quality Levels
Service Levels
Innovation

Supplier Contract Type
- Length
- Terms & Conditions
- Cost Targets
- Performance Targets

Alliance Relationship Model
- Roles/Responsibility
- Type of Alliances
- Interfaces

Risk Assessment

Benefit Analysis / Timing

Migration Plans

Source: Cap Gemini Ernst & Young.

Exhibit 7-9. Step 4: (continued): commodity sourcing strategy.

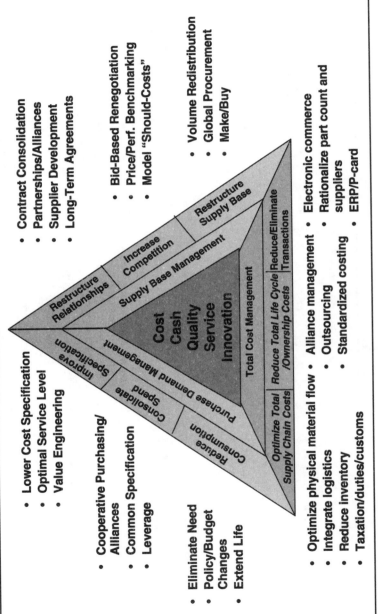

Source: Cap Gemini Ernst & Young.

mance benchmarking, and the modeling of "should costs." Wal-Mart does an outstanding job of modeling "should-costs" with their suppliers. Restructuring the supply base should include volume redistribution, global procurement when feasible, and performing make-versus-buy decisions. A make-versus-buy decision for a health care provider would be the use of their internal IT department to develop and populate Content catalogues.

In *Purchase Demand Management*, the focus should be on reducing consumption, consolidating spend, and improving specifications. We covered the improvement of specifications in the Content section. Ways to reduce consumption are to eliminate need, make certain policy and/or budget changes, and extend the life of commodity groups. For example, an aggressive preventive maintenance program for ventilators/respirators may extend their life cycles, reducing the need for new equipment and spares. One key way to consolidate spend is to develop alliances with purchasing coops. The Global Health Care Exchange is an example of health care providers coming together and consolidating their spend in common commodity groups.

For *Total Cost Management*, the focus should be placed on optimizing total supply chain costs, reducing total life cycle/ownership costs, and reducing and/or eliminating transactions. Optimizing total supply chain costs can be achieved through connecting supply to actual demand, integrating logistics, reducing inventories at each step of the supply chain, and minimizing taxes, duties, and customs clearance issues on global material flow. Alliances, outsourcing, and standardized costing will assist the health care provider in reducing total life cycle/ownership costs. For example, health care providers may outsource their IT department or the preventative maintenance department working on ventilators/respirators or cardiac care equipment. The reduction or elimination of transactions can come from using electronic commerce, rationalizing and standardizing specifications and item counts, and the use of purchasing cards.

✧ *Step 5, Implementation Approach* (Exhibit 7-10), incorporates a framework for Supply Base Management, Purchase Demand Management, and Total Cost Management. All three should be done concurrently. Let's look at the framework supporting each one.

The *Supply Base Management* framework starts with assessing the suppliers for each commodity group. The assessment of the suppliers

Exhibit 7-10. Step 5: implementation approach.

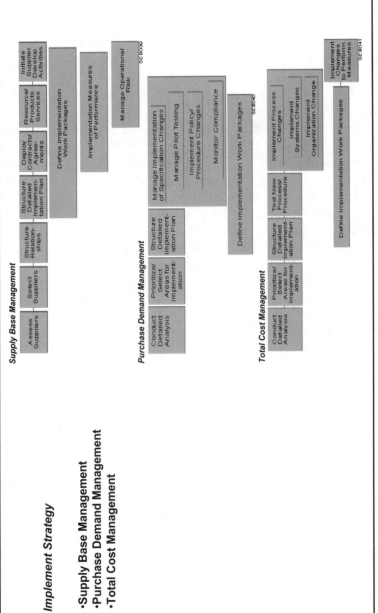

Source: Cap Gemini Ernst & Young.

is then followed by the selection of the suppliers. The structuring of the supplier relationships then feed into a detailed implementation plan. After the detailed implementation plan, the health care provider should deploy the contracts and agreements, dedicate the proper resources to support the products and services, and initiate the supplier development activities. The definition of the implementation work packages should be extracted from the detailed implementation plan, while the implementation measures of performance are developed from the deployment of the contracts and agreements. Finally, the proper resources dedicated to support the products and services should manage the operational risk of managing the supply base.

The *Purchase Demand Management* framework is just as critical as the Supply Base Management framework. The health care provider should conduct a detailed analysis of the purchasing demand by commodity group. Then, using a ranking process (e.g., total dollar spend, total volume, the commodity group cost to total cost percentage, and intangibles, such as the impact on the operation of a shortage of anesthesia drugs), a prioritization and selection should be done. Detailed implementation plans should be completed for reducing consumption, consolidating the spend, and improving and standardizing the specifications of the commodities. These plans need to be followed by defining the implementation work packages. The actual implementation of the plans includes the managing of the implementation of the specification changes (and Content catalogues), managing the pilot testing, and implementing the necessary policy and procedural changes. Last but not least is the implementation of a monitoring process to ensure compliance.

The *Total Cost Management* framework is the missing link to complete the implementation approach. The first three steps in the framework are similar to the purchase demand framework. These steps are: conduct detailed analysis, prioritize/select areas for improvement, and structure detailed implementation plan. However, the focus is to optimize total supply chain costs, reduce total life cycle/ownership costs, and reduce/eliminate transactions. Once the detailed implementation plan is complete, there needs to be the definition of the implementation work packages to feed the testing of the new process and procedures. The learnings from this testing are then incorporated into the implementation of process changes, systems changes, and organizational changes. The implementation of these changes are structured around the specific performance measurements identified in the detailed implementation plan. These performance measurements must also link back to the original objectives established in Step 1, *Opportunity Assessment.*

The Alliance Connection

The benefits derived from a comprehensive Content and Supplier Relationship Management program for a health care provider are huge. Strategic Sourcing experts estimate that the average health care provider can realize between 5 percent and 15 percent cost savings through a Content and Strategic Sourcing program. These savings can be realized without laying off people, and can be achieved while enhancing patient care.

However, very few health care providers are experienced in strategic sourcing, Content technology, the supply chain technology and process thinking, and organizational change to design and implement such a program. Purchasing/buying alliances, strategic sourcing solution alliances, technology investment (e.g., Content) alliances, and joint venture alliances may all be needed for health care providers to realize these savings. These solution-based alliances are frequently governed through the development of a definitive agreement between the alliance parties.

Remember how we discussed in Chapter Three that the Memo of Intent (MOI) was a transition document for alliance parties to get started while the definitive agreement was being negotiated? In a section at the end of this chapter, we will walk through the process to construct a solution-based definitive agreement that serves as an addendum to the overall alliance agreement but covers a specific marketplace solution. It continues the journey began in Chapter Three, using Content and Strategic Sourcing within health care as a representative base.

Keep in mind that there are two cardinal rules to follow when constructing a definitive agreement. The first rule is to know the business terms and requirements driving the development of the definitive agreement. The second cardinal rule is to get your lawyer involved—and the sooner, the better. Many definitive agreements have been well-intentioned, only to go sour due to marketplace changes, business condition changes within one or both companies, or the loss of a sponsoring executive. The time to negotiate the tough language is up front, not after the fact.

Summary

Four "Guiding Principles" serve as the foundation for health care providers to start on the journey toward the achievement of the Adaptive Health Care e-Supply Chain. This journey relies on a strong Content strategy to rationalize and standardize products and services across all hospitals and medical facilities within a health care provider network.

The journey continues with the implementation of the Content strategy that is incorporated into a Strategic Sourcing process. The Five-Step Strategic Sourcing Framework provides a road map for health care providers to follow and achieve strong sourcing results. The Implementation Approach (Step 5) utilizes the Supply Base Management, Purchase Demand Management, and the Total Cost Management frameworks to ensure the establishment of a sustainable, repeatable series of processes that address supplier approaches, demand management, and cost management.

The achievement of the Adaptive Health Care e-Supply Chain is dependent on the selection and use of alliances. The average health care provider knows health care, but Strategic Sourcing expertise, Content technology, supply chain process and technology expertise, and organizational change capabilities are not resident in the core competencies of the typical health care provider. They can be accessed, using the alliance framework and a definitive agreement, to build a holistic plan for the achievement of the Adaptive Health Care e-Supply Chain. With savings of between 5 percent to 15 percent, the opportunity is too great to pass up.

How to Construct a Solution-Based Definitive Agreement

The first paragraph of the solution-based definitive agreement is similar to the MOI. The first paragraph introduces the alliance parties by formal name, includes the headquarters or principal place of business for each party, and establishes the effective date of the definitive agreement.

Remember the *background* of the MOI? The next section of the definitive agreement formalizes the background, and also makes reference to the MOI. For example, if a health care provider, i2 Technologies, and Cap Gemini Ernst & Young entered into a solution-based MOI for the development of health care specific Content and Strategic Sourcing solutions, it would be stated here that all data was owned by the health care provider, all software rights were owned by i2 Technologies, and all implementation solution processes and materials were owned by Cap Gemini Ernst & Young. These items would be identified in attached schedules.

If i2 Technologies and Cap Gemini Ernst & Young were to go to market with the codeveloped solution and implementation materials, then this desire would be stated in this section. This section would also memorialize the mutual intents of the MOI, as stated in the *background* of the MOI.

One major difference between the MOI and the definitive agreement is the transition from nonbinding to binding. The items following this section are those items that the alliance parties agree to be legally binding. Language frequently used at this stage is, ". . . parties do hereby agree as follows:" The items in the MOI now become "articles."

Article I: Joint Solution Development

The *joint solution development* article covers the solution scope, but in more detail than the MOI. For example, the definition of the solution scope may be as follows: ". . . the Implementation Solution will be designed to support Content and Strategic Sourcing processes from the time of item standardization and commonization through the implementation of strategic sourcing strategies. This process includes Content, supplier relationship management, and Strategic Sourcing of health care provider materials and devices." In addition, the solution scope may include a defined role for the specific alliance parties. For example, the solution scope definition may continue as follows: ". . . the Solution Software will be fully enabled by technology based on i2's original software and Cap Gemini's process and organizational behavior implementation methodologies and templates."

This joint solution development includes the requirements definition for the joint solution development and the build-out of the solution itself. The language in the definitive agreement will usually call for the parties to determine (through a joint process) common definitions for the activities and processes. In the case of health care providers and Content with Strategic Sourcing, this would include technology architecture, software applications, and business requirement definitions that would be included in the jointly developed solutions. As in the MOI, the alliance parties may agree to modify their stated definitions as needed from time to time through written notification to one another.

It is also important to specifically identify the responsible alliance party for each section of the joint solution development. The specific number of people dedicated to the joint solution from both parties must be identified, along with their work location and their qualifications. The joint solution development will also include language around the project costs, what party is responsible for what costs, and the overall project cap on the costs. This area is critical, because the return on alliance investments must be measured and communicated.

Article II: Joint Marketing

In *joint marketing*, the alliance parties will agree to the type of marketing to be performed, the specific time period for the marketing activities, and which party will be responsible for each marketing activity. For the definitive agreement, specific names need to be identified as the leaders for the different marketing activities.

In addition, the process and methods must be established for how each party will communicate with the other. This is critical, because this language will guide the behavior and even the subsequent results from the joint marketing activities. This item includes the internal notifications required by each alliance party to their own organizations regarding the definitive agreement. It also includes external publicity, such as press releases and marketing collateral. Unless specifics are known, there may be language that limits advertising and publicity to mutually agreed-upon activities.

As identified in the MOI, there is usually specific language that establishes an active steering committee to review, monitor, and deal with business and relationship issues. These issues can range from progress made towards the agreement targets, joint solution development progress, sales and marketing strategies, relationship conflicts, and needed addendums to the agreement as business conditions change. Specific meeting dates or at least parameters are usually set, along with specific names of leaders from each alliance party that will serve on the steering committee.

One area that must be expanded upon in the definitive agreement is the issue of exclusivity. This issue is significant, because of the legal and operational restrictions it places on a company. To offer exclusivity to an alliance partner, there must be significant benefits that cannot be achieved through another alliance partner. Otherwise, companies can define their relationship as "preferred," with language that defines "preferred behavior" in the marketplace.

The process to select targeted accounts must be included in this section. In addition, the parameters around separate contracting with clients or subcontracting to one another must be addressed. This is critical, because it involves the pricing of the products and services of each alliance partner and determines how each party will be compensated.

Article III: Representations and Warranties

Representations and warranties are commitments made between the parties on a number of items. First, each party represents and warrants that it has the authority to enter into this agreement, and that this agreement does not violate the terms and conditions of any of its other agreements. In addition, each party commits to the other that the material, services, software, or solutions they provide under the agreement do not infringe upon the copyright, trademark, patent, trade secret, or other proprietary right of any third party.

There is also continuing Y2K or Year 2000 language to protect both parties as it relates to any software. In addition, each party should warrant to the other that qualified personnel would perform the services in accordance with the statements of work agreed to in writing by the parties in a professional manner. If a breach of performance on services occurs, one approach for remedy is for the parties to agree that the sole responsibility for nonperformance of services would be the re-performance of the services that caused such breach.

The other item in the warranties and representations section involves third parties or brokers. If brokers are used, then they must be party to the agreement and be bound by the legal warranties and representations specified in the agreement. If brokers are not to be used, then language must specify that brokers and third parties must not be used in moving forward. This is critical to control both confidential information and marketplace perception.

Article IV: Limitations of Liability

In the MOI, *limitations of liability* were covered in the legal issues section. In the definitive agreement, these limitations of liability are expanded and included in a separate article.

Most companies adopt a limitation of damages in their definitive agreements. The limitation of damages disallows claims by either party for lost sales, lost profits, or special, indirect, incidental, punitive, or consequential damages (including injury to business reputation) from all causes of action of any kind. Exceptions to limits of damages include death or personal injury caused by negligence or willful misconduct and breaches of confidentiality or unauthorized use of confidential information. The aggregate liability in the MOI (from $25,000 to $250,000) is similar to that frequently used in definitive agreements. These limits vary from industry to industry, and from company to company.

Another item in *limitations of liability* involves limited recourse. Many corporations have multiple subsidiaries or wholly owned companies. The alliance agreement either includes all of these subsidiaries and wholly owned companies, includes some of them, or excludes them entirely. If a subsidiary or wholly owned company is included, the parent company is solely responsible for its performance. In addition, the subsidiaries and wholly owned companies become party to the agreement and all of its obligations and liabilities.

Article V: Intellectual Property Rights

The *intellectual property rights* article covers the ownership rights of the original materials identified in the *background* of the MOI, and the ownership rights of the jointly developed solution as the original materials are modified. If needed, the alliance parties will grant to each other a license to use each other's knowledge or legally protected copyrighted or patented material as it is used in the joint solution. Usually, the knowledge, know-how, and concepts jointly developed in the joint solution development are co-owned by the alliance parties, unless otherwise specified. For the definitive agreement, the parties should also agree to reasonably assist each other in jointly obtaining, registering, and perfecting the joint materials.

Article VI: Term and Termination

The *term* of the definitive agreement is usually established in increments of years, with the effective date being the start of the term. The term of the definitive agreement either automatically renews for a specific period or is renewed by written agreement by the parties. Otherwise, the term runs its course and the definitive agreement expires.

The *termination* of the definitive agreement is usually warranted through a material breach of the agreement, bankruptcy, or insolvency, or ceases to function as a going concern. In addition, termination is warranted through a merger or acquisition that involves a company that is a competitor to the other alliance party.

If the *term* expires or the definitive agreement involves *termination*, many items (e.g., confidential information and intellectual property rights) survive the ending of the definitive agreement.

Article VII: Amendments and Waivers

In this section, *amendments* to the definitive agreement are usually allowed only through notice and agreement in writing to each other or all parties of the definitive agreement. In addition, the representations, warranties, or conditions set forth in a definitive agreement are allowed to be *waived* only by a written instrument executed by the alliance party doing the waiving.

Article VIII: Independent Contractor Status

The health care alliance discussed earlier did not involve the formation of a joint venture, and therefore did not involve a legal partnership that would result in responsibilities by one alliance party for the actions of the other alliance party. In this situation, the alliance parties are frequently referred to as *independent contractors*. Each alliance party is responsible for the pricing of their own products and services and the compensation of their own personnel.

The issue of exclusivity is covered in this article also. Either the alliance parties grant exclusive rights to each other, or establish a "preferred" but nonexclusive status to each other. In either case, there is usually language that prohibits each party from developing and marketing a similar solution with another party for a specific period of time. As stated earlier, this issue must not be taken lightly. There are costs and benefits to exclusively or nonexclusivity.

Article IX: Confidentiality

An executed nondisclosure agreement (NDA) governs the exchange, disclosure, and use of confidential and proprietary information (see Chapter Four for "How to Construct a Nondisclosure Agreement"). If an executed NDA is in force, then there is reference to it in this article. If there is not an executed

NDA, then one will need to be completed before the definitive agreement is completed.

Article X: Publicity

In *publicity*, both parties will agree on specific, external communications in the form of press releases and other public announcements. All other marketing collateral, advertising, and additional publicity are usually allowed only when mutually agreed to by the alliance parties.

Article XI: Indemnification and Remedies

The *indemnification* language covers the alliance parties indemnifying each other in case the products, services, or materials provided by each party and identified as solely developed by each party infringe on any copyright, patent, trademark, trade secret, or other proprietary right of a third party. Additional language is usually included that provides the indemnifying party the right to defend a claim and control the defense of the claim. Ask your lawyer about the detailed language that governs the rights between the indemnified party and the indemnifying party and the negotiated behavior between the two. In addition, your lawyer can explain any additional *remedies* and the use of "sole basis for claims" language.

Article XII: Miscellaneous

This section is the catchall section. For example, this section addresses the subject of expenses as they relate to the preparation of the definitive agreement and the execution of the agreement provisions, covering whether one party is to pay for all the expenses or whether the parties are to pay their own expenses.

Another subject addressed in this article is *notices*. Notices can be verbal, in writing—hard copy or soft copy—or by e-mail. Usually, Notices become valid when one party verifies receipt of the Notices sent by the other alliance party. There is a signature page that specifies who is to receive the Notices and to which addresses the Notices are to be sent.

There is also language in this article that binds the successors, legal representatives, and permitted assigns to the agreement. Conversely, it also requires that prior written consent is needed to assign the agreement to a third party.

There should be legal language that states that this definitive agreement supersedes the MOI and other agreements based on the same subject matter. In addition, there must be the identification of the governing law (country if global, state if U.S.–based).

Another subject covered under *miscellaneous* is nonsolicitation and nonhiring. Nonsolicitation, which covers the recruitment of personnel from one alliance party to another, addresses only active solicitation. It does not cover the hiring of personnel. A nonhiring clause would prohibit the hiring of personnel as well as the solicitation. Sometimes, the crossover of personnel is beneficial for the definitive agreement and the two companies, whereas other times it can be very detrimental. This subject needs to be openly discussed and agreed-to before the definitive agreement is executed. Nothing can be more detrimental to a working alliance relationship than the hiring of talented personnel by what are supposedly "partners" working under an alliance agreement and a solution-based definitive agreement.

Other miscellaneous items to be covered by the legal team include severability, equitable relief, license agreements, and further assurances.

The signature page follows Article XII. Remember, only authorized personnel with the authority to commit the company can sign the definitive agreement.

The addendums follow the signature page. After the addendums, there is usually a section that defines the dispute resolution procedures in case a dispute arises. This process can range from executive discussions to arbitration. This area can be unpleasant to discuss when there are usually high hopes for the success of the definitive agreement. However, this is why we pay our lawyers the big bucks!

How to Construct a Solution-Based Definitive Agreement Summary

If the definitive agreement looks like a detailed MOI, then the process is working well. The MOI should be negotiated and developed with the definitive agreement in mind. Establishing the bridge between the two should not be difficult if the two documents are completed properly.

Notes

1. Lydon Neumann, Mark Van Sumeren, Amanda Brown, and Jacqueline Lutz, "The New Road to IDN Profitability: Realizing the Opportunity in the Health Care Supply Chain," *A Cap Gemini Ernst & Young Point of View*, February 2001, p. 4.

CHAPTER EIGHT

Software Companies and Consulting Firms: Alliances Viewed from Both Sides

I became involved in software alliances more than twelve years ago when working as a consultant at what was then Price Waterhouse (today, PriceWaterhouseCoopers).* The Unix operating system, coupled with client-server architecture, was starting to be used for mission-critical applications, and businesses were looking to move some of their applications off the expensive mainframe and to a more cost-

*The author of this chapter, Jeff Hook, is a vice president with i2 Technologies in Dallas, Texas. For several years, he led the consulting alliances group for i2. Prior to joining i2, he served as a senior manager of Price Waterhouse. Thus, he has had the good fortune to work on both sides of the alliance fence, so to speak, which gives him a unique perspective on managing alliances between software companies and consulting firms.

effective, user-friendly platform. Oracle had one of the few sets of applications at the time that could be considered mature and robust enough to run on the Unix platform. As part of our marketing efforts, a group of Price Waterhouse (PW) colleagues and I would periodically meet with Greg Brady, who at the time led the south-central sales office for Oracle (Greg is now the chief executive officer for i2). We would meet with Greg and his team to discuss the various accounts we were both working on to try to achieve similar goals. Greg wanted to meet with PW because consulting firms are definitely strong influencers when it comes to the technology decisions made by their clients, and we wanted to meet with Greg because Oracle's sales force was one of the best in the industry. They knew what companies were contemplating a move from mainframe computing, which could lead to potential consulting work for us to help accomplish this migration.

At the time, PW and Oracle did not really have a formal alliance. However, because the two organizations had similar goals of moving customers off the mainframe to mid-range Unix servers, we were able to build personal relationships that allowed us to work together for common sales goals in going to market together. The goals, of course, were revenue-based: Oracle would receive license revenue for software implemented on the new computers, and PW would receive consulting revenue for assisting its customers by implementing the software solution. Years later, at i2, I was asked to try to bring that same "common working spirit" to i2's relationship with its consulting partners.

Eleven Software-Consulting Alliance Lessons Learned

My experience with the PW and Oracle alliance allowed me to learn some valuable lessons concerning alliances that I was able to use in my role at i2. I have summarized my learnings in eleven software-consulting alliance lessons, which are listed below and then discussed in detail.

1. Alliances are structured at the corporate level, but are made or not made at the local, or deal, level.
2. Conflict resolution on key issues must be done on a timely basis.

3. If divisions of a company compete with the alliance partner, trust is constantly in jeopardy.
4. Alliances flourish best when both sides have differentiating attributes and when they determine whether their alliance is strategic or tactical.
5. Tactical alliances can be just as successful at driving additional revenue as so-called strategic alliances.
6. Successful alliances rely on the definition of added responsibilities of both parties.
7. Conflict resolution: Behavior in the field must be monitored.
8. Check your ego at the door!!!
9. Aligned compensation: It helps, but only so much!
10. Leadership builds relationships!
11. Software-consulting alliance programs must be customer-focused!

Let's take a look at each lesson, and at how these lessons impact the success or failure of alliances between software companies and consulting firms.

✧ *Lesson #1: Alliances are structured at the corporate level, but are made or not made at the local, or deal, level.* Please do not misunderstand this lesson. Formal corporate-level alliances can help establish a relationship between two firms and their local offices, can reinforce the proper behavior at the field level, and can even help overcome some miscommunications and misunderstandings at the field level. However, the best corporate intentions with even the most aligned goals will not necessarily cause the proper behavior at the field or client level.

As an example, during my time at Price Waterhouse (PW) we had a formal corporate relationship with J. D. Edwards, an enterprise resource planning (ERP) software company that competes with SAP and Oracle. However, PW's Houston office had very little contact or rapport with the local J.D. Edwards office. That did not stop a sales representative from calling the managing partner of the office to complain that we were not recommending them in certain situations. Because we did not have a rapport at the local level among the people that dealt directly with potential clients, we had simply ignored the corporate alliance that was in place.

Similarly, a major consulting firm that always had trouble working with i2 would always send a couple of their senior supply chain partners to meet with the senior executives and come out of the meetings with what they thought was a general agreement to work together. However, the partners assigned to their clients and projects would frequently decide that the agreement at the so-called corporate level could not influence the decisions made concerning their clients' specific needs. Similarly, this major consulting firm would not spend the necessary time to get their partners and consultants personally involved with the i2 sales force. It has often been said that it's not organizations that do business with other organizations, it's people that do business with people. This is especially true with software alliances!

An Alliance between a Software Company and Consulting Firm: A Paradox in the Making?

Although consulting firms and software companies have some similar goals, they also have conflicting goals that many times get in the way of doing business together. Typically, software companies want to sell a specific solution that can be duplicated, shrink-wrapped, and implemented in a short period of time. Consulting firms, on the other hand, want to appear independent from the solution providers, customize the solution to meet all of their clients' needs, and, by design or consequently, maximize the number of hours billed to maximize their revenue.

Also, because license-based revenue can be recognized by software companies in one lump sum and the sales organization is paid on a quarterly or annual cycle relative to attainment of sales quotas, software salespersons can be very aggressive in trying to close a deal before a certain "drop dead date." Contrast this to the sales behavior of a consulting firm, which typically involves a consulting senior executive dealing with a client senior executive. Consulting sales are usually finalized through a professional letter or proposal rather than by contract. They also do not have the same revenue implications for the immediate period because professional services can only be recognized as revenue when the services are expended. For the consulting professional, when the agreement to proceed slips a day or two it means relatively little since the work will still be performed, only over a longer period. However, a delay of those same few days could mean the difference between a software salesperson making a big commission because of quarterly incentives or a much smaller commission. It could also significantly affect the ability of the software company to achieve its quarterly numbers committed to its investors.

These conflicting goals often result in the software salesperson aggressively pushing for a deal while the consulting partner is viewed as not having the same sense of urgency. This dichotomy of behavior is in many cases exaggerated by the compensation plans and performance metrics of these individuals. Although the individuals may both have similar tenure and overall target compensation, the salesperson is paid a relatively low salary and relies more on commissions paid on deals, whereas the consulting partner typically receives a much higher base but a relatively smaller performance bonus at the end of the year.

Historically, consulting firms have been paid to study a problem before offering a solution recommendation. Of course, to the software salespersons, this time spent studying the problem delays their ability to get a signed contract. They feel that they have already conducted enough analysis to be convinced that their solution meets enough of the requirements to solve the problem at hand—maybe not entirely, but enough to be an improvement over what the customer current has. They typically view the time spent analyzing the "current state" as wasted time that provides very little value in resolving the problem. The salesperson may also view this current state effort as simply educating the consultants on the job, with the real value coming from the determination of the "to be state" using a specific software solution.

✧ *Lesson #2: Conflict resolution on key issues must be done on a timely basis.* For an alliance to work, the companies involved must address the inherent conflicting issues between the companies on a timely basis. One such problem that alliance partners face on an ongoing basis is the competition for a fixed pool of money that clients set aside for a particular program or solution. In other words, the client will set aside a fixed sum of money, either from their capital budget or operating budget, for a specific project. Each party—the software company and the consulting firm—believes that whatever of that amount is spent on the other party is revenue that their own firm will not get. If the client spends most of the budget on services, then there is less for the software solution, and vice versa. This results in the consulting firm getting involved in the negotiation of the software contract, trying to lower the contract amount of its software partner. Conversely, this can also result in the software firm bidding on the solution implementation using their services division to either lower the cost of implementation (often using a different scope of services) or to increase revenue to the software company.

The extreme of this happened during the big ERP wave of the late 1990s in response to the Y2K problem. In the early 1990s when Ray Lane and Robert Shaw were hired by Larry Ellison to revive Oracle, Oracle Consulting was revamped to compete directly with the Big Five (Big Six at the time) for the applications implementation work. This was not received well by the large consulting firms, including Price Waterhouse. The goodwill that had been built between Greg Brady's sales team and PW quickly broke down.

The sales of Oracle's applications solutions suffered because often the large consulting firms would not want to recommend Oracle's solution to clients. This scenario developed because consulting firms would not want to compete with Oracle's services division for the implementation services. This competitive activity for implementation services between Oracle and its consulting firm alliance partners was typically not done at the expense of the customer. If more than one solution (Oracle or a competitive offering) would work for a client, the overall fit of the Oracle solution would be discounted by the consulting firm alliance partner in favor of Oracle's competitor. Competitively, the larger consulting firms would tend to influence a software selection towards SAP or PeopleSoft to avoid this competition for implementation services with Oracle's services division.

❖ *Lesson #3: If divisions of a company compete with the alliance partner, trust is constantly in jeopardy.* Exhibit 8-1 summarizes the differences between the two types of companies—software and consulting—that need to be addressed to make an alliance work. The software salesperson is generally a low-salary, large-variable compensation individual. The consulting person is generally a high-salary, low- to medium-based compensation individual. The quarterly emphasis, while very strong for a software company, is moderate at best for a private consulting firm. (The recent movement to go public by Cap Gemini

Exhibit 8-1. Issues affecting software-consulting alliances.

	Software Sales	*Consulting*
Compensation	Low salary, large variable	High salary, low to medium variable
Quarterly Emphasis	Strong	Moderate
Revenue Recognition	Contract-based	Services-rendered based
Solution Definition	Software focused, somewhat fixed to capabilities of package	Process focused, includes process reengineering, software and organizational change management
Sales Demeanor	Aggressive	Executive, statesman-like

Ernst & Young through a merger and KPMG through an IPO allows for a more intense quarterly focus by these public consulting firms.)

The revenue recognition by a software company is contract-based, while the revenue recognition by a consulting firm is services rendered–based. The solution definition by a software firm is software-focused, and is usually bounded by the capabilities of the software modules. The solution definition by a consulting firm is process-focused, and includes process reengineering or transformation, organizational change management, and software. The sales demeanor of a software salesperson is aggressive and "push-based," while the sales demeanor of the consulting person is executive and statesman-like. Clearly the differences are present.

Bridging the Disconnect

Although there may appear to be a large disconnect between the two sides to the software-consulting alliance equation, there are many reasons for software companies and consulting firms to develop alliance partnerships. Let's take a look at some of these reasons from the software company's point of view:

1. The consulting firms are direct and indirect influencers concerning the software solutions purchased by their client and prospects.
2. The software companies realize they need the consulting firms to understand the software solutions offered by their company if they are going to recommend their software solution (consultants do not recommend solutions that they do not know or that they have no experience with).
3. For popular software solutions, it is difficult for a software company to hire the number of consultants needed for implementations, even if their strategy is to compete with the consulting firms for the implementation.
4. Services margins are typically lower than software margins and can affect the overall gross margin and stock price multiple of the company, which may discourage software companies from focusing on services as a core strategy.

Here are some reasons from the consulting firm's standpoint:

1. There has been, over the last several years, a movement by customers to select packaged software solutions in lieu of customized software solutions. Packaged software solutions are more cost-beneficial and less risky than customized software solutions. In this market, if a consulting firm is going to be in the technology implementation business, it needs to be willing to implement packaged software solutions.
2. One of the reasons a company hires a consulting firm is because the consulting firm typically invests in staying current with the available software solutions offered in the market. The best way to stay current is to have a strong working relationship with the software company and meet frequently with its development organization. The purpose is to learn not only what the current capabilities of the solution are, but what is new with future releases of the products and what is the vision for the future products.
3. Because the capabilities of technology solutions have become so robust in the last few years, even for the nontechnical consulting firms, technology has become a component to the overall solution for many of the problems encountered by clients.

The ERP Fatigue and Its Impact on Software-Consulting Alliances

As they say in comedy, timing is everything. Timing also affected the need for these two types of companies to work together. After the ERP wave of the 1990s, many client companies were fatigued when it came to large information systems implementation projects. Also, many of the client companies were not willing to pay significantly large fees for requirements definition and software selection projects. The client attitude and expectations were that the consulting firms should already know the best and most robust solutions that are available in the market. The software selection process framework shown in Exhibit 8-2 illustrates the traditional process by which consulting firms were engaged by their clients to help them solve their applications system problems.

As the exhibit illustrates, during the first few steps of the process few problems are being solved because the problems, for the most part, are simply being studied. During a longer, drawn-out project such as shown by this traditional approach, the project team can lose momentum and focus. As requirements are defined, scope can expand, drawing out the time frames and increasing the costs. As scope increases, the risk of not achieving all the project objectives increases. The risk is compounded by the fact that many of the promised benefits identified and used to justify the large expenditures associated with the ERP mega-projects were simply not achievable.

Although there were some added capabilities to the systems being implemented to fix the year 2000 (Y2K) problem, for the most part

Exhibit 8-2. Software selection process.

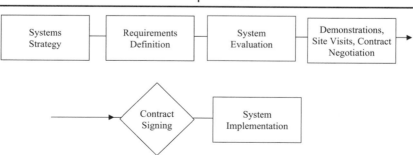

the systems supported the same work flows and functions as provided for by the predecessor systems. And even though many of the projects started out with business process reengineering components to them, frequently this aspect of the project was dropped to accommodate the time pressures associated with the testing requirements and impending millennium calendar change.

From ERP to Value-Based Solutions

To address the change in the market conditions, both software companies and consulting firms started focusing on value and solutions. To accomplish this, the consulting firms moved to solution-based consulting. Taking a clue from their clients, the consulting firms started to inventory the available software companies within specific solution areas—such as Enterprise Resource Planning, Customer Relationship Management, Supply Chain Management, eBusiness Platform—and to select one or maybe two of the best solutions within an area on which to focus proactively. This focus would include marketing and training, as well as reusable implementation templates.

A couple of the major firms have referred to this as establishing a "point of view." By establishing a point of view, a consulting firm is committing their firm to recommend specific solutions to their clients. It is saying to its clients that it has conducted some level of analysis to determine the best solution for its clients in a particular space. This can be done at an overall level across the firm or by industry. As an example, several years ago, it was fairly typical for a consulting firm to choose to use i2 as its point-of-view solution in High Technology and Automotive and to use the solutions from Manugistics for Consumer Goods and Retail.

Periodically, consulting firms will revisit their point of view to determine its appropriateness based on the market dynamics and success of the different firms in that space. Using the above example, it was fairly common for a firm to change its Consumer Goods and Retail point of view to i2 due to the significant wins by i2 at some key customers in the space, such as WWRE (Worldwide Retail Exchange), K-Mart, and Procter & Gamble. Conversely, the tide has started to change in High Technology because of i2's alliance with IBM and Manugistics' wins with Cisco and Microsoft.

This change in approach does not mean that a large consulting firm would not fall back to the previous work flow process if the client requested or allowed it. Nor does it mean that a large consulting firm would not train its people in other solutions and implement them, if asked. It is, primarily, a matter of focus. To achieve the clients' requirements of time to value, consulting firms need to have available resources already trained in the solution selected by the client for implementation. Economically, it is not feasible for a firm to train its consultants in too many solutions that may or may not be used in the future. Thus, the focused solution-based approach allows a firm to specialize its resources and limits the amount of down time that its consultants spend in training—there are not too many clients who are willing to pay consulting fees for the time consultants spend in training.

As Exhibit 8-3 illustrates, moving quickly to implementation facilitated through the solution-focused consulting approach inherently addresses some of the issues between a software company and consulting firm. This affords both parties a move towards stronger alliances.

Turn About Is Fair Play

One of the responsibilities of a software company to its alliance partners is to help them, where possible, differentiate themselves from their competitors. When i2 first established its Alliances Program, we thought it was not our responsibility to help our consulting partners with this. It was our view that i2 was a constant and that it was their job to provide differentiators in how they approached their i2 practice. However, as the program matured, we could see that in exchange for an exclusive or preferred "point of view," added benefit to the alliance could be achieved by a bilateral preference. Because some customers do not allow a software vendor to dictate what, if any, consulting firm should be hired to provide implementation services, i2 could not provide the same level of exclusivity as one of the consulting firms. But in

Exhibit 8-3. Quick implementation work flow.

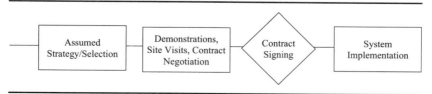

most situations, a preferred status is definitely considered a competitive advantage by the consulting firm.

Inherently, there is more of an investment on the part of a consulting firm to train its personnel in the specifics of a solution that make the comparison an apples and oranges relationship. However, to help a firm differentiate itself from its competitors, i2 for example would allow a consulting firm to participate in the actual development of a certain product or its tailoring to an industry. The firm could then tout this in their sales process that they were more qualified to assist in the implementation because of this added experience. By dividing this up by product or industry, i2 could select a number of firms across the various industries that it targeted, allowing all of the major firms to have some level of expertise or niche that was unique. This also allowed i2 to get an outside perspective to the solution it was developing, and its applicability to the situations was seen by the consulting partner. The personal relationships that were built due to these efforts helped both companies during the implementations that were conducted by the people who contributed to the development efforts (see Lesson #1 earlier in this chapter).

✧ *Lesson #4: Alliances flourish best when both sides have differentiating attributes and when they determine whether their alliance is strategic or tactical.* Early in this book, five different types of alliances were defined. Software-consulting alliances are primarily marketing/sales alliances. To further define them, a key characterization is whether an alliance is strategic or tactical. Strategic alliances require much more investment from the participating parties than tactical alliances. A strategic alliance requires a framework, as well as a governing infrastructure, which need to be communicated, believed, and adhered to throughout the organizations. Although it is possible for an alliance to be strategic for only one of the parties, such an alliance will over time be viewed as lopsided and thus begin to falter from poor execution.

Strategic alliances, if executed well, can effect major changes within an industry sector that can result in the alliance dominating the market share of the segment. An excellent example of a strategic alliance that dominated an industry segment was between Andersen Consulting (AC) and SAP. These two companies joined forces to develop an industry-specific software application based on the R3 version of SAP tailored to the energy industry. With this solution—called ISO

OIL—SAP and AC captured a large percentage of the top oil and gas companies. But like many alliances in the software-consulting segment, this alliance had a limited life tied to the viability and predominance of the software solution.

Tactical alliances are different in that they are much more temporary. In the fast moving world of technology, tactical alliances are much more common than strategic ones. They are often deal-related, brought together at the field level, to provide an integrated solution to a customer or group of customers. Typically, the participants in tactical software-consulting alliances will agree to work together on deals when it makes sense, but they usually do not put in place behavior-changing processes and metrics.

Tactical alliances can be either formal or informal, with or without infrastructure and support personnel and processes to facilitate communication and cooperation. The underlying dedication of the parties makes for whether an alliance is truly strategic or tactical. They are, at times, even orchestrated by a single customer for its own purpose to coerce cooperation between two parties that have not been able to come together by themselves.

Whenever two organizations first begin talking about forming an alliance, everyone will talk about how strategic the relationship can be to both sides. There are high expectations that it will do this and that, providing additional revenue for both companies. But when it really comes down to investing in the infrastructure and support processes, organizations may take a minimalist approach or use poor execution. It seems that many organizations want the payoff before the investment. That is why early "alliance wins" are so important. Early alliance wins, or joint sales wins, give credibility to the expectations expressed during the formative meetings of an alliance. From these wins, support for investments in infrastructure and processes can be provided to executive management for approval.

If you were to evaluate all of the alliances announced between the various software companies and consulting firms, you may be surprised to find how many of the agreements would be touted as strategic. Yet, upon close examination, the characteristics would appear to be and behave more like a tactical alliance.

✧ *Lesson #5: Tactical alliances can be just as successful at driving additional revenue as so-called strategic alliances.* As mentioned above, tactical alliances are often successful in driving specific deals. In addition, tactical deals can drive a sustained deal flow over time when they are anchored by a specific account or client. They can also drive a sustained deal flow when a software salesman and a lead consultant develop a strong one-on-one relationship. There is certainly nothing wrong with tactical alliances when they produce recurring revenues for the two parties!

❖ *Lesson #6: Successful alliances rely on the definition of added responsibilities of both parties.* For an alliance to prosper, each party must do more than just meet the minimum requirements. An ideal alliance would have the following attributes:

1. *Open Communication between Executive Sponsors on Both Sides.* In order to ensure that the alliance companies are strategically aligned, each party should assign an executive sponsor who meets with his or her counterpart no less than twice a year, and preferable quarterly. The outcome of such meetings needs to be communicated to the two organizations, and support staffs need to be assigned specific responsibilities that can be measured, monitored, and tracked. In addition, the executive sponsor needs to be the visible internal champion for the alliance partner.

2. *Open Communication between Organizations concerning Joint Wins, as well as Sales and Implementation Issues.* The momentum of joint sales wins helps to build additional joint wins. Many times joint wins are not communicated appropriately by both parties, thus missing the opportunity to build on the alliance successes. Too often, the win is communicated internally by one company, but only as a win for that company, thanking everyone internally involved without mentioning external influences.

   Open communication mechanisms need to also be put in place so that field sales issues between the companies are addressed and not ignored. If issues are left unresolved, the underlying trust that the alliance is built on begins to break down. A separate mechanism should be established so that the consulting partner can raise chronic implementation support issues that arise during the conduct of the projects. The same forum can be used by the software company to raise issues that are identified through the customer support center concerning issues due to poorly trained consultants assigned to implementation projects. The sooner implementation issues are identified to the other party and discussed, the sooner the issues can be resolved. The issues should be captured in a log and tracked so that none of them inadvertently fall through the cracks.

In addition, there should be a zero tolerance policy for finger pointing when trouble occurs. It is easy for alliances to flourish when times are good. However, the real test of a true alliance is how well the alliance holds up under stress. The behavior of the executive sponsor is critical to the avoidance of finger pointing when stressful situations occur.

3. *Open Communication concerning Software Products and Capabilities.* One of the responsibilities a software company has towards its consulting partner is to help "make them look smart." This includes providing to them as much product training as required for them to successfully implement the solutions provided by the software company. At i2, we have opened up our internal training classes to our partners so that our partners can be subjected to the same amount and quality of training as our own consultants. We also are developing a Web site that contains partner-specific support information concerning the problems being encountered at implementation projects around the company.

Many software companies sell their vision and future capabilities as part of the sales process. In newer areas of capabilities, such as e-business public and private exchanges, this is a necessity so that the customer knows where the solution is headed, and can plan its implementation accordingly. The consulting partners need to also be aware of what are current capabilities and what are future capabilities.

In addition, it is important to have full disclosure between software companies and consulting firms concerning what software exists today and what software is "under construction." Nothing can destroy an alliance relationship faster than a software company "selling a vision" and not having the software developed to either begin implementation or scale the product for adequate implementation.

4. *Confidence in the Security of Each Other's Intellectual Property.*
   Earlier chapters have discussed confidentiality of intellectual
   property, both in the construction of the alliance agreement
   and the development of the nondisclosure agreement (NDA).
   As companies become closer, sharing increasingly sensitive
   confidential information, the risk of that information being
   abused becomes higher.

   We have heard many stories, some substantiated, where
   a consulting firm has taken information received in confidence
   from one software company and discussed it with other software companies. Any breach like this rocks an alliance at its
   core. Formal controls, such as specific language in the alliance
   agreement and the master NDA, should be considered, along
   with education for personnel, so that both sides understand
   the proper way to secure a partner's intellectual property.

5. *Quality Assurance/Quality Control by Both Sides.* A software
   company is concerned about whether an implementation consulting partner can provide quality implementations for its
   customers. Conversely, a consulting company is concerned
   about the reliability and scalability of the software. As part of
   the implementation effort, a consulting partner should include
   in its implementation work plan time for quality assurance
   reviews by the product experts from the software company to
   ensure that the solution is being set up properly. To build its
   partners' expertise, as well as the resulting personal relationships, a software company should invite its strategic consulting
   partners to participate in the testing of new product releases.

6. *Quick and Easy Ramp-Up of Consulting Resources.* One of the
   biggest issues for a consulting firm in working with a fast-
   growing software company is the lack of trained resources.
   Software companies need to provide a training mechanism for
   its partners to ramp up its staff as quickly as possible for as low
   a cost as feasibly possible. This training should be implementation and product oriented. Many times the training provided
   by the software company is the same for all of its partners. For
   some strategic partners, i2 assisted them in establishing their
   own in-house training that provided a competitive advantage
   by integrating the firm's implementation methodology train-

ing tailored to the i2 solutions. As the alliances program at i2 matured, this became a requirement for our strategic partners.

7. *Joint Marketing Program, including Advertising.* To establish and communicate a strong alliance, joint marketing and advertising is an additional step that shows commitment on both sides. This joint marketing should be focused not just on the joint customers and prospects, but also on the employees of both companies. When we asked a managing partner of a major consulting firm whether his joint advertising campaign in *The Wall Street Journal* with another software company had been successful, he responded that no direct business was actually created as a result of the effort. However, he also said that it was some of the best money spent because it showed the employees from the respective firms that the two companies were serious about the alliance. This commitment helped jump-start the relationship and propel his company into one of the premier implementation partners for that software provider.

8. *Joint Programs to Make the Other Party Better.* Because each of the companies within an alliance is selfishly looking out for its own best interest, it is often forgotten that one of the ways to strengthen an alliance is to improve the abilities of the other party. A consulting firm typically has different strengths from a software company, and a mature software-consulting alliance is between two companies that can openly exchange ideas to help improve the other party, as well as improve joint processes and programs.

✧ *Lesson #7: Conflict resolution: Behavior in the field must be monitored.* As identified earlier in this chapter, one of the obstacles to building stronger alliances is improper field behavior. Improper field behavior can range from the field personnel involved in the account not picking up the phone to communicate to working against the alliance in front of the customer by competing with the alliance with another party.

Frequently, improper behavior occurs inadvertently. However, if not properly raised to a level of consciousness, the inadvertent behavior may be assumed to be intentional by the other party. Either overt or covert actions can set an alliance back significantly and require senior management involvement to resolve. If not resolved, the alliance can begin to break down and will eventually dissolve.

The overt actions that constitute improper behavior must be dealt with swiftly and decisively by both sets of executives. Failure to act on overt improper behavior is equivalent to management's sanctioning of such behavior. When this occurs, the integrity of the alliance is in trouble!

✧ *Lesson #8: Check your ego at the door!!!* Let's face the truth about successful software salesmen and consulting partners. They both are successful because they are good at what they do. They are also compensated very well for what they do and what they accomplish. As a result, serious egos are present on both sides of a software-consulting alliance. One of the biggest obstacles to the success of alliances is field-level arrogance that results from unchecked egos. This arrogance can be a staunch inhibitor to the compromise needed between alliance partners to forge timely solutions for clients.

Many companies depend on some level of arrogance to motivate their employees. Pride in a company and in the job that is being done helps a company's self-image. It also helps for the software salesperson and the consulting partner to ask for a price-premium for the best software-consulting solution combination in the marketplace. In addition, pride at work does help feed the motivation or the higher calling of what we all do day-to-day. However, taken to an extreme, uncontrolled arrogance breaks down alliances. This arrogance does not allow trust to build up in the relationships of the individuals and thus the organizations. Because trust is the cornerstone o working together, the sharing of information and the ability to coexist in a sales cycle to achieve the goals of the customer is where we need to be at the end of the day. Complementary goals must be present for an alliance to be considered; trust is essential for it to be successful.

✧ *Lesson #9: Aligned compensation: It helps, but only so much!* One of the leaders of a major software company once told me, "The key to alignment between alliance partners is compensation. It's the payday, and what is in the paycheck, that motivates people!" For software companies in particular, this leader is right on with his comments. The field behavior for a software company is heavily affected by the compensation system. On the other hand, consulting firms appear to partner because the alliance is part of an overall strategy of the firm, supported by management through program dollars tied to training, advertising, and marketing. Typically no additional compensation is offered or required.

For software companies, the situation is vastly different. Many things revolve around the sales representative's compensation system. If the software salespeople, or for that matter any of the supporting organizations, have compensation systems that work against their alliance partners, the alliance will need to try and overcome that resistance in some way. If the compensation mechanism is strong enough, the viability of the alliance could be at stake. The key is to ensure alignment in the compensation system!

In the early 1980s, an alliance between the Oracle Corporation and any of the major consulting firms would have been difficult at best because Oracle sales representatives were paid to sell Oracle Services. For a period of time, this compensation was even quota-based so that any work performed by a consulting partner was actual money out of the hand of the sales representative. Of course, there are not many who will happily sell against themselves. However, there were times when a sales representative would team with a consulting partner to get the deal because the consulting partner was in control of the sales cycle and Oracle Services was not perceived as a competitive threat. In other words, the value of the overall license deal compensated for the sales representative not being paid for the services.

Although the structure of a field compensation system can work quite effectively against an alliance, structuring the compensation system to include incentives to work with consulting partners has only a mild effect on the behavior in the field. The message to the field is clear that the intent is to partner because you are putting your money where your mouth is. However, typically the amount of money at stake is not significant enough to risk picking a losing partner and thus losing the deal.

At i2, we tried several times to incent the field to partner with the alliance partners. This incentive was viewed primarily as added compensation after a deal was done but did not affect the behavior during the sales cycle.

We actually tried several different methods. One commission kicker was offered to the sales representative to engage and work with any consulting partner. We did this believing that if the consulting firm was involved earlier in the sales cycle, the consulting firm could more easily be contracted for the implementation work. In another instance, we provided an extra kicker above and beyond the partnering kicker to incent the sales representatives to work with a specific partner in order to work off a contractual obligation associated with an asset purchase i2 bought from the consulting firm. Although the amounts could add up to significant compensation ($10,000 for both plans), the added incentive had little effect on behavior. The number of sales transactions engaged with partners was not significantly affected, nor was the number of deals conducted with the specific partner.

✧ *Lesson #10: Leadership builds relationships!* What does seem to affect the behavior in the field is management focus on partnering. In one word—leadership! This focus starts with the proper attitude towards the partnering organizations. This attitude then transcends into a true collaboration with the outside firms by doing joint account planning and eventually joint sales calls. Much like in any relationship, when the participants are looking for the value of the relationship, trust builds, and from that success is achieved. Conversely, if the attitude from management is negative, the field senses that partnering is not much of a priority, and thus execution at the field level breaks down and, in the end, there is no real alliance.

✧ *Lesson #11: Software-consulting alliance programs must be customer-focused!*
The best way for an organization to build an Alliance Program is first to understand the purpose and goals of the alliance for the customer. After this is determined, it is then important to understand the purpose and goals of the alliance for the participating organizations. If the end customer is not to receive benefit from the alliance, then the self-serving business reasons will not sustain the cost of a formal alliance program.

Defining a formal Alliance Program shows both your customers and your potential partners the commitment that you have to conduct business through partnering arrangements. It also takes the responsibility and the guesswork away from software salespersons to craft the solution benefits for clients. By defining a standard program, the program sets the guidelines for the cost-benefit commitments to clients, rather than having every aspect of the cost-benefit commitments be recreated and negotiated with each client. It also allows for different levels to be established based on level of commitment of the organizations.

At i2 we recently instituted a "four-diamond" program for consulting alliance partners where the entry level of "one diamond" has few responsibilities and requirements but also receives few benefits. As an organization commits to a higher level (two, three, or four diamonds), additional requirements and responsibilities are asked of both the consulting alliance partners and of i2. Four-diamond partners are able to spend more time with sales, development, and corporate management, participate in more marketing programs, and receive certain training that is not available to the other levels. The intent is that these added benefits, at an added cost, will help build a stronger alliance and provide additional sales to both parties. (The four-diamond program mirrors the construction of an alliance business plan in Chapter Six, which is an attachment to the alliance agreement discussed in Chapter Two.)

To support a formal alliance program, certain standard contracts should be developed that reflect the nature of the requirements and benefits of the program. A formal application process, including a formal review, should be instituted that captures the prospects that want to join the program. (This mirrors the process to approve alliance agreements discussed in Chapter Two.) Because an organization is somewhat defined by the alliances it creates, the review process should be stringent enough to weed out any organizations that are not fiscally sound, that are not willing to live up to the spirit of the requirements, or that fundamentally do not match the business model for which the Alliance Program was established. At i2, because our Alliance Program is targeted at joint marketing and selling, we categorically reject any consulting firm that primarily provides staff augmentation.

The more alliances a company supports, the more personnel and infrastructure is required to support them. In addition, the more alliances a company supports, the less unique their alliance partners become within their organization. At i2, the staff augmentation firms do not meet the target business model and purpose for alliances, and it would cost the company more to process the application and maintain the relationship than it could derive in revenue over the life of the alliance.

Exhibit 8-4 is a detailed example of what some of the require-ments and benefits might be for an Alliance Program for a software company in dealing with consulting firms. The example is intended to be a guideline for software companies and consulting firms.

Summary

Software companies and consulting firms have their differences. How-ever, bridging these differences can have a profound impact on clients, on consulting firms, and on software companies.

The marketplace is rapidly becoming solution-based. These solu-tions include processes, software technology, and organizational be-havior capabilities. More and more, clients are asking for risk-based contract terms that tie their payments for the solutions to actual re-sults. This action places software companies and consulting firms in a solution-based partnership where the risk and the rewards are shared.

The eleven software-consulting alliance lessons have been learned over time, with many having been time-tested in a variety of real-world scenarios. From being customer-centered to the alignment of compensation to trust, these lessons should serve you well when the time comes to implement your own software-consulting alliance. In addition, Exhibit 8-4 will help you frame out your own alliance be-tween software companies and consulting firms.

The key success factors around all of this are execution in both solution sales and solution delivery. These two key success factors don't just happen. They require a strong alliance framework between a software company and a consulting firm to combine best-in-class capabilities for a client-based holistic solution. There is nothing that sells better than success. If software companies and consulting firms follow the chapters in this book and the eleven lessons outlined in this chapter, the odds of establishing a successful alliance are very high.

Exhibit 8-4. Detailed requirements and benefits of software-consulting alliance.

1. REQUIREMENTS	Level 1 Alliance	Level 2 Alliance	Level 3 Alliance
Written, jointly approved alliance agreement with annual business plan with revenue goals and quarterly reviews		√	√
Written, approved practice development plan		√	√
Trained and certified consultants on staff	5	15 (end of Year 1) 30 (end of Year 2)	50 (end of Year 1) 100 (end of Year 2)
Established "Train the Trainer" program		√	√
Use of joint sales methodology		√	√
Use of software company's implementation methodology	√	√	√
Dedicated skills development server		√	√
Creation of joint industry specific solutions			Minimum of 2 industry verticals
Development and maintenance of software knowledge base and information center		√	√
First-level implementation support			√
Senior partner sponsor	√	√	√ (Dedicated)
Sales champions in major geographic areas			√
Sales champions in major industry verticals			√
Development of joint collateral		√	√
Marketing show participation	Booth	Booth	Major Sponsor/ Booth
Target rating on customer performance reviews	√	√	√

(continues)

Exhibit 8-4. (Continued).

2. BENEFITS	Level 1 Alliance	Level 2 Alliance	Level 3 Alliance
Joint selling		√	√
Sales training	50% Discount	50% Discount	No Charge
Implementation training	20% Discount	50% Discount	50% Discount
Demo software (requires product training)	No Charge	No Charge	No Charge
Technical support or demo licenses and practice development	$10,000/year 2 Contacts	$5,000/year 2 Contacts	No Charge
Industry-specific templates, value propositions, and methodologies			√
Executive sponsor			√
Global alliance manager		√	√ (Dedicated)
Consulting services manager		√	√
Alliances presales manager		√	√ (Dedicated)
Regional alliance manager		√	√
Industry account manager			√
Listing on each other's Web site	√	√	√
Profile on Web site with reciprocal link		√	√
Log in to "Partner Focus" Web site	√	√	√

Member of software company's industry leadership program			√
Invitation to annual partner summit		√	√
Joint development of marketing collateral		√	√
Access to collateral	√	√	√

CHAPTER NINE

Know When to Hold, and Know When to Fold

The flight from Dallas–Fort Worth to London's Gatwick airport was smooth and uneventful. As we made our final approach for landing, I noticed that the weather was rainy and overcast, as it always seems to be in London. The pilot announced that the temperature was 10 degrees Celsius, or roughly 50 degrees Fahrenheit, which would be a welcomed change from the weather in Dallas.

After landing, I went through immigration and customs in record time. Since the flight was on time and the process through the airport was so smooth, I felt that I would have a chance for a quick nap before the big alliance meeting. However, as I approached the train station in Gatwick, my heart sank. The trains were not running at all! I knew that the privatized train system in the U.K. was being criticized in the media for numerous problems, but I thought the Gatwick Express was a nice exception to these problems.

With much difficulty, I located a taxi to take me to London. It was from the taxi driver that I learned why the trains were not running. The day I landed was May 1st, or "May Day." London was the target of a coordinated "anti-capitalist" protest that included groups ranging from anarchists to Trotskyists, eco-warriors, the Turkish communist party, militant cyclists protesting the automobile, and animal lovers protesting fur trapping and fur trading.

The estimated 5,000 protesters were outnumbered by the 9,000 police officers, who contained the demonstrations around Oxford Circus, an area in downtown London.[1] In preparation for the demonstration, schools and businesses (except mine of course) were closed for the day. Still, travel was disrupted, major streets were closed, and the damage to downtown businesses was estimated at 20 million pounds, or roughly $30 million.[2]

The police did an excellent job of containing the demonstrators and minimizing the damage. The preceding year the damage had been considerably greater in cost and symbolism (for example, Churchill's statue in Parliament Square had been defaced, causing significant embarrassment to Scotland Yard). This year, the police were ready.

One of the leaders at Scotland Yard, speaking on one of the radio stations in the evening, was praising his police troops, both active and reserve, for a job well done. However, he did say that there had been negotiations with several of the demonstration leaders in an attempt to prevent any demonstrations at all. He said, "I thought we had an alliance negotiated with those bloody hooligans right after last year's demonstrations. Then I found out that they were using the Internet to carefully plan a roving demonstration to maximize damage and confuse our police. At this point, I knew that this alliance was rubbish! We needed to plan for an alternative action plan before we were broadsided."

Alliance Blues

Did you ever have feelings about an alliance partner similar to what the Scotland Yard leader felt about the demonstrators? If you have been in alliance roles, chances are that you have had this sinking feeling with at least one or more of your alliance partners. In early 1996, Deutsche Telekom, France Telecom, and Sprint formed Global One. Global One was categorized as a new company, when in reality it was just an investment alliance. As a result, insiders told me that there was constant fighting among the partners as to who was in charge. I am not sure that they even agreed as to where the home office should be located.

Because there was no separate entity (which is one of the defining factors of a joint venture versus an investment alliance), decisions had to be cleared through each corporate board. The bureaucracy led to decision making by each partner that circumvented Global One. The end came in mid-1999, when Deutsche Telekom made a bid for Telecom Italia without informing its partners. France Telecom already had a subsidiary in Italy, and viewed the Deutsche Telekom move as a competitive threat. Perhaps the executives at France Telecom felt like the leader of Scotland Yard and asked the same question: "I thought we had an alliance with those guys!"

There are in fact five independent and interdependent forces at work with alliances. The first two forces are the organizational dynamics of "Company A" and the dynamics of "Company A's" primary marketplace. The third and fourth forces are the organizational dynamics of "Company B" and the dynamics of "Company B's" primary marketplace. The fifth force is the dynamics of the overlapping marketplace between the two alliance partners. With continuous changes occurring in all five, it is easy to see how alliance partners can grow apart as rapidly as they came together.

Our meeting in London started thirty minutes late, but started nevertheless. Our alliance partner took the first thirty minutes to discuss what organizational dynamics were occurring in their company and their primary marketplace. Our team took the next thirty minutes to discuss the organizational dynamics in our company and our primary marketplace. The next two hours were then dedicated to discussing our progress with the alliance in Europe and our collective ability to harness the dynamics within our organizations. The meeting ended up with an agreement on our collective next steps for achieving our targets for the following quarter.

As I looked out the bay windows from our meeting room, I noticed the endless procession of police and emergency vehicles trying to contain the protesters. My mind wandered to how this alliance or alliance partners in general handle the disbanding of alliances. Will old soldiers never die and just fade away, or will the partners take to the streets to do combat with one another? The words of the Scotland Yard leader continued to ring in my ear, and provided a constant reminder that all alliances, even successful ones, must plan for an inevitable end to their alliances to maximize the benefit and minimize the costs associated with the lifecycle of alliances.

The Lifecycle of Alliance Management

Alliances follow a lifecycle curve similar to that of organizations. Let's try to pull together what we have covered throughout the book under the framework of the organization lifecycle.

The lifecycle of an organization—and that of an alliance—has six distinct stages. These stages are start-up, emerge, high-growth, mature, decline, and disband, as illustrated in Exhibit 9-1. In each stage, there

Exhibit 9-1. Lifecycle of alliance management.

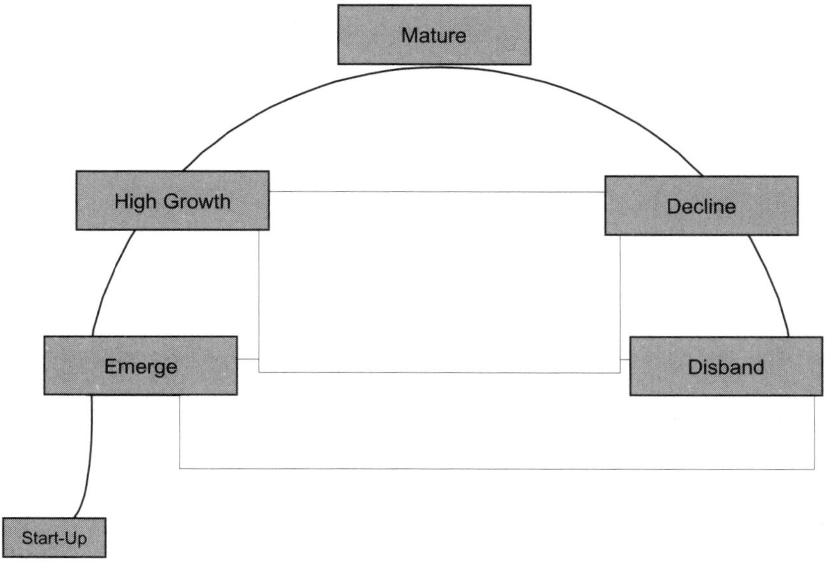

are different legal agreements and a different management focus required of each alliance partner. There are also different "trigger points" that cause an alliance to progress or regress from one stage to another. It is important to address each one, and understand how each stage relates to the other stages.

Start-Up

The start-up of alliances begins with the recognition of need. In Chapter One, we discussed two frameworks, the Framework to Determine the Need for an Alliance, and the Framework to Determine What Type of Alliance Is Needed. Before the start-up of an alliance, the two companies must go through these frameworks.

The anchor of the start-up stage of alliances is the proper definition of the need for an alliance. The business and market strategy, the marketplace scan, the product portfolio assessment versus the marketplace scan, the "build internally" versus "acquire externally," the organizational readiness and speed to market demand, and the decision to proceed to "build internally" or "acquire externally" are all steps in the Framework to Determine the Need for An Alliance. Once these steps are completed and the need for an alliance is confirmed, the companies then must determine what type of alliance is needed. The five alliance types are sales, geographic-specific, solution-specific, investment, and joint venture. Once this process is complete, the two companies are prepared to initiate the start-up of the alliance.

The start-up stage can begin with a Memo of Intent (MOI), which was discussed at length in Chapter Three. The MOI can be used for a specific period of time to allow for the start-up of the alliance and a faster grounding in marketplace activities. For example, in April 2001, Motorola Japan and NTT Software signed a Memo of Understanding (or MOU, similar to an MOI) to develop and provide the "Voice Internet Platform" to Japan. Motorola will provide its Mya™ Voice Platform products, while NTT Software will provide its Japanese language voice application development technology. Although the time frame of the MOU was not announced in the press release, it does allow for Motorola and NTT Software to begin the start-up stage.[3]

Emerge

The emerge stage of alliances is perhaps the most critical of all the stages. It is in this stage that the formal alliance agreement is negotiated and executed. We discussed how to construct an alliance agreement in detail in Chapter Two. This alliance agreement, which lays the groundwork for all other stages in the lifecycle, will govern the behavior of the alliance parties throughout the lifecycle of the alliance. It builds on the foundation of the two frameworks in the start-up stage, and sets the stage for success or failure for the alliance.

The completion of the alliance agreement should have a definite timetable attached to it. The alliance parties can achieve this by establishing a time frame for the expiration of the Memo of Intent. This will force a compromise between the business owners or the lawyers on items that would inhibit the quick completion of the agreement. It may also cause the breakdown of talks on the agreement. This is not necessarily bad, because if the two alliance parties cannot agree on key points in an accelerated fashion, perhaps their collective decision-making capability may be too slow for the marketplace as alliance partners.

One item for a successful emerge stage is quick wins. Nothing sells like success. The alliance leaders must focus on quick wins under a Memo of Intent while the alliance agreement is being negotiated and completed. Quick wins will ensure that the momentum for the alliance is sustained while the lawyers go through their process of negotiating the agreement.

In June 1999, Cisco and Motorola announced their joint venture, Spectrapoint Wireless. Spectrapoint Wireless was to focus on delivering voice, data, and video to businesses over a fixed "last-mile" wireless infrastructure. The two companies spent approximately $300 million to purchase the fixed wireless assets of Bosch Telecom. In mid-2000, Cisco and Motorola canceled the joint venture. According to several press releases and two insider interviews, there were no customers for the new joint venture. It was reported that the equipment was too expensive for the prospective customers.[4] Despite two leading technology companies (and one of the best companies in doing alliances with Cisco) entering into a joint venture in a potentially hot market, the joint venture could not get out of start-up and into emerge. Quick hits with customers just did not materialize.

High Growth

The next stage of the lifecycle is high growth. In this stage, alliances need to start focusing on those activities items that will help produce results for both parties. The development of a business plan guides the activities and enables growth to occur in a structured manner. We discussed how to construct an alliance business plan in Chapter Six.

The alliance business plan includes sales and revenue targets that become commitments by both alliance partners. It also includes the dedication of personnel, the training of personnel, and the marketing efforts that will assist the sales efforts. Depending upon what type of alliance is entered into, there may be other items that are included in the business plan.

Alliances that are lucky enough to enter into a high-growth stage need structure. Structure allows for the growth to be channeled in a direction that supports the intent of the alliance. Uncontrolled growth in multiple directions may produce short-term results but it will also produce confusion within the organization as to why the alliance exists. It will also confuse customers, which is the last thing that any company needs.

As alliance partners use the business plan to focus, there will be more pressure to trade confidential information and work together in an intense manner. As this scenario emerges, there is the need to protect each other when trading confidential information. In Chapter Four, we discussed how to construct a nondisclosure agreement (NDA). NDAs are needed to fortify and augment the confidential information language in the alliance agreement.

Mature

As alliances evolve into the mature stage, there is a need to focus on developing high performance teams. The selection of the right people for alliances doesn't just happen. It takes an understanding of the social styles we discussed in Chapter Five and how they come together in a complementary way to build a high performing team. Conflicting styles produce nonvalue, add strife and politics, and will probably help to create a team that underperforms and one in which no one wants to participate.

People also need to know how to enhance their own selves. Exposure to Stephen R. Covey and his "Seven Habits of Highly Effective People" will help people achieve a "private victory." The "private victory" is necessary to achieve a "public victory" and a positive interdependence with others. Achieving a "public interdependence" is a critical success factor in becoming a high-performing team member.

Another key success factor is shared accountability for common performance measurements. This calls for a mutual commitment to each other's performance metrics and their common performance metrics. With this shared accountability for common performance measurements comes a carefully crafted compensation program. We discussed alliance compensation programs in Chapter Six.

The closer people work together and the more complementary their social styles, the greater chance that the joint alliance teams will sustain the achievement of positive results. In fact, high-performing teams have a chance to generate the positive results that will move the alliance from mature back to high growth.

Decline

Inevitably, one or more of the five forces mentioned earlier in the chapter may cause alliance partners to drift in different directions. Ford and Volkswagen had two alliances that went through a decline stage. In the early- to mid-1990s, Ford and Volkswagen marketed their cars in selected Latin American countries through AutoLatina. At the end of 1995, Ford and Volkswagen parted ways. A friend of mine who was the Senior VP of Marketing for a competing automotive OEM told me that Volkswagen felt that they had a greater product selection and preferred to go to market alone. This was echoed in the many newspaper articles that emerged in the Buenos Aires newspapers in early 1996. During the mid-1990s, Ford and Volkswagen also had a joint venture in Portugal to produce luxury vans. In that case, Ford felt that *they* could produce the vans more economically on their own.[5]

When situations like these occur and the decline stage is entered, it is necessary to determine whether the alliance needs to be disbanded.

Framework to Determine the Need to Disband an Alliance

The Framework to Determine the Need to Disband an Alliance (Exhibit 9-2), which builds on the Framework to Determine the Need for

Exhibit 9-2. Framework to Determine the Need to Disband an Allliance.

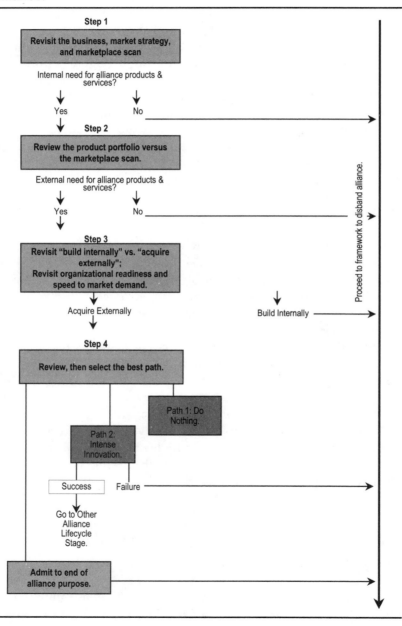

an Alliance discussed in Chapter One, provides definitive options for the alliance partner. Let's take a look at this framework, and how an alliance partner can address an alliance in decline.

✧ *Step 1. Revisit the business and market strategy and marketplace scan.* In this step, the alliance partner will review steps one and two of the original framework. If the business, strategy, the market strategy, or the marketplace has changed, then it should surface in this review. These changes connect to the organizational dynamics and the marketplace dynamics mentioned in the "Alliance Blues" section of this chapter, and may provide the reasons behind the existence of the alliance blues.

If the business strategy, the market strategy, or the marketplace scan surfaced the need for similar products and services being offered through the alliance, go to Step 2. If this review surfaces that the need is no longer present, then go to Disband.

✧ *Step 2. Review the product portfolio versus the marketplace scan.* If in the review in Step 1 it was determined that the need for the products and services of the alliance still exist, then the alliance partner needs to review Step 3 of the original framework. In this step, the alliance partner should review their product portfolio against the marketplace scan. This is a deeper review, and should be more or less a "stress test" against the perceived need surfaced in Step 1.

Several years ago, a major consumer products company was on the leading edge in developing tools to enable category management. In their first big test with a major retailer, the results were both exhilarating and shocking. The category management tool identified both velocity of throughput on store shelves and profitability of each line item. When actual data was used for all competitors, this company placed six line items in the top ten of the category. It also placed the bottom two line items.

Both of the bottom line items were specialty, low-volume line items. They were also copacked, meaning that an alliance partner was "private labeling" these items for this consumer products company. Before this category management tool, these line items were always lumped into a product category from both a sales and profitability standpoints. A Step 1 review would surface the need for these line items. A more detailed Step 2 review would identify the need to discontinue these items. The consumer products company did indeed drop the line items and disband the alliance. It also revamped its product portfolio financials based on a more robust activity-based costing methodology.

If the products or line items pass the review in Step 2, then the alliance partner should proceed to Step 3. If these products or line items do not pass the review, as was the case with the two line items with the consumer products company, then the alliance partner should proceed to Disband.

❖ *Step 3. Revisit "build internally" versus "acquire externally," and then revisit the organizational readiness and speed to market demand.* When products and services pass Steps 1 and 2, then the alliance partner should re-review Steps 4 and 5 of the original framework. Sometimes, alliance partners build up internal capabilities in a specific area during the time frame the alliance is in effect. This may give rise to a decision to "build internally" versus continuing to "acquire externally." If this capability was acquired outside of the alliance, then the alliance partner should proceed to Disband. If the capability was developed through the alliance, then the alliance partner should proceed with caution to Step 4, the last step in this framework. If the capability does not exist and "acquire externally" is still the best option, then the alliance partner should still proceed to the last step.

The alliance partner should also review the company's organizational readiness and capacity for speed to market demand if "build internally" is an option. Sometimes a company has a capability, but is slow to use the capability to meet changes in market demand. This presents a different set of options (e.g., joint ventures, outsourcing) designed to unleash their internal capabilities. The name of the game is meeting the ever-changing customer demand with speed. If an alliance is in decline, then this step becomes the "how" to connect faster and stronger to the market demand.

❖ *Step 4. Review, then select the best path.* If alliance partners determine that the products and services do not fit the business and market strategies or the marketplace of either company anymore, then the alliance partners proceeded straight to Disband. The same held true for the product portfolio review against the marketplace scan. When alliance products and services are in decline, yet they pass the business strategy, the market strategy, the marketplace scan, and the product portfolio review against the marketplace scan, the alliance partners must proceed on a course to move the alliance out of the Decline stage of the alliance lifecycle. There are three options for the alliance partners to choose from and follow.

1. The first path is to do nothing. This option will cause alliances to drift into oblivion, canceled out on a formal basis by the expiration of the alliance agreement and all other legal agreements. By default, the alliance partners will enter into the Disband framework. In my experience, most alliance partners usually follow this path. It is also the least proactive path, and leaves a bad taste in everyone's mouth concerning the value of alliances.

2. The second path is intense innovation between the alliance partners. As mentioned earlier, high-performing teams may be able to find other areas or ways to jump-start growth and renew the alliance growth. This is very difficult to do, but can and has been done. If this occurs, then alliances become even stronger.

    The use of definitive agreements around innovative solutions can help jump-start alliance results. We discussed how to construct definitive agreements in Chapter Seven. The danger here is the use of definitive agreements when there is a marketplace need for the joint solution. Alliance partners can use definitive agreements in each stage of the lifecycle. However, they can be immensely powerful in moving an alliance from decline to either mature or even high growth.

    If the intense innovation path is selected, then the alliance partners should revisit the type of alliance needed (see the discussion of the five types of alliances in Chapter One). In addition, the alliance agreement and business plan may be in need of modification to address the new form of alliance relationship between the two alliance partners.

3. The third path is to admit the end of the alliance, and proceed to Disband. There are situations when an orderly end to alliances will result in positive feelings between the alliance partners and a positive influence on the marketplace. Conversely, there are situations when alliances disband and the partners become intense competitors. For example, Oracle and i2 Tech-

nologies had a very strong alliance at the end of the 1990s. When the alliance ended, Oracle and i2 became intense competitors around the development of public marketplaces. Oracle even announced their intention to develop a suite of Advanced Planning Solution (APS) software, which is the heart of i2 Technologies' base business!

The above framework helps alliance partners address the internal and external reasons for why the alliance is in the Decline stage of the alliance lifecycle, and provides different paths for the alliance partners to choose. This framework is marketplace- and need-focused. As a result, it usually helps each alliance partner be more objective as to which path is needed to get the alliance out of Decline. Too many times, I have seen emotion cloud what otherwise would have been a positive decision for both alliance partners to follow. The decision to get into an alliance should have been one that was made on a strong foundation of market need, internal/external capability assessments, and speed to market. The decision to revitalize an alliance or Disband should be made with the same deliberation.

The process to disband an alliance is one of utmost importance. Unfortunately, it is one that too often is left to the lawyers to handle. Let's take a look at a framework to properly disband an alliance (Exhibit 9-3).

Framework to Disband an Alliance

✧ *Step 1. Identify reasons to disband the alliance.* In the Framework to Determine the Need to Disband an Alliance, there existed several reasons for alliances to progress from Decline to Disband. There was the change in the internal need for the alliance products and services. There was the change in the external need for the alliances products and services. In addition, there was the acquisition of the capability internally to produce the products and services provided by the alliance partner, the drifting of alliances into oblivion, and the mutual agreement of the alliance partners that the alliance should be disbanded.

This step is important, because the reason to disband an alliance

Exhibit 9-3. Framework to Disband an Alliance.

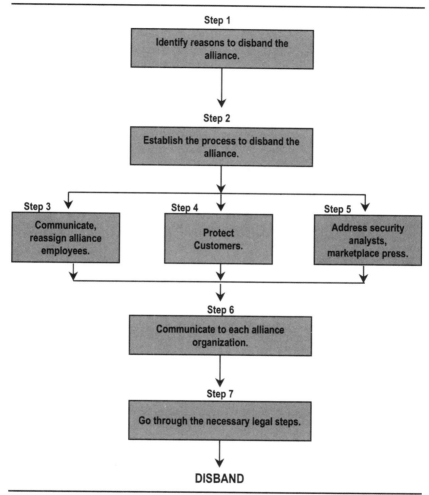

will drive the process to disband. Whatever the reason, it is absolutely critical to specifically identify and isolate the reasons why the alliance is to be disbanded. Honesty is the best course of action. A third party opinion may be needed to get to the actual need to disband.

◇ *Step 2. Establish the process to disband the alliance.* The executives from both alliance partners need to agree on the reason or reasons to disband the alliance. They need to then proceed to map out the process to disband.

Disbanding an alliance involves more than notifying each other of an intent to disband the alliance. There is first of all a strategy for addressing customers, the security analysts and the marketplace press, the employees from both companies working in the alliance, and the organizations themselves. In addition, the lawyers must proceed to do their thing to disband the alliance.

◆ *Step 3. Communicate to and reassign alliance employees.* Executives from both alliance partners should communicate to the employees as soon as the decision is made to disband the alliance. It is important to reinforce the criticality of alliances, and recognize their commitment—physical and emotional—to the alliance effort. Executives must be brutally honest with the employees, because their own credibility is on the line. No one knows the reasons why alliances fail better than the employees working the alliance. Any effort on behalf of the executives to communicate reasons other than the truth will just undermine their own credibility.

The most important question that will be raised by the alliance employees is, "What happens to me now?" There must be a clear plan to answer this question. These employees are perhaps some of the strongest and best-trained employees in the companies, and it is important to have alternative career paths to retain them. It is also important to treat the alliance employees well, because any failure to do so will inhibit the company from enticing others to work in future alliances.

◆ *Step 4. Protect the customers.* Above all else, the alliance partners must protect the customers. Despite the disbanding of the alliance, the alliance partners must work with each customer and make sure that their commitments to the customers are honored and met. If customer commitments are not honored, the ramifications for the base businesses of both companies can be huge.

The customer commitments must transcend the alliance agreement. The run-out process must be established customer by customer, with the executives fully backing the customer commitments in terms of financial and people resources.

✧ *Step 5. Address the security analysts and the marketplace press.* No matter what the real reasons are for the disbanding of an alliance, there is the matter of managing the perception of the security analysts and the marketplace press. It is absolutely critical to be proactive in addressing the analysts and the press. It is also critical to be honest. Further, any delay in communicating the reasons will result in the analysts and the press determining their own reasons for the disbanding of the alliance. In addition, any reasons communicated to the analysts and the press other than the real reasons will result in mistrust.

When possible, the two alliance partners should together address the security analysts and press. This is not always possible. However, the message and subsequent impact of the announcement will be enhanced if the alliance partners deliver the message together.

✧ *Step 6. Communicate to each alliance organization.* It is absolutely essential that each alliance partner organization be notified of the disbandment of the alliance, and that this be done after the notification of the alliance employees. The last thing that employees want is to find out from a general communication to the organization that their alliance and possibly their jobs are being disbanded.

This communication does not need to be elaborate. It does need to be timely and to the point. It also needs to be supportive of the alliance partner and the employees of the alliance.

✧ *Step 7. Go through the necessary legal steps.* The last step is to have the lawyers weave their magic with the alliance. The lawyers need to review the alliance agreement, the definitive agreements, the nondisclosure agreement, all memos of intent, and all other documents associated with the alliance. The lawyers also need to identify every step necessary to disband the alliance.

The other item of note is the responsibility that each alliance partner has beyond the disbanding of the alliance. As we covered throughout the book, there are customer commitments, responsibilities around confidential information, and other accountabilities that transcend the expiration of the alliance agreement. The lawyers must map out all of these, and communicate them to the executives in charge to make sure that all responsibilities are covered. The motto here is, when in doubt, listen to the lawyers!

When Alliances Are Allowed to Drift in "Decline"

A few years ago, I was working in Campinas, a wonderful city that is situated about a two-hour drive from of Sao Paulo, Brazil. Sao Paulo is huge, with approximately 17 million people in the city itself and another 17 million in the rest of Sao Paulo state. The total of 34 million people in all of Sao Paulo state is equal to the total population of Argentina and twice the population of Chile! By contrast, the population of Campinas is approximately 1 million.

Campinas is home to several high-tech firms and a major Brazilian university. The energy in the city that revolves around the high-tech industry and the university is very intense and infectious. The young people are excited about the future of Brazil and their own future. Housing is affordable, and the environment is relatively clean.

I had the pleasure of speaking to a relatively large audience of students at a campus event. The formal topic was on alliances with companies from other cultures. The topic was selected because of the presence of American and Japanese firms in Campinas and because of the strength of the Nordic countries in mobile telecommunications devices. These students desired a career in the high-tech and telecommunications industries, and were very inquisitive about multicultural alliances.

During the open discussion that followed my presentation, I asked the students to voice their opinions about what was working and what was not working with alliances. The feedback I received was what I expected, until I heard from two particular students in the audience.

The first student, Alex, had worked for a high-tech company as a summer intern. His job was to review how his company could improve its sales in France through one specific alliance. He spent two months of his three-month internship in France, after which he had crafted a very unflattering report on the state of this alliance.

This high-tech company had entered into an alliance with another high-tech company at the corporate level. The two companies had complementary and noncompeting products and services. The alliance was designed to encompass seven countries on two continents. The alliances in two of the seven countries were struggling.

When Alex had worked in France in one of these two alliances, he discovered several reasons why this particular alliance was struggling. First, the communications from the corporate offices and the two country offices of the alliance partners were severely lacking. Second, these two companies had complementary products, but had service offerings that were competitive. Third, these two companies had no incentives to work together, since the only alliance performance incentives were with the alliance executives in their respective corporate offices. Last but not least, the two companies that entered into the alliance were from different countries, with France being a third country. (The student intern was from Spain, yet a fourth country!) This alliance was not set up for success at all.

In some respects, this particular alliance was in the Decline stage of an alliance lifecycle. However, in several other respects, it never did get out of the start-up stage. What was most troubling to Alex was the behavior of these two companies.

He discovered that the poorly communicated alliance between these two companies had actually created an open animosity between them. This conflict was demonstrated through competing advertisements, negative comments by salesmen from both companies, and occasional comments in the press, as well as scathing comments made privately by representatives of each company about the other company.

After talking with Alex, I contacted a friend of mine at one of these alliance partners. I asked him point-blank whether any of these comments were true, and whether his company knew of this conflict between the two alliance partners in France. He told me that the company knew of the conflict, but preferred not to act because the rest of the alliance was going very well. The alliance numbers were blended together, so the perception was that the alliance was very successful.

This was disappointing to hear, because the situation in France was very damaging to both companies, who were hurting themselves by allowing this behavior to go on. The lesson with this situation is two-fold. The first lesson is to immediately recognize and address conflict. The second lesson is to recognize when alliances are in decline, and to address the reasons in an organized and expedited manner. As previously discussed, alliances in decline should either innovate and move back up the lifecycle curve, or proceed to disband. In this case, the two alliance partners should have recognized the negative ramifications of the alliance in France, and should have proceeded to disband the alliance in that country. (It was obvious that the animosity between the two companies would have precluded any short-term teaming on innovative solutions to move the alliance into an emerge or high-growth stage of the alliance lifecycle.)

This student intern had an unbelievable summer internship learning experience. There are benefits to know when to restart alliances and when to disband them. There are also lessons learned when people discover the real reasons why alliances drift in decline. The name of the alliance game is success. Sometimes there is greater benefit in recognizing an alliance in decline, disbanding it, and emerging either as friends or as marketplace-neutrals rather than letting the alliance drift. It's always a tough call to make, but a necessary one for the benefit of each alliance partner. There is also an even greater benefit, which is the preservation of a positive attitude toward future alliances within both alliance organizations.

Character and Integrity: Two Cornerstones of Alliance Behavior

The second student that spoke during the open discussion of my on-campus event asked a far-reaching question. This student, who was of Japanese ancestry, asked why alliance partners would not have an honor code and be loyal to each other during good times and bad. He went on to say that the "essence" of the alliance agreement was a commitment to be loyal, and that people working for alliances should have a higher honor code than other employees.

In my travels around the world, I did discover that Japanese companies were very loyal to their business partners. I know of one particular incident where a major Japanese automotive OEM selected a third-party logistics company to handle the imports of parts, subsystems, and systems from Japan to their assembly plants in North America. When the third-party logistics company got into trouble, the Japanese OEM provided financial and human resources assistance in order to help the company turn itself around. It would have been easy to claim a breach of contract and switch to a new third party logistics company. However, the senior executive of the Japanese company who told me this story said that they had selected this third party logistics company as a partner, and they would hope that they would be treated in the same way if they were to find themselves in trouble.

When selecting alliance leaders and employees, companies need to first look for character and integrity. These alliance people come into contact with confidential and proprietary information on a frequent basis. A lot of coverage has been given in this book about language in the alliance agreement covering confidential and proprietary information and nondisclosure agreements. Why does all this effort go into these items? The answer is that companies need to protect themselves against the actions of people with low character and integrity. It is critical for companies to demand that only the people of the highest character and integrity work within alliances.

Another area where character and integrity are critical is with international or global alliances. There are significant business transactions being done around the world where questionable deal making occurs on a routine basis. The employees of companies wear their company name on their foreheads (figuratively) as they do business with partners around the world. When they start doing shady deals, they give the marketplace the perception that this is how their company does business on a routine basis. They not only place their companies at risk, but in several countries (including the United States) they put themselves at risk as well.

When I started living in South America, I was initially appalled at the idea of one-and-a-half-hour lunches. I thought early on that these lunches were an incredible waste of time, and that they allowed employees to escape from their responsibilities of work. After I had been there about a month, one of the salesmen in my office (Carlos) asked me to go out for a beer after work. It was during my discussion with Carlos that I connected the dots with the long lunches.

Carlos told me that in many South American countries, there still exists a mistrust of government officials, the court systems, and the military. The business people develop alliances and do business only with people with whom they have a relationship and whom they can trust. Character and integrity are key ingredients to developing that sense of trust. People develop these relationships primarily over lunch and sometimes dinner. They want to rely on the relationship, the character, and the integrity of their alliance partner to do business together, and to feel protected in a difficult political and social world.

Character and integrity are also key ingredients for consistent behavior. One item I have noticed in working globally is that people do respect consistency in behavior. People also honor consistency in behavior when it is combined with character and integrity. This ties to a sense of trust. Alliance partners want to feel that they can trust their partners both when they are working directly with them and when they are not and their backs are turned.

Honor, Loyalty, and Trust: Three Critical Success Factors

Character and integrity lead to trust through honor and loyalty. The traits of character and integrity are not found in all employees, and must be nurtured in people from a young age. The selection of the right alliance people must include a screen for character and integrity to create this sense of honor, loyalty, and trust between alliance partners. The loyalty between alliance partners may be at risk if character and integrity play a minor role in the selection process for alliance leadership. Perhaps the Japanese student in Brazil was right. I still have several business associates that are friends from South America. I also learned to enjoy one-and-a-half-hour "working lunches" with business associates, and to build the alliance relationships from a level of trust and integrity. I now view a trip through the drive-thru of a fast food restaurant as a missed opportunity to further develop the relationships with business associates.

Moral strength and self-discipline are at the heart of character, and result in a reputation that permeates both the employees in each company involved in an alliance as well as the marketplace. Sound moral principle, honesty, and sincerity are at the heart of integrity. Character and integrity work hand-in-hand, and they produce an environment that evokes honor, loyalty, and trust. The Japanese OEM demonstrated character and integrity by sticking with the third-party logistics company during tough times. It earned the positive reputation it enjoys.

Honor, loyalty, and trust are the critical success factors that govern the behavior within alliances throughout their lifecycles, and they have much to do with how successful alliances can be. Honor involves having high regard or giving great respect to the alliance partner and the agreement. Loyalty involves being faithful during the term of an agreement (and beyond in some circumstances.) Trust is a resulting state of belief or confidence in a partner that pulls together character, integrity, honor, and loyalty. These cornerstones and critical success factors frequently dictate how alliance partners are perceived in the marketplace (and perceive each other), both during the alliance and after it is disbanded.

How Do You Test for Character and Integrity?

The selection of the right people for alliances is critical to their overall success, a point stressed repeatedly in several of the earlier chapters. However, the question that comes up a lot is, how do you test or screen for character and integrity?

One obvious way to test for character and integrity is to strictly adhere to background and reference checks. These checks do have a way of surfacing the character and integrity of prospective employees in a legal and above-board manner.

There is another innovative way that a leading Fortune Global 500 company uses to screen for character and integrity. Working closely with a leading university, the company establishes simulated case studies for joint teams of employees and prospective employees. These simulations are structured in such a way that there will be winning teams and losing teams. They are also structured in such a manner that the winners must resort to questionable, unethical, or illegal tactics to win. The losers recognize the cost of winning, and bow out of the competitive bidding.

This company does not tell the prospective employees that all of them have passed the interview process up to this point, and that the simulated case study is their final step in the hiring process. The prospective employees are also not aware of which team members are actual employees, which team members are university professors, and which team members are prospective employees. Sometimes, this company even uses customers and—you guessed it—alliance partners as team members.

The simulated case study is structured in an intense, winner-take-all environment. Although facilitators are used to guide the process to a "winner" solution, the content of the team solutions is not on center stage during this process. What is critical is how well prospective employees perform under pressure and how rigidly they adhere to the company's code of conduct and stated values. As such, the losing teams that adhere to the code of conduct, demonstrate unwavering character and integrity, and remain loyal to their teams and alliance partners are declared the winners. The winning teams that abandon the code of conduct, choose to do things that demonstrate questionable character or integrity, or choose to abandon their loyalty to their alliance partners to achieve the winning solution are declared the losers. The prospective employees on the losing teams are not hired.

Oddly enough, there are very few instances where *all* the teams choose to lose rather than compromise their codes of conduct, their character, or their integrity. This means that the company knows that they must continue to tighten their background and reference checks in order to achieve a better ratio of "losers and winners." Even so, this is an innovative way to screen out potential bad hires in a simulated, pressurized environment.

Summary

The path to successful alliance management is a journey, not a one-time event. It begins with the Framework to Determine the Need for an Alliance and the Framework to Determine What Type of Alliance Is Needed. Once these frameworks are completed, the process continues with the negotiation of the alliance agreement. The journey continues with the negotiation on memos of intent (MOIs), nondisclosure agreements (NDAs), and the selection and training of the right alliance people.

The construction of definitive agreements helps drive the alliance through the lifecycle of alliance management. As alliances progress through Mature into the Decline stage, it is necessary to revisit the alliance. The Framework to Determine the Need to Disband the Alliance offers an opportunity to either revitalize the alliance or move into the disband stage. The Framework to Disband an Alliance provides an orderly process to evolve the alliance partners into life beyond the alliance.

The traits of character and integrity are the cornerstones for the effective management of alliances. These two cornerstones provide the foundation for honor, loyalty, and trust within alliance relationships.

The journey to alliance management is more than just negotiating press releases. As we will see in Chapter Eleven, leading companies like General Electric and Cisco are successfully and aggressively using alliances to extend competencies and generate speed to market.

Notes

1. Ian Cobain, "Rain Rescues Capitalism From Spike-Haired Horde," *The Times* (London), May 2, 2001, p. 1.
2. David Graves, et al., "Police Quell May Day Threat," *The Daily Telegraph* (London), May 2, 2001, p. 1.
3. www.zdnet.com/news/stocktalk, "Motorola Japan and NTT Software Sign MOU to Design and Deliver VoiceXML Applications in Japan; Collaboration to Provide Japanese Market with Voice Access to the Internet," April 23, 2001, pp. 1–2.
4. www.zdnet.com/news/pressreleases, "Cisco and Motorola Form Joint Venture, June 1999"; www.nwfusion.com/archive/2000/85951 _01-31-2000.html, p. 1; and www.motorola.com/pressreleases, July 2000.
5. Nikhil Hutheesing, "Marital Blisters," *Forbes Best of Web*, May 21, 2001, p. 30.

CHAPTER TEN

Critical Success Factors in Establishing Alliances

As I walked into the room, I noticed a very eclectic crowd. There were professors, department chairs, and even the president of the university. There were also twenty presidential scholars graduating after four eventful years, who were there with their parents and friends. And there were twelve representatives present from the companies that funded the scholarships of the presidential scholars. The conversation was fast, energetic, and at times very intellectually challenging.

Past presidential scholars from this university have become doctors, lawyers, CEOs, chief financial officers, and even actors on Broadway. They come from poor, well-to-do, or average families. They are racially diverse, politically diverse, and have diverse sexual orientations. The one common thread they do have is that they are very intelligent! A second common thread is that they are our leaders of tomorrow.

In the middle of the room close to the punch table, five or six presidential scholars were holding court with three of the company representatives. One representative was an executive vice-president of one of the largest global banks, another was a senior partner in a major consulting firm, and the third was the founder of a successful high-tech start-up.

These presidential scholars were really pressing the company representatives on a number of topics. One of the topics was centered on how successful executives and successful companies establish lasting legacies. This topic was refreshing, because we were at the end of the dot-com bubble, and the career landscape for these presidential scholars had changed overnight. What was a perceived legacy before the dot-com run changed during the dot-com frenzy, has now changed as the dot-com bubble burst. These students were in "seek" mode and wanted to tap the wisdom of these successful executives.

The executives were taking turns tackling the challenge of answering the students' questions. One by one, they covered topics that ranged from consistent performance exceeding expectations to time in position. Their logic was sound, but they didn't appear to be providing the kinds of answers that the students were searching for in their questions.

In the audience was the mother of one of the students. She was a single mother and employed by the United States Postal Service as a freight handler. She had worked extremely hard to put her daughter through school and to raise her with strong morals and a great work ethic. As the students' questions were getting more and more pointed, she suddenly spoke up. She said that the people throughout history who enjoyed a strong legacy well beyond their careers and even their lives had three things in common, and that these three things were:

✧ A strong vision for their organization
✧ A message that combined passion and focus
✧ The absence of a fear of failure

She went on to cite Franklin D. Roosevelt, Winston Churchill, Martin Luther King, Jr., Ronald Reagan, and Margaret Thatcher as examples of politicians with strong, lasting legacies. She also cited

Thomas Edison, Alexander Graham Bell, Henry Ford, Bill Gates, and Sam Walton as businessmen with lasting legacies. The executives looked a little taken aback, as the students nodded and smiled at this woman who was obviously very intelligent and well read, and who had ended up providing a few pointers to the executives in the room.

Picking up on her lead, one student said that many companies had consistent financial performance, but most people do not know or remember the names of the CEOs. Another student said that several companies had CEOs who had been in office a long time, but that the performance of many of these companies was mediocre at best. A third student listed five CEOs who had been in office for a long time, who had produced consistent financial performance with their companies, and who he felt belonged in this premier category of lasting legacies. The five executives, which included three of the men the mother had mentioned, were Henry Ford of Ford Motor Corporation, Bill Gates of Microsoft, Sam Walton of Wal-Mart, Jack Welch of General Electric, and John Chambers of Cisco Systems. The young women at the meeting were touting (and cheering for) Carly Fiorina of Hewlett-Packard, although her tenure has been too short to create a lasting legacy.

The students picked up the pace and started to focus on General Electric, Hewlett-Packard, and Cisco. One common thread that began to appear with the companies being discussed was their aggressive pursuit of alliances. General Electric extensively works with other organizations and companies through their divisions like G. E. Power Systems and G. E. Aircraft, and through their G. E. Capital subsidiary. Cisco Systems collaboratively works with its suppliers and customers in a solution-based environment. Hewlett-Packard has roots with alliances dating back to the 1970s with Canon. In all three cases, these companies actively work with other organizations in an open, collaborative environment to dominate their respective marketplaces.

The original responses from the executives were not entirely wrong. Consistent performance is indeed an ingredient for a strong legacy. Time in position does help the building of a legacy, although it does not guarantee a legacy in and of itself. However, the single mother filled in the blanks. To build a legacy, one needs to have a strong vision, a message that combines passion and focus, and an unwavering commitment to succeed without an overriding fear of failure.

Following a similar path creates the legacy of a successful alliance. Companies that have a legacy of strong alliances have alliances that consistently perform above expectations, leave their people in position for an extended period of time, have a strong vision for their alliances, create a message for their alliances that combines passion and focus, and have an unwavering commitment to succeed with their alliances.

As the students were starting to leave to attend the graduation ceremonies of one of the colleges in the university, I noticed the single mother off to the side. She was in active discussion with the founder of the successful high-tech start-up. I smiled as I realized that she had already begun to build a legacy of her own. It also appeared that she might have an opportunity to move beyond the Postal Service and start a career in the high-tech start-up world.

Critical Success Factors for Establishing Hall-of-Fame Alliances

The discussion with the group of presidential scholars, their parents, and their sponsoring executives was energizing, and primarily focused on the legacies of individuals. However, the same factors that were discussed in support of the legacies of individuals can be applied to the legacies of companies and their success with alliances.

As we have seen throughout the book, there are several critical success factors that support a successful alliance program. Companies that are effective in establishing strong alliances usually embrace the majority of these factors. These critical success factors are:

1. A strong vision for alliances
2. An alliance message that combines passion and focus
3. An unwavering commitment to succeed without the fear of failure
4. The strength of the process to enter into meaningful alliance agreements
5. The knowledge of how to partner
6. The fortitude to stick with alliances through good times and bad times
7. The ability to know when to hold, and when to fold alliances

These seven critical success factors pull together the messages throughout the book, and provide a foundation for executives to build legacies with their alliance programs. Let's take a look at these seven critical success factors in turn, and at how they impact alliance programs.

❖ *Factor One: A Strong Vision for Alliances.* The politicians, CEOs, and founders of major corporations that were cited by the students, sponsoring executives, and parents in the discussion at the university all had strong visions. For this purpose, a vision is defined as the conceptualization of an end state for a particular cause or a particular company. Winston Churchill and FDR shared a vision of winning the war during World War II, and returning the world to one of peace and democracy. Henry Ford had a vision to build the best car manufacturing company. Sam Walton had the vision to be the number one retailer in the world. Martin Luther King, Jr., had a vision that all people would be able to live and work side by side without regard for race, color, or creed.

The establishment of a hall-of-fame alliance program does not just happen. It needs a strong vision to initiate and maintain momentum throughout the lifecycles of alliances. This vision needs to be established by the chief executive officer (CEO) or president of each company. It also needs to be supported by key members of the board of directors.

The strong vision must include the products and services groups that will be involved with alliances. For example, we discussed in Chapters Three and Four different alliances with 3G wireless networks. The product and service group in this case would be 3G wireless technology applications. A strong vision should include a geographic scope (e.g., global, EMEA only, etc.) as well as a definition of "alliance success."

Frequently the definition of "alliance success" is measured in sales and profits. However, strong CEOs also recognize the value of increased customer satisfaction and loyalty as measured through market share. Jack Welch, for example, had a vision that the products sold by General Electric had to attain a number one or number two market-share positions in their respective marketplaces. In addition, strong CEOs also identify the value of alliances in transforming their companies to adapt to the ever-changing marketplace and customer desires, and they weave this into their vision.

Perhaps the greatest benefit to a strong vision for alliances is the recognition of the company's strengths and weaknesses. By identifying and conceptualizing an end state for a product and service group with or without geographic boundaries, and by identifying the definition of "alliance success," the CEO is in essence outlining the company's strengths and weaknesses. The CEO is also identifying how alliances will complement the company's strengths by augmenting the company's weaknesses in key areas. This action is necessary for CEOs and their companies to take advantage of fast-paced opportunities and respond to fact-acting threats.

✧ *Factor Two: An Alliance Message That Combines Passion and Focus.* The political and business leaders discussed earlier all had passion and focus to go with their vision. They also had an ability to communicate their message to their constituents, and demonstrate their passion and focus. How many of you remember learning about (or actually hearing) Winston Churchill's speech rallying his countrymen during the darkest times of World War II? How about Martin Luther King, Jr.'s "I Have a Dream" speech? Or Ronald Reagan's "Tear down this wall, Mr. Gorbachev" speech. Many of us also remember Sam Walton doing the hula dance on Wall Street. Most of us have to resort to the history books to remember Henry Ford's message, "The customer can have any color of automobile he wants, as long as it is black!" Passion? Focus? They all had it. They also had the ability to communicate their messages with their passion and focus.

In my travels around the world, I have found that successful companies are almost always led by CEOs with passion and focus. Most of these CEOs have the ability to communicate their messages and convey their passion and focus. This is critical for alliances, because frequently alliances are not in the mainstream of the day-to-day business operations for these companies. The objective of alliances is to develop new channels and new businesses that will rapidly become part of the mainstream business operations. This passion and focus helps elevate the vision of alliances to a level of importance and acceptance within the CEO's company.

The acceptance of alliances into the mainstream of the day-to-day operations of companies is important for three reasons.

✧ First, to get support for alliances throughout the organization at all levels

❖ Second, to entice the top performing employees into leadership positions with alliances

❖ Third, to mobilize the organization to utilize alliances to drive additional sales, profits, and market share in a rapid manner

One company that I worked with a few years ago decided to elevate the status of alliance management in their organization. The CEO placed the alliance leader role as an official pass-through position for promotion. This one move validated alliance leadership, and created instant popularity and demand within the rising executive ranks.

❖ *Factor Three: An Unwavering Commitment to Succeed without the Fear of Failure.* Companies around the world take many different approaches to risk . Some companies risk everything on a new model or the next generation of technology. Other companies have risk management groups that are extremely conservative when dealing with any risk. Northern European companies usually take a lot less risk than Silicon Valley companies. Japanese companies study the factors driving risk and aggressively manage these factors. One company that I am familiar with has the reputation of avoiding all risk. Their executives have even nicknamed their risk management group "No Fear, No Risk." Most companies fall in between these extremes when it comes to risk.

Throughout the book, we discussed why companies come together and form alliances. From complementary core competencies to a rapidly changing marketplace, the reasons are usually rooted in the need to access new markets, new channels, new products and services, or new solutions—faster than a company can do it on its own. The key word is new. Anything that is new carries a certain amount of risk. Add on the realities of working with other companies, other cultures, and other people who have different performance incentives, and the probability of entering into a "no-risk" alliance is very low.

A no-risk approach means the complete avoidance of any possibility of failure. What if Babe Ruth, Roger Maris, or Mark McGuire had taken the attitude that they wanted to avoid failure? Power hitters in baseball strike out at least twice as many times as they hit home runs. For example, Babe Ruth struck out 1,330 times and hit 714 home runs. Sam Walton was a Ben Franklin franchiser before he took several of his stores and started Wal-Mart Stores. Mr. R. H. Macy failed several times before his "Macy's" store in New York was a success. Fred Smith nearly went bankrupt with Federal Express before he realized success. No risk and a fear of failure? Not with these guys. No risk means no access to opportunity, and no opportunity means no growth!

As we discussed in Chapter Nine, one of my hall-of-fame alliance companies took a risk and formed an alliance that failed. Cisco Systems took a risk when they established their alliance with Motorola and formed Spectrapoint Wireless. If Cisco had followed a path of no risk, no failure, then they could have avoided failure with Spectrapoint Wireless. However, they would have missed out on all of their other successful alliances. According to insiders, they also would have missed out on the development of their real-time order management system, which today processes approximately 70 percent of their orders without human intervention.

The fact is that alliances have risk. The lesson here is that executives must first sharpen the pencil on the benefits of alliances, and then focus on how to mitigate the risk with alliances. The process to enter into alliance agreements and manage them throughout the alliance lifecycle is all about taking advantage of opportunities while mitigating risk. So what about the fear of failure and no risk? Alliances are about accelerating growth. The best way to avoid risk is to do nothing. The choice is yours.

❖ *Factor Four: The Strength of the Process to Enter into Meaningful Alliance Agreements.* The process to enter into alliance agreements and manage them throughout the alliance lifecycle takes time, effort, and commitment. We have visited the Framework to Determine the Need for an Alliance and the Framework to Determine What Type of Alliance Is Needed, which were introduced in Chapter One. We also reviewed the construction of a strong alliance agreement, the use of nondisclosure agreements, the development of memos of intent, and the use of definitive agreements. We also reviewed the Framework to Determine the Need to Disband an Alliance as a way to mitigate risk.

The strength of the process to enter into meaningful alliance agreements is critical to the success of alliances. It takes a strong commitment from the CEO, supported by adherence to the process by his or her direct reports, to ensure that the right resources, time, and commitment are made to the process. This is important, because alliances are not the mainstream for most companies. Without this senior executive support, there will be the tendency for middle-level managers to redirect resources from the alliance process to more tactical, immediate tasks. The process is just like a pipeline—you get out of the one end what you put in on the other end. The redirecting of resources will only result in a weak process that produces haphazard alliances—and disappointing results. This is a poor way to maximize growth opportunities and mitigate risk.

One way to reinforce the strength of the alliance process is to hold executive reviews on the process itself. Another way is to assign a top executive as a "Chief Alliance Officer" reporting to the president or CEO. A third way is to create a process performance metric in the performance appraisal and incentive programs of each executive. Whatever the combination of these or other ways, the executive reinforcement of a strong process to enter into meaningful alliance agreements is a critical factor that will drive alliance success.

✧ *Factor Five*: *The Knowledge on How to Partner*. We reviewed several ways for companies to approach how to become an alliance partner, varying from people processes to joint compensation incentives. There is an immense opportunity for collective learning when companies try different methods to become alliance partners.

How can companies turn this opportunity for collective learning into knowledge of how to partner? One of the answers lies in a strong knowledge management program. Such a program should be structured to capture all templates and knowledge objects to be reused in the future. These objects include completed frameworks, alliance agreements, nondisclosure agreements, memos of intent, and definitive agreements.

Other contributions to the knowledge program should be success stories. These success stories should detail the process of how a successful alliance was created, the performance metrics used, and the value delivered to clients as well as the alliance partners. Client testimonials and alliance partner testimonials should be included in these success stories.

Perhaps a greater contribution to the knowledge management program is the construction of "failure stories." There are significant lessons to be learned when alliances fail. The failure stories should recap the process to initiate the alliance, the factors driving the need for the alliance, the performance metrics, and the understanding from clients, the alliance partner, and other executives as to why the alliance failed.

The key here is to capture this information as it occurs. Too often the knowledge of why alliances succeed or fail resides only in the heads of alliance leaders and clients. Over time, the failure to formalize and centralize this information allows this valuable knowledge to dissipate. People retire or die, memories fade, and people change jobs. It is critical to formalize the capturing and reuse process of this knowledge to improve the chance for success with future alliances.

Another way to improve the knowledge on how to partner is through a formal 360-degree feedback process. Alliance employees and alliance partners need to be able to provide feedback to the executives. This feedback needs to be done in an anonymous, open environment, which may necessitate a third party to facilitate the feedback process.

The capturing of all this information is important. The final step is to convert this information into knowledge. Whether it is the job of the chief alliance executive or an alliance employee, the question is what to do with the captured information. The answer is to design a strong alliance process, and convert the captured information into reusable objects and templates to be used in the alliance process. These reusable objects and templates may indeed change, enhance, or speed up the alliance process while improving the overall success rate for alliance partnerships.

Knowledge that is created from information relies on reusable knowledge objects and templates. It also relies on experienced alliance leaders to recognize the value of information captured from alliance employees and partners. Tenure in alliance leaders will help sharpen their skills in recognizing and determining value drivers for successful alliances. The combination of recognizing value drivers for successful alliances and the conversion of information into reusable knowledge objects leaves only one item to be addressed. This item is communication.

Communication is extremely important for companies learning how to partner. This communication is in two flows. The first flow is an internal flow on what alliances work for what reasons and what alliances do not work and why. The second flow is an external flow.

When the two are combined, the company needs to make the modifications necessary to address the deficiencies and improve the process.

One company that I know continuously tries to craft press releases on how great their supply chain alliances are and the wonderful results they are achieving as a result of these alliances. The company's recently retired vice president of supply chain has gone on the lecture circuit and is even an adjunct professor at a major university touting the unparalleled successes of his company. However, both the employees and this company's alliance partners have privately and publicly stated that their supply chain operations have never been in such bad disrepair. Many have never heard of the "knowledge objects" that appear in the press releases, nor do they have any training programs in the field to prepare people to incorporate new ideas into their everyday job duties and responsibilities. In this case, the internal flow of communications does not match the external flow of communications. People do know what the real situation is with their supply chain, but that message is not reaching the CEO's office, and the needed modifications are not being addressed to improve the process. As a result, the alliance and its results are both suffering.

❖ *Factor Six: The Fortitude to Stick with Alliances through Good Times and Bad Times.* From 1997 to March 2000, it was easy for executives to declare victory in alliances with high-tech companies. The market capitalization of companies, especially dot-coms, went to dizzying heights substantiated by nothing more than the small "e" my executive friend liked so well. Between March 2000 and mid-2001, the compression of price-to-earnings (PE) multiples brought the market capitalization of most of these technology companies plummeting back down to earth. (Unfortunately for many, they plummeted six feet under!)

If the alliance process has been properly followed, the values of most of these alliances should still play themselves out. (I know one alliance executive who established over thirty alliances between January 1998 and April 2000. All but one of these alliances are still producing positive results!) Executives should have the fortitude to stick with alliances and a strong value proposition even when times get tough.

The message to an alliance partner should be one of commitment. Of course, results do matter. Alliances that go into the decline phase of the lifecycle of alliances must be addressed. However, when alliances are established using a strong process and maintain a strong value proposition, they should not be disbanded just because of difficult economic times. Alliances should be part of a company's overall strategy, and should be approached as a strategic effort. Fair weather treatment of alliances will discourage companies from developing alliances and discourage top employees from working within alliances. This goes back to the strength of the process to enter into meaningful alliance relationships. The CEO must be aggressive in the management of the alliance process through good times and difficult times.

One company I know had an alliance with a small company that has a valuable piece of technology. The NASDAQ drop that started in March 2000 reduced the short-term need for technology solutions that incorporated this technology. This company decided to give written notice to their small alliance partner because they had a difficult time justifying the alliance, given the drop in solution sales. The small company first accepted the written notice canceling the alliance agreement, and then proceeded to develop an alliance with the company's primary competitor. Within a year, the market rebounded for this particular solution. For the cost of having an alliance leader in the budget for less than a year, this company lost access to a market-leading solution. Worse yet, this company lost access to the market-leading solution to its competitor!

❖ *Factor Seven: The Ability to Know When to Hold, and When to Fold, Alliances.* As we discussed in Chapter Nine, the ability to know when to hold and when to fold alliances is a critical success factor for successful alliances. In Factor Six, we covered the fortitude needed to stick with alliances during good times and bad times. However, senior executives need to learn how to differentiate between good alliances in bad times and alliances in decline.

Alliances in decline need executive attention. The framework to determine the need to disband an alliance will help executives address alliances in decline. It will also help them initiate the innovation process to help move the alliance from decline to mature or high growth.

Saying goodbye to alliances is hard to do. There is a lot of goodwill built up between alliance partners. The employees of the alliance sometimes identify with their alliance partner as strongly as they identify with their own company. Separation can be traumatic for all involved. The separation should be done with the same care and compassion that went into establishing the alliance. This is even more critical when two companies that are separating become competitors. The legacy of a company is built step by step, and any misstep can cause damage to the perceived image of the company.

Summary

Strong alliances don't just happen. They are created one alliance at a time. The companies creating strong alliances have a strong vision for alliances and send an alliance message to their employees and the marketplace that combines passion and focus. They also have an unwavering commitment to succeed without the fear of failure, and insist on strength of the alliance process to enter into meaningful alliance agreements.

The companies that create strong alliances also learn to develop the knowledge on how to partner. They have the fortitude to stick with alliances through good times and bad, but can distinguish between an alliance in decline and a good alliance in bad times. They also know when to disband alliances when they are at the end of the alliance life cycle.

One common thread throughout all seven critical success factors is integrity. We discussed the need for character and integrity during the book. Companies that diligently work at preserving character and integrity in their operations usually make the best alliance partners. The global marketplace is changing so fast that there is no time to engage in researching the accuracy or intent of the actions of a partner. In addition, if you cannot trust your partner, you must ask yourself who are your real competitors? The companies that demonstrate an uncompromising commitment to integrity spend more time focusing on marketplace opportunities and maximizing value for their alliance partners.

There are several companies who have effectively pursued alliances to accelerate growth, develop innovative solutions, and penetrate new marketplaces. In my opinion, two of these companies have established themselves as the best of the best when it comes to world-class alliance programs. These two companies are General Electric and Cisco Systems. Chapter Eleven will cover in detail why these two companies were chosen to be in my "Alliance Hall of Fame."

CHAPTER ELEVEN

The Alliance Hall of Fame

During the past several months, I have asked over 150 people involved with alliances in over 100 companies from all around the world what companies had the best alliance programs. The responses identified many companies, with several companies being mentioned repeatedly. Hewlett-Packard, Siebel Systems, Marriott International, Sony and Toyota in Japan, BP Amoco in the U. K., and the Usinor Group in France all surfaced in multiple responses. Each of those companies was very active with alliances in their respective marketplaces to drive innovation, create new solutions, or access new markets.

Throughout all of this research, it became clear that two of the companies had clearly distinguished themselves with alliances above and beyond all of the rest. These two companies are General Electric and Cisco Systems. Although a case could be made for any of the other companies listed above to be in the Alliance Hall of Fame, I chose General Electric and Cisco Systems for a few key reasons. Let's take a look at each company, and learn why they have earned entry into the Alliance Hall of Fame.

The General Electric Company

The General Electric Company (GE) is one of the world's largest diversified services, technology, and manufacturing companies. It had revenues in FY2000 of about $130 billion, with net earnings of about $13 billion. *Fortune* has identified GE as the "Global Most Admired Company" in the years 1998, 1999, and 2000. *The Financial Times* identified GE as the "World's Most Respected Company" in the same three years.[1]

General Electric was the most frequent response to my question, "What company would you like to develop an alliance with?" In addition, there are three main driving forces behind my vote for General Electric to be one of the two winners in the Alliance Hall of Fame: building an e-Culture, some personal experiences, and the GE Values. Let's take a look at each of these forces at work at General Electric.

Driving Force Number One: Building an e-Culture

In the past couple of years, General Electric has been diligently working on incorporating the impact of the Internet and the Web into the daily business lives of all GE employees, suppliers, and customers. The intent of this e-initiative effort is to accelerate the awareness and use of the Web to the point where it permeates every aspect of their business lives and is no longer just an initiative.[2]

There are four major components to GE's building an e-Culture. These four components are:

1. e-Workplace
2. e-Learning
3. e-Metrics
4. e-Boardroom

e-Workplace

General Electric is pursuing an e-Workplace through expanding their internal online resources and simplifying its information streams. The intent of an e-Workplace is to fundamentally change how its organization communicates.

One way that GE is pursuing its e-Workplace is through the development of a strong Intranet. Through this Intranet, GE is focused on developing online information that is available real-time to its employees. It provides personalized news and content delivery as well as providing a company-wide productivity center of tools and resources. In addition, GE provides one shared global platform with its Intranet.[3]

Another way that GE is pursuing its e-Workplace is through the use of project collaboration tools. These tools are designed to strengthen GE's relationships with its customers through providing faster information and customer service efficiencies. This is accomplished through online Extranets designed specifically for customer interactions. This single repository of information for customers also provides a channel for two-way communications, facilitating immediate feedback. Most importantly, these project collaboration tools provide for continuous cooperation during engineering, manufacturing, and installation cycles.[4]

The impact that e-Workplace has on alliances is huge. Many of GE's customers feel that they are alliance partners with GE. The easy access to collaborative information provides for a powerful sharing of knowledge across GE's extended enterprise supply chain to its suppliers and customers. If alliances are intended to provide a common set of products and services with one face to the marketplace, then collaborative sharing of information and knowledge must occur.

In addition, people who work for GE feel connected to their customers and to one another. One division manager told me that he feels part of a close-knit family despite the fact that the company has over 300,000 employees, numerous alliance partners, tens of thousands of commercial customers, and millions of consumers worldwide!

e-Learning

GE is focused on assisting its employees to create and access the wealth of knowledge and collective learnings of all employees. The ability of employees to create and access knowledge (Launch and Learn) varies according to the amount of training, exposure to best practices, and support for learning from top management. The GE e-Mentor program provides for reverse mentoring for top management, regular meetings on e-business learnings, and discussion groups to share best practices.[5]

One Home Depot department manager in Florida credits the discipline surrounding GE's e-Learning as a major contributing factor in getting his appliance program off the ground. The e-Learning helped his GE partners to pull together best practices on appliance delivery, appliance hook-ups, and appliance service plans in a rapid manner to allow him to open up his store with a full-service appliance center.

e-Metrics

Through the application of e-Business strategies to core business processes, GE is driving the improvement of the immediacy of its optimization capabilities based on real-time metrics. To accomplish this, GE is committed to digitizing its entire company. Business-level metrics are tracked and reported, with a focus on speed and productivity. The e-Metrics are designed to also drive the creation and access to knowledge and best practices.[6]

One former business unit leader, speaking about the creating and sharing of knowledge with alliance partners, said that in the GE culture, everything needs to evolve around metrics. The faster the meaningful metrics were available, accessed, and shared, the better his business unit performed. In addition, his alliances performed better when meaningful metrics were provided on a timely basis.

e-Boardroom

GE uses its Intranet to facilitate a CEO communication forum for all employees, sharing business-critical information and corporate messages real-time.[7] The sharing of information and access to the CEO combine to reinforce the top management commitment to major programs and alliances. As far as alliances are concerned, there is no doubt about top management support for major alliances. When in doubt, alliance leaders can simply ask the CEO!

Driving Force Number Two: Personal Experience

In November 2000, I was in the market to buy a new dishwasher for my parents, who live in Florida and are in their eighties. They bought their last dishwasher twenty years ago. Their health is relatively poor, so speed in shopping is important.

During my research on dishwashers, I noticed that GE had a major alliance agreement with Home Depot. There was a new Home Depot store close to my parents that had just opened a few months earlier. With my eighty-three-year-old mother in tow, I went to the Home Depot store to look at dishwashers.

When we arrived there, it was a few minutes after eight o'clock in the evening. The appliance store worker had just clocked out, but the department manager was more than willing to help us. He was very patient with my mother, showing her the dishwashers that he had in stock in the store. He then went to the kiosk, and showed my mother the types of dishwashers that were in inventory at their warehouse. He explained the delivery process, the installation process, and the service plans associated with each dishwasher.

The appliance program was very customer-centered, and was all-inclusive with a solid available-to-promise capability. My mother and I liked three models—two made by GE and one by a competitor. On the printouts provided by the department manager, I noticed that the delivery and installation would be done for all three by GE. When I asked the department manager about this, he then confirmed that GE had worked collaboratively with Home Depot to establish the alliance program, including the delivery and installation services provided by GE. Even if we wanted the competitor's dishwasher, it would be delivered and installed by GE.

After our research, I purchased a GE dishwasher. It was installed on time and without incident. The new dishwasher looked so great that my mother said that she now needed to redo the rest of the kitchen appliances. Diane Ritchey, the executive editor of *Appliance Magazine*, told me in an interview that in her opinion installation and service are more important than speed of delivery in driving major appliance sales. Based upon my personal experience, I would have to agree with her!

The Home Depot department manager was extremely supportive of the GE alliance partnership. He said that without GE, Home Depot could not have entered the appliance business as fast or as completely as they did. He also said that even though Home Depot sold competitor dishwashers, he had complete faith that GE would deliver, install, and service the dishwashers with quality and timeliness.

It appears that the e-Culture at GE was a contributing factor to the Home Depot/GE alliance. The use of the e-Workplace, e-Learning, e-Metrics, and e-Boardroom contributed to the creation and sharing of knowledge around a solution-specific alliance. The use of kiosks to access a centralized inventory allowed Home Depot to sell appliances they did not have in stock. I know, because I bought one.

The building of an e-Culture at GE contributes to the strength of its alliances. There is another driving force behind the success of alliances at GE. This driving force is the General Electric Values. Let's review these values and their impact on alliances.

Driving Force Number Three: GE Values

If you have the pleasure to talk with employees at GE or their alliance partners and customers, you will find that the GE Values permeate everything they do. Let's take a look at the GE Values as identified on the GE homepage, and how they impact their approach with alliances.[8]

The GE Values start off with the following introductory phrase:

All of us . . . always with unyielding integrity . . .

There are nine statements that make up the GE Values. These statements guide the behavior of all employees. In addition, several of these statements can be seen in the annual reports, on their Intranet, and on their Web site. (Note: There is the integrity word again!)

✧ *Value One: . . . are passionately focused on driving customer success.* One thing that can be said about GE employees is that they are passionately focused on driving customer success. The GE philosophy is to achieve a number one or number two market share position in every market segment through making their retailers extremely successful and their customers extremely satisfied. We have to look no further than the Home Depot example. GE worked with Home Depot to make them successful in the appliance retail business. As a result, they have people like the Home Depot department managers singing their praises to individual consumers like myself. Results do matter, and alliance results need to be win-win. Focus on customer success will ensure this win-win result.

✦ *Value Two: . . . Live Six Sigma Quality. . . . ensure that the customer is always its first beneficiary, and use it to accelerate growth.* If GE employees are passionately focused on driving customer success, they are equally passionate about their Six Sigma Quality process. The Six Sigma Quality process uses six steps (Recognize, Define, Measure, Analyze, Improve, and Control) to drive improvements in processes. The objective is to reduce variability within these processes so that products are produced defect-free to customers.

GE started its Six Sigma Quality program in 1996. The program is anchored by actual customer expectations. In the "Letter to the Share Owners" in the *1999 GE Annual Report*, the following quote is made under the Six Sigma Quality heading: "The objective is not to deliver flawless products and services that we think the customer wants when we promised them—but rather what customers really want when they want them."[9]

The General Electric Six Sigma Quality program has (you guessed it) six key concepts.[10] These concepts are:

1. Critical to Quality: Attributes most important to the customer
2. Defect: Failing to deliver what the customer wants
3. Process Capability: What your process can deliver
4. Variation: What the customer sees and feels
5. Stable Operations: Ensuring consistent, predictable processes to improve what the customer sees and feels
6. Design for Six Sigma: Designing to meet customer needs and process capability

(GE is more than willing to share its philosophy on Six Sigma. Connect to the GE Web site at GE.com/corporate, click on Roadmap, and select "What is Six Sigma? The Roadmap to Customer Impact.")

One customer representative who also referred to his company as a GE alliance partner said that they originally thought their joint solution development would be done at the GE world headquarters. Instead, GE sent its teams to his company's locations, using the Six Sigma Quality process but utilizing his company's processes. In fact, he told me that after his own teams became immersed in the Six Sigma Quality process, the joint teams actually went on-site a few times to his company's customers (that is, GE's customer's customers).

This customer representative said they never once visited the GE headquarters. However, because of the GE e-Culture, they never felt isolated from either the headquarters or their central knowledge repository.

✧ *Value Three: . . . Insist on excellence and be intolerant of bureaucracy.*

Bureaucracy breeds slowness. One thing that will kill alliances is a slowness to react to the marketplace. Excellence at all levels contributes to elimination of waste. The combination of the two reinforces the quest for speed in adapting to the marketplace with its extended enterprise alliance partners. A passion for driving customer success and living the Six Sigma Quality process to drive this customer success leaves little room for dealing with internal, nonproductive bureaucracy.

✧ *Value Four: . . . Act in a boundaryless fashion . . . always search for and apply the best ideas regardless of their source.* The name of the game with alliances is to pursue the best ideas regardless of the source of the ideas. The ideas that are surfaced outside of the company call for a combination of core competencies to deliver these ideas. One GE executive told me that this value directly supports the first value. If ideas can drive customer success, the GE culture is to pursue these ideas to develop the needed solutions to drive customer success. The fact that the idea was surfaced outside of GE would call for the initiation of alliances to create and deliver the solutions with these ideas.

✧ *Value Five: . . . Prize global intellectual capital and the people that provide it . . . build diverse teams and maximize it.* With the innovations in technology and the swiftness of change around the world, there is the creation of intellectual capital occurring in all corners of the globe. The General Electric Values call for the identification and recognition of this intellectual capital, and also call for the establishment of a culture that values diversity and maintains the flow of intellectual capital regardless of the source.

This value is critical, because it casts aside the "not invented here" syndrome that many companies fall into over time. It is also critical because more and more alliances are global. The creation of intellectual capital can come from alliance partners from all over the world.

The building of diverse teams allows for the free flowing of ideas that support the creation and use of intellectual capital. The building of diverse alliances allows for the free flowing of intellectual capital that supports solution-specific alliances.

⬧ *Value Six: . . . See change for the growth opportunities it brings . . . e.g., e-Business.*
Change is omnipresent. People can view change in one of two ways. Change can be a major threat to the status quo for people who enjoy a particular advantage with a current state. The problem is that change will happen, regardless of how much we may like the current state. Change can be a major opportunity for people who see that change is inevitable and that there is an advantage to be the first to embrace change.

GE stresses that change should be seen for the growth opportunities it brings. Change may also necessitate alliances to augment core competencies needed to adapt to change. The GE executives whom I know are all focused on blending quarterly execution to meet specific profit and loss targets with a longer-term quest for customer-driven growth opportunities. This customer-driven mentality makes these executives open-minded about change. It also allows for the acceptance and embracing of change throughout all levels of GE.

⬧ *Value Seven: . . . Create a clear, simple, customer-centered vision . . . and continually renew and refresh its execution.* A strong vision for alliances is the first critical success factor for successful alliances. Imbedded in the GE Values is the value to create a clear customer-centered vision. The GE value also calls for the continuous renewing and refreshing of its execution. We discussed in the critical success factors for alliances the need to have the CEO establish and reinforce the vision for alliances. GE establishes this need in their GE Values for the entire organization. As such, the GE leaders are supported in their efforts to create and execute to a strong vision with their alliance partners through their GE Values.

⬧ *Value Eight: . . . Create an environment of "stretch," excitement, informality, and trust . . . reward improvements and celebrate results.* For all of us, "stretch targets" are nothing new. The combination of excitement, informality, and trust with the stretch targets creates an environment of performance achievement with organizational support. The rewarding of improvements and celebration of results with alliance partners is critical to maintain momentum with alliance partners. For example, the Home Depot department manager told me that they had a mini-party with their GE partner when they sold their first appliance from the store that was not in stock in the store. (My dishwasher was not the first one.)

❖ *Value Nine: . . . Demonstrate . . . always with infectious enthusiasm for the customer . . . the 4 E's of GE . . . the personal Energy to welcome and deal with the speed of change . . . the ability to create an atmosphere that Energizes others . . . the Edge to make difficult decisions . . . and the ability to consistently Execute.* This value comes through in all that GE does in the marketplace. It permeates its employees, its solutions, and its inner workings with its customers and alliance partners.

The Home Depot department manager told me that the GE people he worked with had an incredible amount of energy for their joint solution. He said that this energy rubbed off and energized his own workers, and that the extended group came together to focus on executing the solution on day one of the new store opening. He also told me that the GE people had the edge to make the tough decisions about including competitor products side by side with GE products.

The General Electric Company: Summary

From building an e-Culture to the GE Values, the General Electric Company has what it takes to develop Hall-of-Fame alliances. According to my research and my conversations with people all around the world, this company is viewed as being tops in ability to work with other companies to create positive change in the marketplace.

Although my personal experience was driven by the need to replace a twenty-year-old dishwasher, it was remarkable to experience a GE alliance in action. It also came at a time when I was doing research on best-in-class alliance programs, so the signals were very evident. In addition, the comments from the Home Depot department manager almost mirrored the philosophies of the GE Company. The indoctrination was so complete, that at times I felt that the department manager had just finished a career working for GE. Clearly, GE has earned the title of "Global Most Admired Company." It has also earned a spot in my Alliance Hall of Fame.

Cisco Systems, Inc.

Cisco Systems, Inc. (Cisco) is the global leader in the creation of networking solutions for the Internet. It had revenues in FY2000 of about $19 billion, with a mid-2001 market capitalization of approximately $125 billion. Cisco was founded in 1984 by a group of scientists from Stanford, shipped its first product in 1986, and grew to a global leader with over 34,000 employees by the year 2001.[11]

Fortune has identified Cisco Systems as the second "Global Most Admired Company" in the year 2000 and the fourth "Global Most Admired Company" in 1999. *The Financial Times* identified Cisco Systems as the "World's Seventh Most Respected Company" in 2000. Other achievements include the "#3 Best Company to Work For" by *Fortune* for the year 2000, and one of the top "100 Best Corporate Citizens for 2001" by *Business Ethics* magazine.[12]

Cisco sets the stage for leadership in alliance management through its stated objective in its FY2000 annual report. In the company profile, Cisco states that its objective is to provide its customers with more efficient and timely exchange of information that results in driving cost savings, process efficiencies, and closer customer relationships with customers, prospects, business partners, suppliers, and employees.[13]

Cisco was second only to GE in response to my question, "What company would you like to develop an alliance with?" In addition, there are three main driving forces behind my vote for Cisco to be one of my two winners in the Alliance Hall of Fame. These three main driving forces are: alliance philosophy, alliance structure, and alliances in action. Let's take a look at each of these forces at work and why Cisco deserves to be in the Alliance Hall of Fame.

Alliance Philosophy

Cisco lives and breathes by its stated alliance philosophy. This philosophy is titled "Partnering to Shape the Future." Let's look at this philosophy.

> Our strategic alliances are designed to help deliver a cus-
> tomer-centric, total solutions approach to solving prob-
> lems, exploiting business opportunity, and creating
> sustainable competitive advantage for our customers. This
> shared commitment to deliver solutions and services, en-
> compassing products, applications, systems integration, and
> best practices, will help make our customers successful as
> globally networked organizations in the new economy.[14]

There is an uncanny similarity to GE's approach and connectivity
to the seven critical success factors for successful alliances. The customer-centric approach, the joint solution development, and the objective to help make their customers successful through the creation
of sustained competitive advantage—all parallel the GE approach. In
addition, this philosophy has a strong vision, a focused message, the
willingness to enter into meaningful alliance agreements, and the ap-
pearance of an absence of the fear of failure.

Alliance Structure

Cisco has selected fourteen companies as strategic alliance partners.
These companies are Callisma, Cap Gemini Ernst & Young, Compaq,
EDS Corporation, Hewlett-Packard, IBM, Italtel, KPMG, Microsoft,
Motorola, Netigy, Oracle, Sun, and ThruPoint. Each of these compa-
nies has dedicated alliance personnel working with one another with a
specific mission and set of solutions that are jointly developed for the
alliance. These strategic alliances are anchored by the strategic alliance
philosophy, and are supported by the chairman and CEO of Cisco,
John Chambers. Let's take a look at a few of these alliances, and how
Cisco structures its alliances with them.

Alliances in Action

Cisco/Hewlett-Packard

The Cisco/Hewlett-Packard (HP) global alliance brings together
the global leader in creating networking solutions for the Internet
(Cisco) and network management (HP). The alliance objective is to
bring the best in network performance to joint customers through
bringing together computing and networking, data and voice, and

Unix and Windows NT. The joint customers are targeted as telecom service providers, enterprise users, and consumers.[15]

Hewlett-Packard and Cisco have committed to create "The Smart Way to Manage Cisco Environments." This involves significant integration of the HP OpenView Network Node Manager 6.X and the CiscoWorks2000 family of products and the Cisco device-specific Event Correlation circuits from LOGEC Systems. The expected joint customer benefits include decreased network management complexity, faster problem resolution, and increased uptime.[16]

The Cisco/Hewlett-Packard global alliance is clearly a solution-specific alliance. It involves sales, the geography is global, the industry is telecommunications, and the solution is specifically identified. There is a strong vision for the alliance, supported by focused, strong comments from both Carly Fiorina of HP and John Chambers of Cisco Systems, whose commitment to the alliance is definitely visible with their comments appearing on the Cisco Web site just below their respective pictures. There appears to be a strong process to enter into their global alliance, because of the presence of a global alliance mission statement and a description of the joint solution being developed.[17]

Will this global alliance enter into the high-growth stage of the lifecycle? Only time will tell. However, there appears to be a very strong and organized start to this solution-specific alliance with several of the critical success factors present. Market-dependent, the chances are very good for a successful global alliance.

Cisco/Microsoft

The Cisco–Microsoft global alliance brings together the global leader in creating networking solutions for the Internet (Cisco) and the worldwide leader in software for personal and business computing (Microsoft). The alliance vision/mission jointly announced ". . . a shared vision of the Internet and networked applications as the primary information technology platforms around which organizations will create sustainable competitive advantage in the future." The global alliance was announced to cover a broad range of technology areas, including multimedia, security, and directory services.[18]

Among the specific initiatives that spawned from this broad alliance was the Cisco/Microsoft solution-specific effort around application service providers (ASPs.) This initiative, announced in October

1999, focused on the collaboration necessary to provide ASPs with end-to-end solutions for deploying outsourced applications and services. Specifically, these end-to-end solutions focused on midsize companies in corporate purchasing, business management, and customer relationship management. Selected ASPs entered into development alliances with Cisco and Microsoft, resulting in these ASPs offering their application hosting services on the Windows NT Server platform, Microsoft QSL Server tm 7.0 database, Site Server Commerce Edition, and Cisco networking solutions.[19]

The Cisco/Microsoft global alliance is clearly a solution-specific alliance with a series of investment alliances around specific initiatives (e.g., ASP collaboration). It is a solution-specific alliance in the area of technology, with a series of investment alliances around specific initiatives (e.g., ASPs). There is a strong vision for the alliance, supported by focused, strong comments from both Bill Gates of Microsoft and John Chambers of Cisco Systems. As with HP, the commitment to the alliance is definitely visible, with the CEOs' comments appearing on the Cisco Web site just below their respective pictures. There also appears to be a strong process to enter into their global alliance, because of the global alliance structure and the presence of a global alliance vision/mission statement with an executive summary. On the evidence of the number of press releases and initiatives, this alliance appears to be in the high growth stage of the alliance lifecycle.[20]

Will this global alliance stay in the high-growth stage of the lifecycle? Only time will tell. However, this alliance between two global leaders appears to be very strong and well organized. Given the strength of these two global leaders and their respective CEOs, I would place my bets on a long and successful global alliance partnership for years to come.

Cisco/Cap Gemini Ernst & Young

The Cisco–Cap Gemini Ernst & Young global alliance brings together the global leader in creating networking solutions for the Internet (Cisco) and one of the largest management and information technology consulting firms in the world (CGE&Y). This is a special alliance to highlight, because it hits close to home for the author. The alliance has a strong vision, manifested through its mission statement. The mission statement is as follows:

> *Alliance Philosophy*: From strategy to implementation, the mission of the strategic, corporate alliance between Cap Gemini Ernst & Young and Cisco Systems is to accelerate the development of innovative, transferable Internet-based solutions that enable customers to take control of present and future business opportunities with confidence. Together, this alliance brings a cohesive understanding of what it takes to succeed in the new globally connected economy.[21]

The alliance is an investment alliance that focuses on five sets of solutions. These solutions are Network Infrastructure Solutions (NIS), Networked Value Chain (Supply Chain Management), Broadband Services Network Management (OSS/BSS), eCRM (Customer Relationship Management), and Workforce Optimization.

Cisco and CGE&Y partnered on the Network Infrastructure Solutions (NIS), which focuses on network gap assessment, design, and building of infrastructures for all industries. This is a solution jointly developed with Cisco and other ecosystem partners, such as EMC and Oracle. The Networked Value Chain (NVC) collaboration focuses on the communications with business partners through a standards-based connectivity infrastructure. This connectivity allows for the integration of multiple and disparate supply chains through the NVC communicators. (See Chapter Four for further information on the Networked Value Chain.)

The Broadband Services Network Management (OSS/BSS) combines best-of-breed applications around an information business architecture to allow service providers to take new broadband services to market quickly. The eCRM solution provides pre-integrated intelligent contact center software to enable companies to manage its customer experiences more effectively and cost-efficiently. The eCRM initiative is a joint solution development effort to establish a repeatable, go-to-market customer care solution set through the use of intelligent software, thought leadership, and network infrastructures. Workforce Optimization solution focuses on the productivity increase of employees through web-based applications, such as employee directories, time and expenses, workforce portals, etc. Other ecosystem partners include Corechange, Extensity, and Oblix.[22]

The Cisco/Cap Gemini Ernst & Young global alliance is clearly an investment alliance that includes sales and joint solution development in a global environment. Although the emphasis is on joint solutions for multiple industries, there is a heavy emphasis on the telecommunications industry.

What is it like to lead a global alliance with Cisco? Let's hear from Lilly G. Chung, the CGE&Y alliance vice president for the Cisco Alliance:

> Cisco's commitment to its ecosystem partners permeates throughout the company. It is part of the Cisco culture as they "walk the talk." This does not come easy. There have been many defining moments when Cisco debates internally about the value of partners. However, the ecosystem prevails. It has been a great partnership between Cap Gemini Ernst & Young and Cisco, and it is based on three major premises:
>
> ♦ Share a common vision.
> ♦ Balance of short-term and long-term results.
> ♦ Trust of each other.
>
> The Cisco and Cap Gemini Ernst & Young alliance team members are very tight. It is virtually impossible to tell who is from which firm. We speak the same vernacular, we execute on a joint business plan, and we have fun together!

Cisco Systems Summary

Cisco has a very strong alliance structure. They focus on developing alliance partnerships that are customer-centric, with joint solution development on next generation capabilities using the Internet. They also develop alliances with best-in-class companies.

Cisco's alliance structure calls for a strong vision and mission for the alliance, with support from the CEOs of both alliance companies. They take the CEO support for alliances very seriously, placing the photos of the CEOs with their supporting quotes right on their Web site. Cisco also has a passion for its alliances, as manifested through its approach and its dedication to joint solution development with its alliance partners. They demonstrate a strong knowledge on how to partner, and have demonstrated the ability to know when to disband an alliance.

The recent slowdown in spending by telecommunications companies is a direct result of the huge amount of debt that has been incurred in the industry, such as the telecom debt problem discussed in Chapter Three. This slowdown is slowing the growth rate of Cisco in a significant way. However, many security analysts are pointing to Cisco's marketplace focus on driving innovation with alliance partners as one of the key reasons for their continued confidence in Cisco's future.

Conclusion

Hall of Fame alliances do not just happen. As we have seen, they take a dedicated approach to the seven critical success factors for alliances. In addition, as both GE and Cisco have demonstrated, they require passion for customer-centered solutions using the joint capabilities of key alliance partners.

Throughout the book, we have outlined the alliance frameworks, agreements, documents, and success factors necessary to create lasting alliances. We have also reviewed company examples of what worked, what didn't work, and lessons learned. Alliances are easy to set up, but hard to set up properly. This book was designed to provide a road map for the journey to successful alliance management. The journey will only be as strong as the preparation before beginning the journey. However, don't wait too long before starting your journey. The competition is already working on the next best marketplace solutions while you sleep. Let the journey begin!

Notes

1. www.ge.com/GEfactsheet, May 20, 2001, p. 1.
2. www.ge.com/e@GE/Buildingane-Culture, p. 1.
3. Ibid.
4. Ibid.
5. Ibid.
6. Ibid.

7. Ibid.
8. www.ge.com/news/podium_papers/ourvalues.html, p. 1.
9. www.ge.com/annual99/letter/letter_three.html/#sixsigma, p. 1.
10. www.ge.com/corporate.htm/roadmap/thesixsigmastrategy, p. 1.
11. www.cisco.com/annualreport2000, p. 2.
12. www.cisco.com/warp/public/750/awards/company.html, p. 1.
13. www.cisco.com/annualreport2000, p. 2.
14. www.cisco.com/warp/public/756/partnership/, p. 1.
15. www.cisco.com/warp/public/756/partnership/hp/overview.html, p. 1.
16. www.hp.com/print.asp?catidf/749elelev = partners, p. 1.
17. www.cisco.com/warp/public/756/partnership/hp/overview.html, p. 1.
18. www.cisco.com/warp/public/756/partnership/microsoft/alliance, p. 1.
19. www.microsoft.com/presspass/press/1999/oct99/endtoendpr.asp, p. 1.
20. www.cisco.com/warp/public/756/partnership/microsoft/alliance, p. 1.
21. www.cisco.com/warp/public/756/partnership/cgey/overview.html, p. 1.
22. www.cisco.com/warp/public/756/partnership/cgey/solutions.html, pp. 1–2.

Index

Adaptive Health Care e-Supply Chain, 154–159
  accountability, 155
  content management, 157–158, 161–162
  end-to-end integration, 159
  guiding principles of, 155–159
  strategic sourcing, *see* strategic sourcing
  variability reduction, 158
Advanced Mobile Phone System (AMPS), 50
Advanced Technical Fighter (ATF), *see* F-22 Raptor fighter
agreements
  alliance, *see* alliance agreement
  memo of intent, 65, 68–72
  nondisclosure, 93–96
  solution-based definitive, 179–187
alliance agreement
  amendments, 46
  approval process for, 28–31
  and authorization, 37
  business need review, 28, 30
  and competing products, 43
  construction of, 27–28, 35–47
  damage limitation under, 46
  definition section of, 36
  general provisions of, 45–47
  and intellectual property rights, 42–43
  intent of, 35
  legal compliance review of, 30
  nonassignment of, 46
  and notices, 45
  and partners' responsibilities under, 37–39
  and proprietary information, 44
  provisions for nonsolicitation, 45
  and publicity, 47
  and severability, 46
  term and renewal of, 40

  termination of, 40–41
  waiver of, 46
  and warranties under, 39–40
Alliance Hall of Fame
  Cisco Systems, Inc., 261–266
  General Electric Company, 252–260
alliance partners
  former competitors as, 108–109
  key traits in, 232–236
  relationship of, 41–42
  selecting the right, 27, 34, 85–90, 235–236
alliance performance steering committee, 31
alliances
  agreement, *see* alliance agreement
  business plan for, 143–149
  commitment to success of, 33, 244–245,
    248–249
  compensation alignment of, 206–208
  critical success factors for, 232–236
  declining, 221, 249
  defined, 3
  disbanding, 226–229
  emerging, 218–219
  of former competitors, 108–109, 119–122
  Hall of Fame, *see* Alliance Hall of Fame
  high-growth stage, 219–220
  ideal attributes of, 202–205
  impact of e-Workplace on, 253
  importance of in health care, 160
  importance of local relationships in, 191–192
  intermodal, 132–134
  lifecycle of, 217–221
  mature, 220–221
  need for, 11–16
  need to disband, 221–226
  partners, *see* alliance partners
  and personality tendencies, 112–114
  software-consulting, 192–195

269

alliances (*continued*)
  start-up, 218
  success factors for, 241–249
  tactical *vs.* strategic, 200–202
  types of, 4–8, 16–19
  vision for, 242–243
alternate dispute resolution, 46
American President Lines railroad, 131–132
America Online (AOL), alliance with Nokia, 57–58
Andersen Consulting, alliance with SAP, 200–201
Apax Partners, alliance with Ericsson, 60–61
appliances, online sales of, 10
AT&T Wireless, alliance with NTT DoCoMo, 59–60
automated guided vehicles (AGVs), 62
automated storage and retrieval system (ASRS), 62
Avres, Scott, 138

Boeing
  alliance with General Dynamics and Lockheed, 108, 119–122
  proposal to build F-22 Raptor, 107
Boston Consulting Group, and Brandwise.com alliance, 4–5, 6–7
Brady, Greg, 190, 194
Brand Central program (Sears), 9
Brandwise.com alliance, 5, 6–7
  rise and fall of, 8–9, 11
British Telecom, 63
Broadband Services Network Management, 265
business partners, defined, 41–42
business plan construction, 143–149

Caltex Australia, alliance with TNT Australia, 138
Canon, alliance with Ericsson, 53
Cap Gemini Ernst & Young (CGE&Y)
  alliances with i2 Technologies, 4, 5
  alliance with Cisco Systems, 264–266
  Five-Step Strategic Sourcing Framework, 163–176
  Networked Value Chain, 78–80, 81
Cart-to-Cart shopping (Maytag), 9
CGE&Y, *see* Cap Gemini Ernst & Young (CGE&Y)
Chambers, John, 240, 262, 264
character, as key trait in alliance partners, 232–236
Chief Alliance Officer, 246
Chung, Lilly G., 266
Cisco Systems, Inc.
  in Alliance Hall of Fame, 261
  alliance partners of, 262
  alliance philosophy of, 262
  alliance with CGE&Y, 264–266
  alliance with Hewlett-Packard, 262–263
  alliance with Microsoft, 263–264
  alliance with Motorola, 219
Commerce One, as Covisint partner, 25, 26
commodity profile process, 168, 169

confidential information
  covered by alliance agreement, 44–45
  covered by nondisclosure agreement, 94–96
consulting firms
  alliances with software companies, 192–195, 211–213
  point-of-view solutions of, 198
Cotton, Charlie, 109–111, 114, 115
Covey, Stephen R., 110, 220
Covisint, successful establishment of, 25–26

DaimlerChrysler, as Covisint partner, 25, 26
Danzas Group, alliance with NextLinx, 138
Deutsche Telekom, 216
Digital AMPS (DAMPS), 52

Ellison, Larry, 194
enterprise resource planning (ERP), 194, 197
Ericsson
  alliance with Apax Partners, 60–61
  alliance with Canon, 53
  alliance with Sony, 89

F-22 Raptor fighter
  artist's rendition of, 116
  design proposals for, 101–102, 106
  key characteristics of, 103–104
  requirements for, 105
  teaming agreements to build, 108–109
Farrill, Craig, 64–65
Federal Trade Commission (FTC), and Covisint review, 25
Fiorina, Carly, 240
Five-Step Strategic Sourcing Framework, 162–177
Ford, Henry, 240, 242
Ford Motor Company, as Covisint partner, 25, 26
Foster Brewing Company (Australia), alliance with Molson Canada, 6
framework
  to determine need for alliances, 11–16
  to determine need to disband alliance, 221–226
  to determine type of alliance, 16–19
  to disband alliance, 226–229
France Telecom, 216
Frito Lay
  Myers-Briggs profile used by, 110
  and networked supply chain, 109–111
  and scan-based trading, 88
Fujitsu, 89

Gates, Bill, 240, 264
General Dynamics
  alliance with Boeing and Lockheed, 108, 119–122
  proposal to build F-22 Raptor, 107
  study of fighter characteristics, 102–104
General Electric Company
  in Alliance Hall of Fame, 251–252
  e-Culture of, 252–254
  GE Values, 256–260
  Six Sigma Quality program, 257
  vision for alliances, 259

General Motors, as Covisint partner, 25, 26
General Packet Radio Service (GPRS), 52
geographic-specific alliances
  Caltex Australia and TNT Australia, 138
  compensation strategy for, 141
  defined, 5–6
  Nokia as leader of, 58–59
  rationale for, 17, 18
  selecting the right partner for, 87
Global One, 216
Global Positioning Satellite, *see* GPS technology
Global System for Mobile Communications
  (GSM), 51–52
governing law, 45
Grumman, proposal to build F-22 Raptor, 107

Hays Fourth Party Solutions, 140
  alliance with i2 Technologies, 140
health care
  Adaptive e-Supply Chain, 154–159
  hospital procurement, 152–153
  purchase demand management, 175, 176, 177
  strategic sourcing in, *see* strategic sourcing
  supplier sourcing approaches, 168, 170–172
  supply base management, 172–175, 176, 177
  total cost management, 175, 176, 177
Hearst, and Brandwise.com alliance, 4–5, 6–7
Hewlett-Packard, alliance with Cisco Systems,
  262–263
High Speed Circuit Switched Data (HSCSD), 52
Home Depot, and scan-based trading, 88

i2 Technologies
  alliances with CGE&Y, 4, 5
  alliance with Hays Fourth Party Solutions, 140
  eCatalogue, 162
  four-diamond program, 209
independent contractors, defined, 42
Industrial Brance de Organizacion Techint,
  138–139
integrity, as key trait in alliance partners, 232–236
intellectual property rights, 42–43
intermodal traffic, 135
Internet connectivity, as benefit of mobile services, 76–77
investment alliances
  AT&T Wireless and NTT DoCoMo, 59–60
  compensation strategy for, 142
  Danzas Group and NextLinx, 138
  defined, 6–7
  rationale for, 17, 18
  selecting the right partner for, 87–88
J. D. Edwards Company, 191
J. B. Hunt
  alliance partnerships, 134
  and driver shortage, 136
  and regional feeds, 133–134, 137
  transformation into intermodal company,
    132–134, 136
Joint Strike Fighter Demonstrators, 116, 117

joint venture alliance, compensation strategy for,
  142
joint venture alliances
  defined, 7
  Ericsson and Apax Partners, 60–61
  rationale for, 17, 18
  Ryder System and Toyota Tsusho America, 139
  selecting the right partner for, 89–90
Juniper Networks, alliance with Nortel, 14
Justice, Stephen, 102, 105, 119, 120

Keirsey, David, 111
Keirsey Temperament Sorter, 111–114
  used at Frito Lay, 110, 114–115
Kent International Freight Services, Ltd., 137
King, Martin Luther, Jr., 242, 243

Lane, Robert, 194
Less-Than-Truckload carriers, *see* LTL transportation
linehaul costs
  of LTL carriers, 125
  of truckload carriers, 129
Lockheed
  alliance with Boeing and General Dynamics,
    108, 119–122
  proposal to build F-22 Raptor, 107
LTL transportation
  cost components of, 125–128
  Roadway Express relay system, 127, 128

Maytag.com, Cart-to-Cart shopping, 9
McDonnell Douglas
  alliance with Northrop, 108
  proposal to build F-22 Raptor, 107
memorandum of intent, 65
  construction of, 68–72
  for Motorola and NTT Software alliance, 218
Microsoft, alliance with Cisco Systems, 263–264
mobile commerce, benefits of, 75–78
mobile phones, worldwide ownership of, 61
Molson Canada, alliance with Foster Brewing
  Company, 6
Motor Carrier Act (1980), 127
Motorola, alliance with Cisco, 219
Motorola Japan, 218
Myers-Briggs profile, 110

networked supply chain, *see* Networked Value
  Chain
Networked Value Chain, 78–80
  and 3G wireless networks, 80–82
  Cisco-CGE&Y collaboration, 265
  and health care supply chain, 154
  and real time order management, 84
Network Infrastructure Solution (NIS), 265
NextLinx Corporation, alliance with Danzas
  Group, 138
Nokia
  alliance with AOL, 57–58
  focus on digital cellular market, 14
  geographic-specific alliance of, 58–59

nondisclosure agreement (NDA), construction of, 93–96
nonsolicitation, 45
Nordic Mobile Telephone (NMT), 50
Nortel, *see* Northern Telecom (Nortel)
Northern Telecom (Nortel), alliance with Juniper Networks, 14
Northrop
    alliance with McDonnell Douglas, 108
    proposal to build F-22 Raptor, 107
NTT DoCoMo, alliance with AT&T Wireless, 59–60
NTT Software, 218

Oracle Corporation
    alliance with PriceWaterhouseCoopers, 190
    in competition with consulting firms, 194
    as Covisint partner, 25, 26
Osborne, Bart, 102
over-the-road costs, *see* linehaul costs

Personal Digital Communications (PDC), 50
Personal Handyphone Systems (PHS), 50
personality tendencies, 112–114
PriceWaterhouseCoopers, alliance with Oracle, 190
proprietary information, 44

QUALCOMM, alliance with Schneider National, 137

Renault/Nissan, as Covisint partner, 25, 26
Ritchey, Diane, 10
Roadway Express, LTL relay system, 127, 128
Rockwell, proposal to build F-22 Raptor, 107
Ryder System, alliance with Toyota Tsusho America, 139

sales alliances
    compensation strategy for, 141
    defined, 4
    Kent International Freight Services, Ltd., 137
    rationale for, 16–17
    selecting the right partner for, 86
    Virgin Mobile and One2One, 56
SBC Corporation, 89
scan, focus, and act process, 90–93
scan-based trading (SBT), 87–89
    and 3G mobile devices, 88
    at Home Depot, 88
    at Wal-Mart, 88, 159
Schneider National Inc., alliance with QUAL-COMM, 137–138
Sears, Brand Central program, 9
Shaw, Robert, 194
Six Sigma Quality program, 257
software companies, alliances with consulting firms, 192–195, 211–213
software selection process, 197

solution-based definitive agreement, construction of, 179–187
solution-specific alliances
    AOL and Nokia, 57–58
    compensation strategy for, 141
    defined, 4–5
    rationale for, 17–18
    Schneider National and QUALCOMM, 137
    selecting the right partner for, 86
Sony Corporation, and alliance with Ericsson, 89
Spectrapoint Wireless, 219
spend analysis, 166
Sprint, 216
strategic sourcing
    commodity profile process, 166–168
    commodity sourcing strategy, 172–175
    implementation approach, 175–177
    opportunity assessment, 164–166
    plan, 164, 165
    strategic direction, 168, 170–172
supply chain, *see* Networked Value Chain
supply market analysis, 168

teaming agreements, 108
Telecom Italia, 216
terminal costs, 125
3G wireless networks
    and customer relationship management, 82–83
    incremental value of, 85
    and Networked Value Chain, 80–82
    and real-time order management, 84
    and scan-based trading, 88–89
TNT Australia, alliance with Caltex Australia, 138
Total Access Communication System (TACS), 50
Toyota Tsusho America, alliance with Ryder System, 139
truckload carrier, cost components of, 129–131

Unix operating system, 189–190
U.S. Air Force
    Aeronautical Systems Division, 101
    Flight Dynamics Lab, 101
    "Red Baron Study," 103

Virgin Mobile, alliance with One2One, 56
Vodafone, 63

Wal-Mart, and scan-based trading, 88, 159
Walton, Sam, 240, 242
Welch, Jack, 240, 242
Whirlpool, and Brandwise.com alliance, 4–5, 6–7
wireless networks
    defined, 51
    development costs of, 62–65
    first generation (1G), 50–51
    fourth generation (4G), 54, 55
    second generation (2G), 51–52
    third generation (3G), *see* 3G wireless networks
    U.S. usage of, 52
Wolfe, Chris, 138